Entrepreneurship
A Tools-oriented Approach

Entrepreneurship: A Tools-oriented Approach

George Abe

Published by:

 Vandeplas Publishing, LLC – August 2020

801 International Parkway, 5th Floor
Lake Mary, FL. 32746
USA

www.vandeplaspublishing.com

ISBN: 978-1-60042-512-7

ENTREPRENEURSHIP
A Tools-oriented Approach

George Abe

TABLE OF CONTENTS

FORWARD

Much has been written about the tremendous success young entrepreneurs have had in have disrupting entire industries worldwide. The likes of Bill Gates, Steve Jobs and more recently Mark Zuckerberg, Travis Kalanick and lesser known, but just as important successes, Jenn Hyman (Rent the Runway), Wendy Kopp (Teach For America), John Zimmer (Lyft) and Miguel McKelvey (WeWork) have inspired a new generation of entrepreneurs worldwide.

These entrepreneurs were in their twenties when they started. Indeed, the young are daring, open to new ideas, don't mind breaking things and have little to lose. Much of what is written about young entrepreneurs focuses on idea generation, problem solving, personality and entrepreneurial mindset. Surely these are important ingredients for success and readers learn from, and enjoy, success stories.

This book takes a different tack.

Our view is that entrepreneurship is not just for the young. Although spectacularly successful entrepreneurs have started billion-dollar companies often without the benefit of a university degree, evidence suggests that mid-career professionals have advantages of their own in pursuing entrepreneurship. Recent scholarship suggests that work experience, a good Roladex and some savings can be used to their advantage.[1] Moreover, there is strong interest by mid-career professionals in pursuing entrepreneurship. They seek to strike out on their own after some frustrations of corporate life or to improve the performance of the company they're already in.

Rather than dwelling on success stories, great ideas and mindset, our approach is to take tools-oriented approach. Our intent is for readers to become familiar with terminology, legalese, computations and methods used by entrepreneurs, lawyers, advisers and investors when forming and financing a new company.

The author has taught an entrepreneurship course for MBAs and law students at UCLA since 2003. There is intense interest among students in their 30s and 40s in entrepreneurship, particularly those students in the part-time and executive MBA programs. They already have substantial professional experience when they begin their MBA studies which means their interests in, and questions about, entrepreneurship differ substantially from their younger counterparts.

It is their issues and questions which motivate this book.

---

[1] "Age and High-Growth Entrepreneurship", Pierre Azoulay, Benjamin Jones, J. Daniel Kim and Javier Miranda. NBER Working Paper 24489, April 2018. https://www.nber.org/papers/w24489

I am indebted to various colleagues and students at the UCLA Anderson School of Management who provided encouragement. Particular thanks go to my old friends and colleagues Shana Berg, David Geller, Jeff Lawrence, John Miller and Jean-Noel Moneton, who provided insights on their entrepreneurial adventures.

Particular thanks go to Emily Loughran, who taught me all I know about intellectual property matters.

Most of all I'd like to thank Michael Adams, whose punctilious review made this text more readable than it otherwise would have been.

Chapter 1 – Scope and Approach

(It's better to know some of the questions, than all of the answers
– James Thurber, American humorist)

When asked whether he would invest in an entrepreneur who has never started a Company before or one who had failed, Don Valentine, partner at Sequoia Ventures said, "The trouble with the first-time entrepreneur is that he doesn't know what he doesn't know. After a failure he does know what he doesn't know and can beat the hell out of people who still have to learn."[1] Entrepreneurs need to know the right questions.

Add to the fact that entrepreneurship is highly idiosyncratic, (meaning what works in one situation may not work in another similar situation), it's no wonder that entrepreneurs are dazed and confused after they start their businesses. This book is largely about questions. Some high-level questions we address are:

- What are common misconceptions entrepreneurs have?

- Where do ideas come from? How do you know if you have a good one?

- What's the best way to survey the market before beginning work on something that people may not want?

- What are key risks and what should you do about them?

- How do you raise money? What is the fundraising process? Why do investors say "No"?

- What do deal documents look like? For example, what are term sheets and convertible notes? What are key provisions of each?

- How should the entrepreneur think about valuation?

---

[1]   https://www.vcconfidential.com/2007/11/wisdoms-of-sequ.html

- What are the administrative and legal steps required to start a company?

- How do you pick milestones? What is the relationship between milestone selection and fundraising?

- When should the Founder step aside to make way for new management?

- How should you think about the hiring process and compensation of Founders and early employees? What types of equity compensation should you consider?

- How do you protect your intellectual property? How do you monetize your intellectual property or acquire someone else's intellectual property?

- What can you learn from history?

- Is learning entrepreneurship valuable even if you don't plan to start a company?

Having said this, if your proposed business is simple and low cost (including opportunity cost), like a lemonade stand or mobile app, you are probably better off just doing it and learning on the job rather than reading books. On the job training can be faster, cheaper and more instructive than reading. However, if the business is more complex, then some preparation improves your odds of success, or, more likely, reduces your chances of an expensive failure. Therefore, we address the early stages of relatively complex businesses. By "complex businesses" we mean businesses that (1) require fundraising, typically in multiple rounds, or (2) require the acquisition of, or monetization of, intellectual property or (3) involve a spinoff, or divestiture of a small company from a big one or (4) involve an acquisition of a small company.

This book diverges from entrepreneurial writing in the popular press in these respects.

- We use old cases, with the view that old cases demonstrate persistent issues of entrepreneurship across multiple domains and throughout history. Technology changes, human nature doesn't.

- We discuss failures with the view that students learn more from failure than success.

- We don't spend much time on "entrepreneurial mindset". What is the meaning of "entrepreneurial mindset" when people of all types around the world and throughout history have succeeded and failed with different mindsets and personalities? Except for common sense human factors (hard work, dedication, ability to learn), we don't think there is a consistent message regarding "mindset". And, anyway, you don't need a book to learn about common sense.

While we agree that the likes of Rockefeller and J.P. Morgan would find kindred spirits in the billionaire youthful entrepreneurs of today, this book addresses a wider audience. We also consider high-performing lifestyle businesses that are not intended to exit via IPO or trade sale.

- We spend little time discussing the hot investment themes of the day. Products come and go. Our intent is to present tools which are more enduring and independent of current vogue.

This book is intended to be practical. We try improve your odds of survival by indicating warning signs, fatal flaws, tools, samples, contractual terms, techniques and historical lessons. This book is largely about questions, not answers. Our view is that there is no formula for entrepreneurial success. You have to know the right questions and figure things out as you go.

The scope of this book covers the period in the life of a startup company from the time a Founder has an idea, through product development, market introduction and at least 2 rounds of fundraising. Our objective here is to coach the entrepreneur through early gestation until such time as the company has reasonable prospect of standing on its own feet.

WHAT'S DIFFERENT ABOUT AN ENTREPRENEURSHIP EDUCATION?

Apart of the standard MBA curriculum in finance, marketing, accounting and so forth, what can they learn in an entrepreneurial class that they don't get in the core classes?

- Mechanics of starting an entity

- Legal formation, choice of legal entity, team building, equity compensation, Founders' agreement

- Entrepreneurial strategies

Entrepreneurs face strategic decisions that have a different emphasis than their big company colleagues. Selecting or developing an idea, selecting milestones, financing without access to conventional financing, differentiating founders from early employees.

- Management succession

  Certainly, CEOs of large companies get replaced. But Founders of startups get replaced often for different reasons. We'll take a look at some reasons and address why many Founders are more apt to voluntarily leave or be forced out, more so than big company CEOs.

- Fundraising

  Startup companies raise cash differently from large companies who have access to commercial banks. We'll deal with government funding, crowdfunding, angel financing, venture capital, venture debt and similar vehicles more suited to small companies with high risk.

- Cash management

  Startup companies are nearly always starved for cash. This provides a different perspective on cash management and the relationship of cash to profits and assets.

- Different ways to think about valuation

  The classic tools used in corporate finance are typically not useful when valuing startup companies. Classic valuation techniques such as discounted cash flow, net present value, weighted average cost of capital are use only sporadically when there is little cash flow or profits. So how else what investors and entrepreneurs place a value on their company?

AUTHOR'S BIASES

The approach herein relies on these:

- History is important. Mark Twain famously said "History doesn't repeat itself, but it does rhyme". We agree. Much is to be learned from old cases. While technology, population and laws change, human nature does not. Thus, the same mistakes tend to be made repeatedly. We want to emphasize issues, questions and situations which are enduring.

- More is learned from failure than successes. Bill Gates famously said "Success is a lousy teacher". We agree. Success is often the result of a particular confluence of events which occur fortuitously. But the conditions for failure occur more frequently. It is instructive to see what mistakes were made by others so as to help the new entrepreneur in pattern recognition.

- Ecosystem is important. Success and failure are not just about you. Ecosystem must be supportive in order to win. That means markets, investment climate, culture and customs of an industry and supply chains are largely out of the control of the entrepreneur. It is important to recognize a bad ecosystem and act accordingly.

- Numbers are important. Some entrepreneurs have a phobia about numbers. Our view is that entrepreneurs, or someone on the founding team, must be comfortable with numbers in order to under term sheets, debt and stock options, all of which have a key bearing on the economics of the firm.

- Unicorns (billion-dollar, game changing startups that are disrupting entire industries) are important, but so are small businesses. Much of the popular and trade press is focused on disruptive game changers. Companies that become global behemoths. These unicorns make for interesting reading. However, we also consider the importance of small businesses that have more modest goals, like provided a living for the founder and employees and serving the community. This book is targeted to both small businesses as well as unicorns.

- Entrepreneurship is more than starting an enterprise from nothing. Our definition also includes spinoffs and acquisitions, which are often preferred paths to entrepreneurship for persons in mid-career.

- Entrepreneurs should have a grasp of the legal framework in which they operate. Thus, we will review laws, regulations, contracts and non-contractual agreements that entrepreneurs can expect to encounter at multiple stages of the founding and growth. Our objective to remove the mystery of the jargon reflected in various documents.

- There are very few "answers" to key issues of entrepreneurship. James Thurber famously said "It's better to know some of the questions than all of the answers". We agree since we believe there are no pat answers. What works in one situation but may not in another, similar situation. Should the entrepreneur be first to market? Sometimes yes, sometimes no. Should the entrepreneur employ a "Minimum Viable Product"? Sometimes yes, sometimes no. So, what is important is your ability to ask the right question. Our intention is to help identify the questions and provide tools for you to figure it out yourself.

Given this approach, now we turn to some content. The first of these will be clarification of the misconceptions many first-time entrepreneurs have.

SOME COMMON MISCONCEPTIONS OF ENTREPRENEURSHIP

- You must be "first to market".

There is a lot of writing about the need to be first to market. Indeed, such pioneers are often big winners. By being first, you have an early monopoly, can establish the rules of the market, attract innovative staff and create an impression of market leadership which is attractive to investors. However, more often than not being first can be problematic...

Consider the cases of WordPerfect, Visicalc, Friendster and Creative Tech Nomad, all of which paved the way for Fast Followers and failed to get to the finish line.

WordPerfect was originally released in 1979 and thus was a pioneer in the field of word processing software. However, over time it lost its leadership position. Today it is a distant follower to Microsoft Word.

Or take the case of Visicalc. Visicalc (shorthand for visible calculator) was the original spreadsheet for personal computers. It too was released in 1979. It ran on Apple personal computers and was considered the "killer app" for Apple. However, it was eclipsed by Lotus 1-2-3. By 1985, Visicorp, the developer of Visicalc, was bankrupt. Today of course, the industry standard is Microsoft Excel.

Or take the case of Friendster. Friendster was released in 2002 as a social networking platform. Within a few months of it had 3 million users aided by a $12 million investment from key venture capital firms, like Kleiner Perkins. However, it was eclipsed by MySpace and eventually Facebook.

Finally, consider the SaeHan MPMan, which was a South Korean developer of consumer electronics. In 1998, SaeHan arguably had the earliest MP3 player which it introduced in 1998. Other early MP3 players were the Creative Labs Nomad (Singapore) and the Diamond Multimedia PMP300 (Los Angeles). However, these early entrants soon attracted the attention of Apple which introduced the iPod in 2001.

It is often said that "pioneers get arrows". Pioneers are targets. They show a vision, take risks, let others what products work and educate users. All these cost money, which startups don't have. The strategy employed by many successful entrepreneurs is to be a Fast Follower. Fast Followers observe what the pioneers are doing, look for mistakes, notice there are buyers and exploit the market after the Pioneers pave the way. Sometimes being first to market is the winning strategy, sometimes it isn't. This is an example of how idiosyncratic entrepreneurship can be.

- Having no competition is great.

A corollary to the first to market hypothesis is that having no competition is a good thing. It can be said that if you have a product and nothing like it exists, you are first to market therefore are the Pioneer. Again, this can be good or bad.

If an entrepreneur says there is no competition, then the entrepreneur is exposed to two possible critiques. The first is that the entrepreneur hasn't look hard enough.

Another reason is that others, possibly more informed than you, have looked at your market and decided to pass. Or course, companies make mistakes all the time by passing on opportunities. But the experience and market research of potential competitors should not be discarded out of hand. Competition means implies market validation. If there is no one interested in the market, there may be a good reason.

Entrepreneurs should always ask themselves, "Why hasn't this been done before?".

- You must have a breakthrough product to create great big company

In fact, what is more common is that great products and companies are just a few degrees away from prior products and companies. This is a slight variation on the Pioneer/Fast Follower discussion. Let's look at the arc of product development from the transistor radio to the iPod.

In the 1950s, the transistor radio solved a key consumer problem. Until that time consumers could listen to radio, but the radios were not portable. They were connected to a power cord and used vacuum tubes. It didn't take much creativity to believe that mobility was, or could be, a market driver. Hence, the transistor radio was a logical extension to what already existed. The problem was that the transistor had not been invented yet. This is an example of the importance of ecosystem, in this case, supply chain. The technology had not evolved yet to where a transistor radio could be made, although it could be imagined. This changed with the invention of the transistor by Bell Labs in 1947. By 1954 transistor radios were made by Sony in Japan and a joint venture of Texas Instruments and Industrial Development Engineering Associates. Interestingly, the US venture ceased operation and soon Sony had major market share.

However, the transistor radio had a problem. The consumer could not select music. The consumer could select the radio station to be listened to, but the disc jockey selected individual songs. User selection was the next problem to attack. This Sony addressed, in part due to their strong position in radios. Sony introduced the Walkman in 1979 which played cassette tapes and, shortly thereafter, the Discman which played compact disks. These products solved the problem of user selection. Users could choose the songs they want to hear by inserting a cassette or CD into the device. With these innovations, the user had both portability and user selection.

However, the Discman, in particular, had several problems. It was sensitive to vibration which causes skipping in the playback of music. Another problem was its battery consumption, and a third was its size. While it was portable, it could not comfortably fit in a man's shirt pocket or a woman's purse because it needed to accommodate a CD. Finally, although the user could choose music, each CD had a relatively small amount of music which it could play before another CD had to be inserted. The storage capacity and, hence, dimensions of a CD was dictated by the desire of Akio Morita, then CEO of Sony, that a single CD hold all of Beethoven's 9th symphony. Such is how design parameters are sometimes decided.

The solution to the CD player problem was to remove the CD and replace it with a hard drive. This was done by the early MP3 players, SaeHan, Creative Labs and Diamond Multimedia. With all due respect, it didn't take a lot of imagination to believe hard drives were better than CD-ROMs. There were fewer moving parts which meant less energy consumption and no skipping. The problem was that a suitable hard drive did not exist. There was no hard drive that had the capacity to hold a lot of music and is small enough to enable the MP3 player to fit in a man's shirt pocket.

Enter Apple and the development of the original iPod in 2001. Apple didn't have any of the elements need to create a small consumer electronics product. No operating system, no reference platform, no software to transfer music to the player and, crucially, no hard drive. The supply chain wasn't cooperating.

Independent of all this, Toshiba, then a leader in hard drives, was experimenting with new designs. In 2000, they developed a 1.8 inch diameter hard drive that could hold 5 Gigabytes. Interestingly, Toshiba didn't know what to do with this invention. It was an experiment. This was a case of a big company taking a product-first approach. That is, develop the product first, then hope that a market emerges. Big companies with deep pockets can do this. Jon Rubinstein of Apple saw the product fit immediately. He asked Steve Jobs for $10M to have exclusive rights to all the drives Toshiba could make. Within a year, released the first generation iPod in October 2001[2].

---

2   This story is told in detail in Walter Isaacson's biography of Steve Jobs, called "Steve Jobs".

The point of reviewing this history is that from the home radio to the iPod, the transition to the next product seems self-evident in retrospect. Progress is evolutionary, not revolutionary. If products are too revolutionary, consumers often won't embrace them. Consumer understanding of a new product depends in large part on familiarity with a prior product. In the chain of events depicted above, most of the new product already existed in the prior product. Each subsequent product solved a problem with the prior product.

In addition, the chain of events depicted above shows it is instructive to understand the supply chain problem. Often an innovator has an idea of what to do, but the parts needed to fulfill the vision don't exist. It was very patient of Apple to wait for someone to develop the right disc drive.

- People will always buy a "better" product.

There is an old adage that says, "build a better mousetrap and the world will beat a path to your door". Sometimes yes, sometimes no. Often an inventor will create a product that competes with an incumbent product. Your new product is more productive, less expensive or more attractive. However, it is also often the case that people won't buy it. Why wouldn't people buy a better mousetrap? Consider the following.

- Existing buyers don't view the problem as serious enough to warrant a change.
- Existing buyers are in a loyalty program or are purchasing on subscription, which increases switching costs.
- Existing buyers don't want to change their behavior. They know how to use current products. One reason some (older) people won't buy a new car is they don't want to relearn where all the buttons are.
- Existing buyers like the company there are dealing with. Maybe the current company doesn't have the best product, but buyers have received good customer service and feel loyal to the supplier.
- Something better is coming, so buyers will wait. This is called "market overhang".

Users live today without your product. In many cases, they are constrained by habit, are satisfied with what they have and don't want to change their behavior, even for something slightly better. We call this "buyer inertia". Good enough is good enough.

- A single product can make a company

Entrepreneurs are often too enamored with their innovation. Innovations are rightly a source of pride. However, innovations often have short lifespans. Except for strongly branded products like WD-40 and CocaCola, other products are subject to being supplanted by competitive products or technological or regulatory shifts which can cut the product life short. What are you going to do after obsolescence?

Products are not companies. This is a common misunderstanding among first-time entrepreneurs who think that just because they have an innovative product, they therefore must have a company. A company more than a single product. A company is a mechanism for making new products. You need a roadmap.

- It's all about the money

Entrepreneurship is hard. Sometimes just money isn't enough motivation. Successful entrepreneurs are more likely to be missionaries than mercenaries. A mercenary is someone who does something they may not like just for the money. A missionary is someone who does something regardless of the money because they are internally driven to get something done.

The great motivator for entrepreneurs is to do something you think is important that only you can do. Before Steve Wozniak joined Steve Jobs to found Apple Computers, he was perfectly content working at Hewlett Packard. But Steve Jobs convinced him that if he (Woz) didn't make great personal computers, it wouldn't happen. That's what drives great entrepreneurs. They bring something important to the world that others either can't or won't do.

- It's all about me.

The vision and drive of the entrepreneur is a necessary condition for success, but it isn't sufficient.

Over 30 years ago, Robert Reich, then of Harvard, noted that "in a global economy the Big Ideas pioneered by American entrepreneurs and the techniques for executing Big Ideas, travel easily around the world. If a company is to win in an environment with global competition, it needs the talent and creativity of all their workers, not just a few dynamic inventors and CEOs". This was in a piece he entitled, entitled "Entrepreneurship Reconsidered: The Team as Hero", Harvard Business Review, May-June 1987. We agree. The Horatio Alger Myth may have worked in 19th century America. But these days, it won't.

You need a team to scale; you can't do it alone. I periodically poll past students about the key problem they encountered after starting a company. They most often say team building, even more so than fundraising. Good storytelling can get you money but it won't fix team problems.

- Discount the role of luck

E. B. White once wrote, "Luck is not something you can mention in the presence of self-made men." The problem with not acknowledging luck is that a successful entrepreneur believes it is all due to his/her brilliance and hard work. With that attitude, hubris and the feeling of invincibility ensue. This leads to cockiness and not looking hard enough for Fatal Flaws, or Achilles Heels.

Success results from the confluence of a number of external factors as well as the insight and hard work of the entrepreneur. Ecosystems, markets, supply chains, laws, regulations, investment climate, weather, political conflict all can cause problems. In short, events beyond the control of the entrepreneur are also necessary for success. Modesty and gratitude are not only good public relations but, more importantly, preserve good judgement.

Obviously, you can't rely on luck. You need to be prepared when luck happens. It would be sad if, when your ship comes in, you are hiking in the mountains. But you are totally devoid of good luck, your chances are not good.

- Some steps in entrepreneurship are easier than others. Troubles happen by overlooking the hard parts.

Easy	Hard
Invent something	Raise money, scale up production, sales and customer service
Start a company	Grow a company
Work alone	Build a team
Take charge	Become a leader
Study new entrepreneurial theories	Learn from history
Initiate sales	Build a brand
Fail	Learn from failure

Table 1-1. What's hard about entrepreneurship

Inexperienced entrepreneurs understand the steps in the left-hand column but often are unaware of, or overlook, the steps in the right-hand column.

For example, take the problem of scaling. It is relatively easy to make one of something. But it is an entirely different matter to make millions of the same thing with consistent quality, on time and on budget. Scaling up involves completely different skills than invention. And it is in scaling that companies make money.

Another key point is leadership. Some entrepreneurs confuse giving orders with leadership. Proper leadership involves building trust, sharing a common vision and sensitivity to human relations. True leadership goes far beyond simply giving orders. That is where many entrepreneurs fail.

Finally, it is hard for people to learn from their failures. Entrepreneurs put a lot effort into their failed starts. So, a proper post-mortem is hard. But it is necessary before trying the next time.

Having dealt with the doom and gloom of misconceptions and mistakes, we end this chapter on a high note.

LEARNING ENTREPRENEURSHIP IS USEFUL, EVEN IF YOU DON'T PLAN TO START A COMPANY.

Here's why.

- Knowing entrepreneurship helps you learn to work with limited resources.

- Knowing entrepreneurship helps you learn to partner with small companies. You have a better understanding of what they are thinking.

- Corporate entrepreneurship is an emerging topic of interest for large companies who seek to be more agile or resilient. Many of the topics learned by startups can be useful for corporate entrepreneurs, also known as "intrapreneurs".

- Big companies divest, or spinoff, entities frequently. You may find yourself in a spinoff from a big company and thereby become inadvertently employed by a startup. Knowing some entrepreneurial tools may be useful to your spinoff.

- You may lose your job, or just become tired of it. Knowing entrepreneurship is the best form of job security.

- In an article written at the University of Pennsylvania Wharton school of Business, it is mentioned that, controlling for money, entrepreneurs seem to be happier in their careers then their investment banking peers. "Why MBA Entrepreneurs Are Happier Than Their Peers", Knowledge@Wharton Today, August 23, 2012.

Reasons for this satisfaction vary. Some like the creativity. Some like the independence. However, a key reason for satisfaction was that there was something that needed to be done, and no one else was doing it. Therefore, they have to do it. That sounds like a good motive being an entrepreneur.

ENTREPRENEUR'S ADVANTAGES OVER BIG COMPANIES

Entrepreneurs are rightly concerned about competing against big companies. After all, big companies have certain advantages over entrepreneurs, especially economies of scale and brand recognition.

However, entrepreneurs have advantages of their own. There are the obvious advantages of low overhead, agility and faster decision-making. But these aren't always decisive. For example, fast decision-making isn't always an advantage if you make bad decisions quickly. Here are some less obvious advantages of startup companies.

- Entrepreneurs can custom fit their companies into a niche that big company are aware of, but won't address. Big companies need businesses that are material to their financial results. Therefore, some markets which are perfectly fine for a startup would be too small for a big company. Small companies compete well in niche markets.

- New companies don't need to satisfy an embedded base of customers. While it is true that keeping a customer is much cheaper than selling a new one, embedded customers can sometimes prevent a company from introducing new products.

- The maximum amount of money the entrepreneur can lose is the invested capital. Failure by a big company can cause reputational risk and a loss in market capitalization that exceeds the investment in the new product. Therefore corporate entrepreneurship can be riskier for a big company than for a startup.

- A corollary to this point is that big companies tend to slow their rate of innovation. A study by Wharton and INSEAD showed that when new companies go public, the rate of innovation slows down[3]. This is due to greater investor scrutiny, lower tolerance for failure and the inability to bury mistakes.

Entrepreneurs should not be deterred merely by the presence of big companies in their product space. By asking the right questions, entrepreneurs with constrained resources can compete.

TAKEAWAYS

- Entrepreneurship is highly idiosyncratic. What works in one circumstance may not work in a similar circumstance.

- Rather than learning "answers", you should have questions and tools to find your own answers.

- There are common misconceptions about entrepreneurship which need reconsideration.

- Startups have key advantages over big companies.

- We hope you walk away with vocabulary, processes, strategies, tools, checklists and questions. You should be better prepared to start a relatively complex startup, implement a minimum set of processes and provide yourself the best form of job security.

---

3 "Ready to Take Your Startup Public? Hold That Thought", https://knowledge.wharton.upenn.edu/article/ready-take-start-public-hold-thought/

CHAPTER 2 – ENTREPRENEURIAL PROCESSES

("READY, FIRE, AIM")

The subtitle of this chapter ("ready fire aim") reflects the intended or unintended battle cry of many entrepreneurs. This chapter introduces the idea that process, which means that getting ready and aiming first, is a good advice. The notion of process is uncomfortable to many entrepreneurs. One of the reasons people become entrepreneurs is to avoid staff meetings, paperwork, analysis and the like. However, in order to maximize the outcome of hard work, some process is useful. To start thinking about process you have to think about issues first before pulling the trigger.

"WHAT'S THE BEST WAY TO SURVEY A MARKET BEFORE WORKING ON SOMETHING PEOPLE MAY NOT WANT?"

This was asked by an engineering student in the first day of class and is illustrative of the type of question that those without marketing training have about starting a business. We suggest three options. The first is using Classical MBA Techniques, the second is Minimum Viable Product (MVP) and the third is Product First Strategy, or just forget about analysis and Just Do It.

Classical MBA Techniques	MVP	Product First Strategy
Analyze markets	Conduct experiments	Product First based on instincts
Focus groups Surveys Interviews Funded market research Conjoint analysis (underutilized)	Expose elements of your product Get feedback 'Pivot' and try again	Polaroid Camera Google Glass Segway iPod Cryptocurrency
Find out what the market says. Give the market what it says it wants	Conserves cash while the entrepreneur finds a product/market fit	Highest risk Potential highest reward
Do buyers know what they want?	Can you get good feedback? When to stop pivoting?	Can you stand the risk? Can you create a market?

Table 2-1. How to Survey a Market Before Starting a Company

CLASSICAL MBA TECHNIQUES

We first discuss Classical MBA Techniques. In this method the entrepreneur analyzes markets by conducting secondary and primary research. <u>Secondary research</u> involves gathering printed matter from the library or off of the Internet. This is information that somebody else already knew and published. Therefore, secondary research doesn't tell you anything that someone else doesn't already know.

However, secondary research is necessary as a first step in analysis. It can tell you what has failed before, who the key players are, where you should go for primary research, what questions to ask interviewees and sources for more information.

Therefore, the purpose of secondary research is to provide the basis for <u>primary research</u>. Primary research involves discovery, uncovering information that few people, if anyone, know. This means experiments, interviews and direct observation. Often the secret to success in business is to know something that nobody else knows. This is what you're trying to do in primary research.

The purpose of classical MBA techniques to find out what the market says and then give the market what it says it wants. The problem is that many buyers don't know what they want or provide conflicting wants. Or, they'll tell you something they think you want to hear just to be nice. Sometimes what they want is unrealistic or ephemeral or too simplistic, such as lower price. When feedback is vague, contradictory or lacking in commitment, classical techniques aren't very useful.

MINIMUM VIABLE PRODUCT (MVP)

Another approach to understanding the market is taking an MVP approach. This technique is in vogue due to recent literature on the Lean Startup approach. MVP involves conducting experiments and therefore is a form of primary research. Rather than performing exhaustive market analysis, the entrepreneur conducts experiments by introducing a minimum version of their product into the market. By exposing elements of your product to the market, the entrepreneur is able to obtain feedback. Using the feedback, the entrepreneur pivots in a new direction by modifying the product and re-introducing it into the market. Eventually the entrepreneur is able to find a product that fits a market.

MVPs are intended to conserve cash while looking for a product/market fit. Often this is the most sensible approach for product development and market entry, but not always. Here are some questions about the MVP approach.

- Is the market is already proven, or inevitable? If so, is an MVP necessary at all?

- How do you design the MVP? What's included/omitted from the MVP?

- When do you pivot and in which direction?

- Are you willing to expose your idea to Fast Followers? Fast Followers can get the gist of your product and introduce a product of their own.

- Will you put intellectual property at risk? Product introduction, even in rudimentary form, can cause patent application problems.

- You may get conflicting feedback from market about your MVP. Some respondents will tell you to pivot one way, others in equal numbers will tell you to pivot another way. How do you resolve that?

- How do you price the MVP? Do you give it away? What do you prove by giving it away?

- Will people use your MVP and give you candid feedback when they know it's not the real thing?

- When do you stop pivoting and start a serious product launch?

- Each experiment takes time and money. Do you have the time and money to pivot repeatedly? Maybe it would be better to go to market directly and save time.

Despite these questions the MVP approach is a useful technique in many circumstances, especially for online products where pivoting is cheap and quick. It has taken root in the entrepreneurial literature and is a common way to approach product design. But it may not be useful in every circumstance. Think SpaceX.

One tip we offer is to make it easy for customers to complain on your website. If you have an e-commerce site or mobile app, the last thing your customers to do is to complain on Yelp or Facebook or some other public venue. Allow them to provide feedback in the comments section on your landing page. This feedback can be valuable and is better kept to yourself.

The case of Henry Ford's quadricycle illustrates these questions. In Figure 2-1 we see Henry Ford sitting atop a vehicle which looked like a four wheeled bicycle, called the quadricycle. Was the quadricycle an MVP?

Figure 2-1

What the quadricycle had, and didn't have.

- It had:
    - 2 seats
    - 4 horsepower motor; top speed of 20 mph
    - Price tag of $200

- It did NOT have:
    - A roof
    - A trunk
    - Distance capability or speed of a horse
    - Shock absorbers
    - A reverse gear; it couldn't go backwards without turning around.

So that begs the question, was the quadricycle an MVP for the Model T Ford?

If it was not an MVP, what would have been the MVP for the Model T Ford?

PRODUCT FIRST. WHEN IS IT THE RIGHT STRATEGY?

Having discussed classical MBA techniques and minimum viable product we now turn our attention to the Product First approach.

The Product First approach means forget about market analysis, go with your instinct and Just Do It. Entrepreneurs who take this approach believe they will create markets with their product. They believe, often rightly, that consumers don't know what is technically feasible and therefore cannot be relied on for product guidance. Examples of these would be the Polaroid camera, Google Glass, Segway and iPod. Some of these succeeded; some didn't.

Clearly this is a high-risk approach because you have no market support. Nobody said they wanted your product. You have to believe that when you show it to them, they'll buy it.

However, if your entry cost and opportunity cost are low enough, this could be the lowest-cost entry. Classic MBA techniques and the MVP approach take time and money. The Product First strategy has the highest potential reward if you're able to create or disrupt markets. You have the possibility of creating a game changer. The market is all yours since there is no competition. This approach has the highest risk and the highest reward. Entrepreneurs taking this approach must ask if they can create a market and do they have enough cash to survive until the market understands what they have.

Advocates of this approach include:

* Edwin Land (Polaroid, 1972) - "We don't do market surveys. We create markets with our products"

* Steve Jobs (Apple, 1982) - "Did Alexander Graham Bell do any market research before he invented the phone?"

* Tim Cook (Apple, 2015) - "Apple's job is to create products people didn't know they wanted"

Having said this, we should add that entrepreneurs who take the Product First approach don't ignore marketing completely. There are two functions of marketing; market assessment and market strategy.

Market Assessment asks:	Market Strategy asks:
Are there buyers? Or could there be buyers?	How do you get to these potential buyers?
What's the price they will pay?	Placement. Where do you sell it?
What's the total addressable market (TAM), computed as the product of number of customers times price?	Promotion. Advertising.

Table 2-2. Marketing Functions

While it is true that Land and Jobs didn't spend too much time on assessment, or claimed not to, they did pay a lot of attention to market strategy. Assessment is analytic. Strategy is action oriented. Not every entrepreneur does the assessment but all successful ones are strong on strategy.

When is "Product First" the right approach? Consider these conditions.

- Market is proven or inevitable, e.g. cure for cancer.

- High initial profit margins; early pricing power.
    Often the early segment of the market is not as price sensitive as the majority market.

- Cost of failure, including opportunity cost, is low. So why not take a chance?

- When early entrants can preempt scarce resources. There could be materials that you can control. Or maybe a location when starting a restaurant. Or preempt the supply of drivers for ridesharing.

- Quick network effect in Winner-Take-All markets. Ridesharing is an example of a market where the first company in wins. When Uber or Lyft or Grab or Didi enter a new city, their first order of business is to control as many drivers as they can. More drivers attract more riders, who in turn attract more drivers. The circular effect of drivers attracting riders who then attract more drivers, etc., makes it difficult for followers to gain traction. A major reason why Uber retreated from China was that Didi, who started ridesharing in China just a few months before Uber, was able to control a large number of drivers just before Uber got there.

- When there is a moat, like a patent, which prevents others from competing.

- When there are no Fast Followers to exploit your early mistakes.

Let's summarize some of the pros and cons the "Product First" approach.

Pros	Cons
Intuitive and fun	Your intuition may wrong
Capitalizes on your superior skill	Lack of market support means you may spend a lot of time and money on marketing
The product's first market, you have a monopoly, at least for a while	Buyer inertia. You can run out of money trying to convince the market, before the market realizes your brilliance
It's a must for some startups. For example, fads, markets with early network effects, like ridesharing	Investors may not have your vision; they have inertia just like buyers.
Good if users cannot pivot to a fast-follower	Pioneers get arrows, usually in the back since pioneers are out front
Pre-empts scarce resources	Resources usually don't stay scarce for very long
Can create a market. This strategy is for game changers and disruptors	

Table 2-3. Pros and Cons of the Product First Strategy

To summarize our comments about "What's the best way to survey a market before working on something people may not want?", the entrepreneur has 3 choices;

- Market analysis using classical MBA techniques,
- MVP, and
- "Product First" strategy, or Just Do It.

How do you choose among the three? When building a scorecard, consider these questions.

- Is the market proven or inevitable?
- Do buyers know what they want?
- Can the market provide informed feedback?
- Do you have enough information already?
- Can you afford to conduct experiments and change direction?
- Can fast followers learn from your MVP?
- Is it OK to risk everything without market information?
- Can you afford marketing and sales cost to wait for the market?
- Can you create a game changer?

There is no one-size-fits all answer to the question of market entry strategy. The answer is, it depends. But now you have some questions and tools to answer the question for yourself.

We now turn our attention to another process question, that of milestone selection.

Once the entrepreneur is convinced there is, or could be, a product/market fit, the entrepreneur needs to decide on a set of milestones to achieve ultimate company success. You don't get to your pot of gold in one step. Entrepreneurial success is a multi-step process. Milestone selection is about identifying the sequence of steps necessary to get from the idea to the pot of gold.

Milestones can take various forms. They can be product events, like completion of a prototype or obtaining regulatory approval. Or they could be marketing events, such as obtaining feedback from an MVP. Or they could be financial events, such as raising a certain amount of money. In all cases achieving a milestone is marker of company progress.

Table 2-4 shows 3 examples of milestones. These are Prototype, MVP and Beachhead Market entry. A <u>Prototype</u> is a preliminary version of your final product which demonstrates functionality. It is not necessarily the lowest cost or best performing or best looking version of your product. But it does show what the product is supposed to do and provides a point of departure for final product development.

A <u>Beachhead Market</u> consists of your first customers. Who are the first people to buy your product? We sometimes refer to as the "lowest hanging fruit". There are 3 characteristics of a beachhead market. First, the beachhead market must be winnable by a small company. Secondly, the market must be defendable. Finally, the beachhead market must provide a path to adjacent markets for sales expansion.

For each of these 3 milestones, we identify its purpose, activities in achieving that milestone, what to do next when the milestone it is achieved and whether the milestone is achieved with an internal or externally facing business functions.

	Prototype	MVP	Beachhead Market Entry
Purpose	• Does it work? • Does it do what it's supposed to do? • Cost?	• What do potential buyers think? • Will they accept the price?	• Sell to lowest hanging fruit • Sell to buyers with immediate needs
Key steps	• Fix bugs • Reduce costs • Get a comfortable form factor or user experience	• Product introduction and experimentation • Get feedback and pivot	• Sales analysis • Find new markets • Market traction and stabilization
Next steps	• Customer feedback	• Packaging • Quality • Scaling • Secondary features	• Adjacent markets • Product roadmap
Functional leadership	• Product development • Engineering	• Marketing (External focus)	• Sales

Table 2-4. Samples of Milestones

The following diagram illustrates the process. On the left, there is the idea. Your objective is to get to the Pot of Gold. What's the best way to get there?

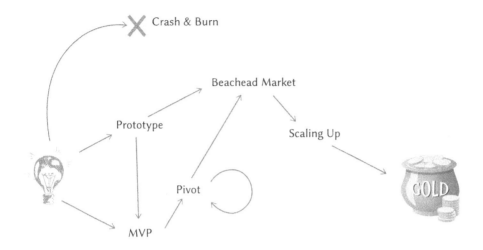

Figure 2-2 Milestone Selection

In Figure 2-2, you start with the idea at the left. What's the first milestone you should select? Prototype or MVP and how do you choose? The choice is largely a function of available resources, how much information you need and the status of product development.

Let's say you choose to do the Prototype. From there you can go to the MVP or take the more aggressive leap the Beachhead Market. If you are successful in getting to the Beachhead, then you have reduced the number of milestones you need to traverse. From the Beachhead you scale up then get to the Pot of Gold.

The entrepreneur could also try to get to the Beachhead as a first step. This further reduces the number of steps to get to the Beachhead. But if you can't make it all the way to the Beachhead, you could crash and burn. The penalty for that is severe. You've sold some equity and have nothing to show for it. The entrepreneur loses leverage when asking for more money. Money is raised on unfavorable terms in order to complete the next milestone. At worst, the company fails.

Here are some requirements about milestone selection.

- Is the milestone clear? Could the investor, or you, know if you have succeeded in reaching it?

- Is the milestone attainable? Can you reach it with the resources you have?

- Is the milestone meaningful? If you hit the next milestone, so what? On the basis of hitting the milestone, can you raise more money?

Milestone selection is industry-specific. For example, if you are developing a new therapeutic drug, then you will have milestones for each phase of FDA testing. Likewise, for semiconductor you may have milestones for tape out, design win and design in.

{Design Win versus Design In}.

"Design Win" means you won a competition and are selected to be the vendor of choice for a company that will use your component in its product. An example is an antenna developer being selected by a cell phone manufacturer. With "Design In", however, the money doesn't come in until the component is designed into the cell phone. It is a more financeable milestone.

Likewise, a Beta Test shows more progress than an Alpha Test. A Beta Test involves outside users. An Alpha Test involves inside developers and thus is less convincing.

There is no need to know all your milestones in advance. Milestone selection is an incremental process. You pick the next milestone based on where you are and how much resource you have.

FINANCING STRATEGY

Milestone selection it is crucial because is tied to financing strategy. Entrepreneurs mistakenly ask investors for "one year of funding". Is this a good idea, or not? No, since you haven't said what you'll do with the money. Investors can't tell if the money was used successfully so there is no accountability for the performance of the management.

Therefore, when you ask for money, you must say what it will be used for. What specific progress will be made with the investment? What milestone(s) will be achieved?

What if you cannot raise enough money to get to your next desired milestone? Then you need to readjust your milestone. There must be alignment between your next milestone and how much money you raise.

In addition to asking for enough money to attain your next milestone, you should ask for a cushion as well. People miss their milestones. People tend to go over budget. You should allow for extra six months of financing just in case. We'll talk more about this when we discuss fundraising.

Milestones that are unclear, unattainable or meaningless make it difficult to raise money.

ECOSYSTEM OVERVIEW

Another part of the entrepreneurial process is to understand your entire ecosystem, not just the market. Milestone selection and therefore financing plan should be informed by analysis of the ecosystem. An overview is in Figure 2-3.

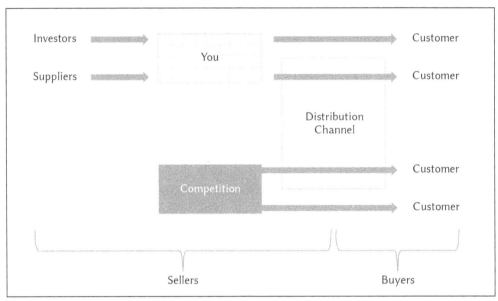

Figure 2-3. Ecosystem Schematic

Your startup company is in the yellow box. The startup accepts inventory and services from suppliers as well as investment capital. In turn, the company produces product and sells to customers directly or through a distribution channel. Likewise, with competitors sell through the same distribution channels and compete directly for end customers. The set of all customers for both the startup and its competitors constitutes the buyers, or market. The set of all suppliers, competitors and distribution channels comprise the sellers.

The success of the startup, in the yellow box, is as dependent on its suppliers as its buyers. Without a functioning, dependable and cost-efficient supply chain, you can't service a market at scale. This is often overlooked by entrepreneurs who focus only on market demand. Feasibility analysis must include analysis of supply chain. For example, airlines are certainly dependent on a supply of jet fuel to operate. However, a crucial supply element is the number of gates at major airports. Without a supply of gates, then planes can't land. Some airports are at capacity in the number of jumbo planes that can be serviced. It's not obvious to the outside observer that gate capacity is a factor in supply chain.

Another point, often overlooked, is the crucial role of distribution channels. In some industries, suppliers can't sell to end users. The distribution channel serves as a necessary intermediary. Entrepreneurs can see the end user demand, but getting to the end user through a channel can be difficult, since channels have their own requirements for carrying product. Industries where these intermediaries play a key role are in hospital supply (Johnson & Johnson, McKesson, American Hospital Supply) and food service (Sysco, US Foods).

The end market may be a monopsony. A monopsony is the inverse of a monopoly. In a monopsony there are very few buyers who are collectively being serviced by many suppliers. For example, there was a lot of innovation by semi-conductor manufacturers in the early 2000's to make mobile phones with extended battery life, better geographic range and higher speed data rates by inventing new types of antennas. The problem was that there were just a handful of cell phone manufacturers; Nokia, Ericsson, Motorola. If one of those few didn't buy product from any of dozens of inventors, those innovators could not survive. It's not good to be in an ecosystem where you are one of many sellers and there are very few buyers.

You can also see from this diagram that there may be hidden sources of competition. The Competitor in the grey box of Figure 2-3 is a company that does the same thing you do. It is also possible that suppliers and/or customers may try to compete against you as well. For example, Apple initially purchased integrated circuits for their computers from Motorola, and then Intel. Finally, they decided to make their own ICs, thereby competing against their supplier. When companies who are customers in a supply chain move upstream to compete against suppliers, we'll call that Backward Integration. When suppliers move forward to compete against their customers, we'll call that Forward Integration. It's not good to compete against your customers but some companies do.

The point here is that an entrepreneur must analyze all these actors, not just buyers, in the ecosystem in order to determine whether a business idea is feasible. Too many entrepreneurs overlook the supply chain and distribution channels and sources of future competition.

BIG FISH, LITTLE POND OR LITTLE FISH, BIG POND?

Now let's move on to market entry. At the beginning of the life of the startup, the entrepreneur can choose to enter big markets or small markets. If you want to be a big, venture capital backed company headed for a big exit, you attack large markets. But it can also make sense to attack small or niche markets. These can support worthwhile lifestyle businesses.

What are some of the pros and cons of each?

- Investors like big ponds. You're not getting their money if you jump into a small pond. But keep in mind that big ponds attract lots of competitors. If you start out as a little fish in the big market, you may stay little.

- On the other hand, by being a big fish in a little niche market, you have less competition and more pricing control. Margins can therefore be more dependable. Niche markets are often ignored by strong competitors due to their small size which restricts long term growth.

- Do you think you can grow your pond? You can possibly get big starting in a niche market but you need a strategy to grow your market or find an adjacent market. Finding an adjacent market is easier if you have already succeeded in another market previously.

- Do you plan your exit or are you OK with the lifestyle business? If you are OK with a lifestyle business, then a niche market is OK. Investors are not interested in lifestyle businesses, but so what!

FOCUS ON ONE THING OR HAVE A PLAN B?

It may be that the entrepreneur has looked at the ecosystem and is still undecided between two equally attractive businesses. Due to indecision, there is a temptation to work on two ideas in parallel. That's a bad idea for the following reasons:

- Entrepreneurs have insufficient resources for one business, let alone two. Don't spread your resources among different ideas, projects, hunches. Concentrate your firepower on one target. You only need to win once.

- Your competitors are putting 100% into their business, while you are putting in 50%.

- Doing multiple things conveys a lack of commitment to investors. Investors are not impressed with the lack of focus.

Of course, it is proper to have backup plans for certain tactical steps, for example in sales and operations. But these are all in support of a single business.

Our message is to choose. If you choose the wrong business, wrap it up quickly and move onto the next business. Entrepreneurship is a serial process, not a parallel process. Do one thing at a time.

These are just a few examples of entrepreneurial processes. In addition, processes are required for:

- Idea generation
- Risk assessment
- Entity formation
- Team building
- Fundraising
- Intellectual property protection

We will deal with these in future chapters.

TAKEAWAYS

- Before "ready, fire, aim", consider some processes before starting out.

- Milestones drive financing. Choose your next milestone based on where you are and how much resource you have to get to the next milestone.

- Entrepreneurship is not just about you. Team and ecosystem count. That's where the opportunities and threats come from.

- Work on one thing at a time. Entrepreneurs work in serial mode, not parallel. Choose.

SELF STUDY

Questions

1. Would a small-scale assembly line to build Model T cars have been a Minimum Viable Product for Henry Ford, circa 1900? Say, an experimental assembly line which produces just a few cars a day in an assembly line process. Would that be an MVP? Why or why not?

2. Why is online retail particularly amenable to the MVP approach?

3. What's the difference between MVP and beachhead?

4. What's the difference between MVP and rapid prototyping?

5. What would be omitted from the MVP of a B2C e-commerce website?

6. Why do some industries, like hospital supply, or food service to restaurants and hotels, find it necessary to use distribution channels, rather than having providers sell directly to end customers?

7. Would the quadricycle have been an MVP for Henry Ford? If not, what would have been an MVP? What would the MVP have?

8. If your client asks you to do something that is not in your business plan, should you say yes or no?

Answers

1. No. An MVP is supposed to help find a product or <u>market</u> fit. The assembly line was an operational improvement to increase productivity. Ford was not in the business of selling assembly lines.

   Instead, his MVP for the Model T would have been to make a few, by hand. The consumer can see and understand the product. Sell them for a price which he could meet with his assembly line. Then see what the market said about not having reverse gear or not having a roof or a trunk.

2. The cost of pivoting is low. Buyers can visualize the product easily and give good feedback. It's relatively easy to decide which features to omit from the MVP. These types of startups are capital constrained and need to conserve cash when doing product development.

3. An MVP is an experiment with no plan to be a "real" product. It exists primarily as a data gathering method to determine market acceptance. A beachhead is a commitment to an introductory but real market. It is not an experiment.

4. Rapid prototype typically tests only functionality and ability to solve problem. There is little market response to pricing, positioning, promotion.

5. Some things to omit from the MVP of a B2C website.

   Scaling - it doesn't have to support a lot of traffic.
   Blog – you are too busy to offer opinions.
   Analytics – there is nothing to analyze yet.
   Order processing – you can process them manually.
   Recommendations – they are hard work and what will you learn by providing them?
   Language translation – to begin with, one language is enough.

6. Too many SKUs and too many sales people to deal with. Using a channel simplifies acquisition for the hospital or the restaurant.

7. It's not an MVP since it didn't have enough features and was much cheaper than a Model T.

   His MVP would have a roof and trunk and more speed and range. He would have built a few by hand and sold them for about the same price as if they were built on an assembly line. He needed to learn if there was a market for a Model T at the price he was anticipating.

8. Probably not since it would defocus you and may affect your brand. You may not have the skills required to do something you didn't plan on. The money may be nice but there is a cost to losing focus.

("I want to be an entrepreneur but I don't have any ideas. How do I get one?")

When this question was raised in class, my silent reaction was "if you don't have any ideas why do you want to be an entrepreneur?". Being your own boss or trying to get rich may not be sufficient motivation to endure the rigors of entrepreneurship. You need an idea that animates you and is compatible with your ecosystem and circumstances. We classify ideas into two broad categories. The first category involves situations in which a product and market already exist. The second involves starting something entirely new. Since the first category already has a product and market, it is overlooked by would-be entrepreneurs. However, inheritance, acquisition of a small business or a spinoff from a big company have many advantages for people with a business background.

WHEN A PRODUCT AND MARKET EXIST

Most would-be entrepreneurs don't think much about inheritance, acquisitions and spinoffs as paths to entrepreneurship since those paths appear to lack creativity. But maybe they should consider these, particularly if they're in it just for the money or the autonomy. Consider these pros and cons of these modalities.

	Pros	Cons
Inheritance	• Culture well defined. • Low cost entry	• Culture well defined, could be a problem • Family problems, nepotism
Acquisition	• Capitalizes on business experience or MBA skills • Many businesses are for sale. Can be choosy.	• Financing • Undisclosed problems. Sellers may try to inflate the valuation of their company.
Spinoff	• Capitalizes on business experience or MBA skills	• Financing • Parent company reluctance to divest. Are they losing their crown jewels? • Appearance of disloyalty by the promoters of the spinoff. Agency problem.

Table 3-1 Pros and Cons of Overlooked Entrepreneurial Options

The presence of a product and market reduces the business problem to strategy and operations and therefore takes a lot of the guesswork (and maybe also the fun) out of starting and running a business.

INHERITANCE

Inheritance is a common form of becoming your own boss. Since the heir is not party to starting the company from the beginning, inheritance is not often considered. Nevertheless, a large percentage of family businesses are passed on to heirs all over the world and for good reason. Market and product risk problems are a solved. The company culture is well defined and the cost of entry for the heir is close to zero, except for maybe opportunity cost. Of course, the company culture could be a negative as well, but if the company is long-lived, then this should be less of a problem.

For example, the extended McIlhenny family in Louisiana has been operating their family Tabasco business since the mid-19th century. In India, the Birla and Tata families have been operating giant conglomerates for well over a century. Well-run family businesses passed down through generations can become long-lasting and very large.

There is ample scope for creativity when inheriting a company. The "elders" may not be familiar with new technologies. There can be great satisfaction, and profit, in upgrading a well-functioning family company with modern technology and business models.

Of course, there are some issues; culture is usually well-defined in a family business, and that could be good or bad. There are the obvious problems of nepotism and family disputes which add drama to the enterprise. However, many of the pains of starting a business are avoided and the manager of the family business can be on a fast track to growth.

{Shinise (shin – ee'-seh.}

{The prevalence of very long-lived, albeit smaller, companies is particularly prevalent in Japan. The Japanese language has a word and Kanji character for long-lived companies. The word is shinise (老舗)

There are over 26,000 companies in Japan which are 100 years or older. Nearly 500 Japanese inns (ryokan) are over 200 years old. Gekkeikan, a brand of sake' now sold in the USA, was founded in 1637.

What makes for long-lived businesses? For the most part, shinise start out as family owned and are passed through inheritance. Eventually inheritance becomes problematic due to lack of heirs or interest, so others are brought in. Food processing (manufacturing of shoyu (soy sauce) or sake'), hospitality (Japanese inns, or ryokans), restaurants and retailers of classic Japanese arts, like calligraphy, washi paper and tatami mats are common types of shinise.

A key to longevity is that shinise target local needs which in turn provide long lasting community support. These aren't just businesses. They become a cultural institution that belongs to the community. Rather than growing a business, the emphasis is staying in business to serve the community. To do so, the company must evolve with the community. So long as the community exists, the company will stay in business. Part of this community involvement is to treat employees as family. Worker pay isn't the highest but for shinise, there is lifetime employment. When workers die, many shinise have annual memorial rites for departed employees for up to 50 years, as is true in many religious traditions.

Another common thread is to avoid raising outside capital, even debt. Grow organically. Keep control. Lack of outside capital, aversion to growth and local community support are key to longevity for many shinise.

Shinise have survived wars, economic ups and downs and Westernization. They constitute an interesting variation on business practice and could provide insight on how small businesses anywhere can survive.}

ACQUISITIONS

The more common, but similar, approach to idea generation is small company acquisition. Many mid-career professionals have some savings with which they can acquire a small business. Small businesses have product(s), customers and a team. In many cases, small businesses are under-managed. They have survived by sheer will and hard work. There wasn't the time or training to implement financial planning, marketing, operations optimization and strategy. A little bit of these can go a long way to improving the prospects of a company that has been managed by common sense and tenacity for years. Many students ask, if they have some money, are they better off buying a business or starting a business. In many, if not most situations, they are better off buying a business. More will be said about this in chapter 18.

SPINOFFS

Spinoffs are another interesting method of idea generation for people with some business back-ground. A spinoff means the creation of new company by the divestiture of a business from a larger enterprise. The initiative to create a spinoff can come from top management or from line management (in a bottoms up approach). Spinoffs, like acquisitions, benefit from a good command of finance, marketing and operations. Since spinoffs have a headstart while being inside a large organization, this type of entrepreneurship has a good track record of success. More will be said about spinoffs in a chapter 19.

We consider acquisitions and spinoffs to be particularly interesting forms of entrepreneurship for people with a formal business education. Since the product and market exist, the new management can focus on growth. So, there is particular value in understanding operations, marketing, sales management, strategy and human resources.

Inheritance, acquisitions and spinoffs all involve taking over an existing business. However, when most students think about entrepreneurship, they think about creativity and starting their own thing from scratch. To start your own thing, you need your own ideas.

Sources of Ideas To Start Your Own Thing.

Here's a list of various techniques we will be discussing.

- Transplantation
- Exploitation of a fad
- Improving operations of an existing enterprise
- Declining markets with long tails. Last man standing.
- Disruption. Demographic, societal, technology
- Find a problem

Transplantation

Transplantation means taking an idea that works in one market and doing it somewhere else. An example of this would be the Williams Sonoma retail outlet for kitchenware. Charles Williams, a resident of Marin County, California, had an interest in cooking and travel. On a trip to Paris he noticed a store that sold pots, pans, kitchen utensils, basically everything you need for the kitchen and dining room. It was all very high-end, suitable for the cuisine of France. Would something like this work in Marin County where there was an appreciation fine dining and wine? He gave it a try. One thing led to another. Williams Sonoma has become a familiar name in this niche.

Starbucks followed a similar path. Howard Schultz, in his job as an espresso machine salesman, went to Italy to find out why so many espresso machines were sold there. He observed the coffee house culture, and saw that Italians are happy to pay more for a good cup of coffee if they have a nice environment to enjoy it in. At the time, coffee shops in the US emphasized low cost and high turnover. When the idea first occurred to Schultz in Italy, he asked himself, "Would this work in the US?". After many of twists and turns, now Starbucks is a behemoth.

Here are some pros and cons of transplantation.

Pros	Cons
Successful model for someone else.	The conditions for success elsewhere may not apply to your ecosystem. Not every detail transplants well.
Product, market and the business model are observable and therefore easily understood	The original entrepreneur can expand to compete in your domain.
No need for creativity. Someone else is doing it already	Little proprietary information to protect
	Why hasn't this been done before where you are? Do others know something you don't know?

Table 3-2 Pros and Cons of Transplantation

FADS

A similar approach would capitalize on fads. Fads come and go quickly so the entrepreneur must move quickly before the fad dies out or before others capitalize on the same fad.

Pros	Cons
Market is proven. Otherwise it wouldn't be a fad	Bad timing. Fads move fast. You might be too late already.
Product, market and the business model are observable and therefore easily understood	Need a rapid product development. Puts a premium on development and operations. Can you execute?
No need for sustainable advantage. It will be over quickly	Fads have short life spans. Therefore, it is difficult to get big and difficult to raise money.
No need for creativity	Little proprietary information to protect
Customers are not too picky	Others see the same fad and will compete

Table 3-3 Pros and Cons of Fads

To capitalize on a fad, the entrepreneur must make quick operational decisions. Among these are outsourcing development, parallel sales channel and having a quick exit or shutdown. For the nimble entrepreneur who is okay with a modest enterprise, this is a fairly low-risk approach.

Improving Operations of an Existing Industry

Mature businesses deliver services using operations that have been honed over many years. However, as technology and consumer tastes change, mature companies run the risk of falling behind on operational improvement. Or new segments can be addressed with mature products, provided there are operational changes.

An example of this would be Southwest Airlines. In 1960 Southwest Airlines was a relatively mature business. However, the new CEO named Herb Kelleher saw the need for a low-cost domestic airline service. To make the service feasible he would need to reconfigure operations and reduce some customer services, thereby making the bet that customers will accept a reduced level of service in exchange for lower fares.

One way to lower operating costs was to have entire fleet of airplanes flying the same aircraft, the Boeing 737. By making all the airplanes the same, training and maintenance costs could be reduced. Also, it gave him more leverage with the Boeing aircraft company.

One reduction of customer service was the elimination of assigned seating, which reduced computer costs. It also meant that passengers had to line up on a first come first served basis, which was derisively referred to as cattle car service. But Southwest's calculation was correct, passengers will put up with waiting in line at the airport to get lower fares. The result was that Southwest, unlike, United, American, Delta and nearly every other major air carrier in the United States, avoided bankruptcy.

Declining Markets

Declining markets are rightly viewed with skepticism by those considering starting a company. However, as an entrepreneurial strategy this approach could work if the number of competitors declines faster than the number of customers. So, there could be a widening gap between supply and demand when supply drops faster than demand. If you are left as the only company serving this market, it could be an opportunity.

An example of this would be the vinyl record retail business. Vinyl records have long given away downloads and streaming music. However, vinyl records continue to have a hard-core following of people who prefer the analog sound of vinyl records and prefer the full-size artwork of an album cover. Search online for 'revival vinyl records' will show a number of articles which indicate vinyl records will be sold for a while.

Pros	Cons
Competitors exit faster than the market declines, thereby widening the gap between supply and demand	No upside. Can't get big.
Laggards can be persistent loyal	Difficult to finance
Customers not price-sensitive. There is little competition.	Supply chain dries up. Parts and suppliers difficult to find or too expensive.
No need for creativity	Bad timing. Maybe too late already.

Table 3-4. Pros and Cons of Declining Businesses

Of course, this is not a scalable story nor is it a story that attracts financing. However, it could be a lifestyle story for entrepreneurs who don't need outside financing, or want to indulge their hobby and love this business.

Disruption

Social, demographic or technological disruption levels the playing field in many markets. Industry leaders lose their dominant position, which provides an opening for entrepreneurs. Chaos is normally good for nimble and well-managed startups.

For example, digital photography disrupted the photography industry. Dominant players Eastman Kodak, Fuji Film and Agfa were quickly outmaneuvered by Apple and other new entrants. Flash memory disrupted hard drives. Streaming audio disrupted CDs and downloads. Technology disruptions create new markets, or take the low end of existing ones, and thereby shift the cost profile of an entire market.

Likewise, social disruptions often introduce chaos of a more long-term nature. Aging and urbanization provide opportunities worldwide. The opening of Vietnam and Myanmar spurred all kinds of new businesses there, providing ample opportunity for Western consumer goods.

Leveling the playing field provides opportunities for new entrants, and entrepreneurs should look for disruption and chaos for possible ideas.

Pros	Cons
Incumbents have relatively little control. No one knows more than anyone else.	You probably don't have any more skills than those being disrupted
Incumbents are tied to existing markets and products. They lack flexibility and can't react to disruption.	Hard to determine long term effect of disruption. Everything is too new.
Where home runs and game changers happen. These markets can get very big.	The market may not want disruption. Buyer inertia applies.
	Hard to acquire resources

Table 3-5. Pros and Cons of Disruption

Find a Problem

Problem solving is often considered the best source ideas. If someone has a problem, they will pay to have the problem solved.

Pros	Cons
Fills a need people will pay for. Buyers are highly motivated	Entrepreneurs tend to overestimate the seriousness of the problem
Some problems are readily apparent. People understand the problem and are waiting for a solution	Other problems may not be obvious to the buyer. The market needs to be trained.
	Others are attacking serious problems already.

Table 3-6. Pros and Cons of Problem Solving

How to classify problems?

It's useful to understand the nature of a problem before deciding whether to solve it or not. We will consider two ways to classify problems. The first is who has the problem. The second is how serious a problem is it.

Who has the problem?

- Problems you have.

    Problems the entrepreneur, or a loved one has, tend to be taken more seriously by the entrepreneur and thus provides long-term motivation - a key ingredient for entrepreneurial success. It doesn't have to be a life-threatening problem. The founder of Instacart hated grocery shopping, so he set about to solve his problem. But for him it was important enough to start a company to fix it.

- Problems others have.

    These could be serious problems. But since you don't have the problem, you may not be as familiar with it, or care as much. Someone who has the problem may compete and have a slight edge in knowledge and familiarity. Nonetheless, it makes sense to look at problems that a lot of people have.

- Problems others don't know they have. This is basically the Product First Approach. Solving these types of problems means convincing the marketplace that they have a problem, which can be expensive. You may be right in the long run, but you may not have sufficient cash to be around when the market turns.

    "Apple's role in life is to give you something you didn't know you wanted" – Tim Cook 2015

How serious is the problem?

- Life saving, like a tourniquet

    If you have a life-saving product, demand for it is highly inelastic, so you can adopt a value-based pricing model. This means pricing according to the value to the customer rather than the cost of production or competition. Demand is said to be inelastic since demand is not responsive to price change. Even as price goes up, demand stays where it is. A liter of water at the neighborhood market costs a dollar or two. However, the same liter of water costs a lot more in the Sahara desert at noon in July. Entrepreneurs should look to provide tourniquets.

- Pain relief, like an aspirin

  Aspirin solves a real problem. But if its price is too high, buyers will live their headache for a while.

- Preventive, like vitamins

  Vitamins are good for you but people can go a long time without them.

- Just fun, like candy

  Candy is bad for you, but people buy it anyway.

The point here is that entrepreneurs tend to overestimate the importance of the problem they intend to solve. Entrepreneurs often think they have a tourniquet when they really have aspirin or vitamins. This causes them to believe where is demand when there isn't any or they misprice their products. Entrepreneurs should ask themselves, "Do I have a tourniquet, an aspirin, vitamins or candy?".

Eli Broad was an entrepreneur who used the problem solving approach. When asked his secret to success, he described his screening process:

- Will it matter many years from now?
- Can someone else do it better?
- Can I get the resources?

In a very long career, two big ideas passed this simple screen. KB homes and SunAmerica both exited for over a billion dollars, and in different fields.

{**Entrepreneur Hall of Fame**}

Our definition of a member of the Entrepreneur Hall of Fame would be someone who started two hugely successful businesses in two different industries. Bill Gates only started one, so he wouldn't be in this Hall of Fame, not that he would care.

Eli Broad would be in it. KB Home was in home construction serving a middle-class mass market. SunAmerica was in financial services. Other candidates? How about Richard Branson (music and airlines), Elon Musk (payments and electric autos), Steve Jobs (computers and movies)?

A less obvious choice would be Patrick Brown. He founded the Public Library of Science (plog.org) which disrupted the scientific publishing business. He later started Impossible Foods (https://impossiblefoods.com), one of the major plant-based protein companies with sales worldwide.

Finally, one can add Sandra Lerner. She was co-founder of Cisco Systems and later founded the cosmetics firm Urban Decay which she later sold to LVMH. You can't get much more broad based than data communications equipment and makeup.

Members of this Hall of Fame tend to be Problem Solvers, even if buyers don't know they have the problem at the beginning.

Armed with these problem characteristics let's take a look at our problem-solving approach shown in the following diagram.

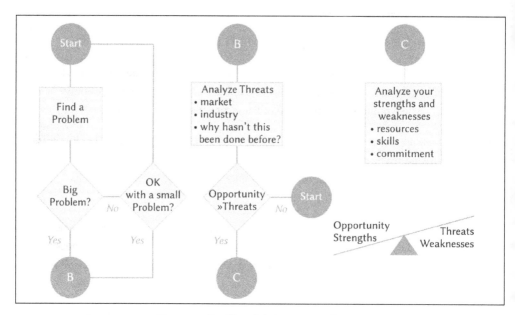

Figure 3-1. Problem Solving Approach.

Notes about this schematic:

- The first step is to find a problem, preferably one you have, or someone close to you has. This provides motivation. Then do some research to decide if the problem is big enough to justify your investment of time and energy.

- At Step B, look at your ecosystem for opportunities and threats. An opportunity is the gap between demand (which should be big) and supply (which should be small). How do you measure demand? You can observe it. If demand is visible, you may be too late but observation gives good information. You can ask people. That's market analysis. Or you can ignore measuring demand and take it on faith that you can create it. That's what Edwin Land of Polaroid believed, correctly.

- Likewise, with supply. You can observe it or you can ask people. Are there competitors now? Or will there soon be competitors?

- Threats come from competitors, a small total available market, an uncooperative supply chain or an inhospitable investment climate. Look for all these threats.

- Only after a look at the ecosystem, then you can look at yourself. Do you have the resources, talent and commitment to see this through? Are you the right person? Can you get the resources needed?

  A common mistake entrepreneurs make is to perform self-assessment before analyzing the ecosystem. This wastes time. You may start a business that caters to your strengths, only the find the world doesn't have a place for you. Look at the world first and then determine where you fit in and how to acquire the necessary resources.

- After all the data gathering, you balance the opportunities and strengths against threats and weaknesses. You are looking for an unfair advantage. The mistake many entrepreneurs make is that in their desire to be an entrepreneur, they kid themselves into thinking they should proceed even though it's a close call. You don't want a fair fight or a level playing field. "If you find yourself in a fair fight, you didn't plan properly" – David Hackworth, US Army Colonel and military journalist.

A Note on 2-Sided Markets

The term "two-sided markets" refers to markets served by platform companies, exemplified by Uber, Airbnb, etc. These are companies that don't hold inventory. Instead, they are software platforms that link suppliers to buyers. For example, in the case of ridesharing, the suppliers are the drivers and the buyers are the passengers. They are said to be two-sided since these companies "sell", or recruit, the suppliers as well as the buyers. If you go to your Uber or Lyft app on your phone, you'll see offers designed to recruit drivers, as well as riders.

Because they are asset light, there is the mistaken view (widely held) that these markets are low cost to enter. Not true. The seeding process to recruit the suppliers is expensive. How does Uber/Lyft get riders if there are no drivers? You need to get the drivers before there are riders. Therefore, the drivers must be subsidized, for a while. This is a subsidy that costs the platform company dearly. Once the drivers come on board, the riders will come. This in turn helps to recruit new drivers, then new riders and the virtuous cycle is in motion. But before that, the entrepreneur must consider the time and money it takes to create network effects when deciding to enter a two-sided market.

Ideas Need Timing

Ideas need proper timing: a good idea at the wrong time loses.

Consider the case of the pop-up toaster. It was invented in 1919, patented in 1921 by Charles Strite (US patent #1,394,450). The marketing problem he had was that there was no commercially available sliced bread when he invented his toaster. People sliced bread manually. It wasn't until a Otto Rohwedder patented machines to make sliced bread years later. Only then could consumers buy sliced bread at a store. Sliced bread was first marketed as Wonder Bread in 1930 by the Continental Baking Company. Strite was about 10 years too early, but he probably had fun, which is what keeps a lot of entrepreneurs going.

In 1973, the Xerox Star computer used a mouse as a data entry device invented at the Stanford Research Institute. A little later, in 1975, the graphical user interface (GUI) was invented at Xerox in 1975. Unfortunately, for Xerox, neither invention made money for them because there were not enough personal computers in existence to make these inventions profitable. Likewise, with their invention of videoconferencing.

Placeware was the earliest incarnation of what we now call groupware or videoconferencing. Now we are familiar with GoToMeeting, WebEx, Zoom and the like. But before these was Placeware by Xerox. Unfortunately, in 1997, there was not a ubiquitous, high-speed, on-demand, network infrastructure which could support videoconferencing so Placeware couldn't find a place largely due to bad timing and an uncooperative ecosystem.

On the other hand, AT&T's inventions of the transistor, laser and communications satellites all proved useful for AT&T. These inventions were perfectly timed to solve the operational problems of AT&T. Not only were these inventions useful for AT&T but they soon spread around the world and into other industries.

Geographic Clustering

Not only do ideas need good timing, they may need to be in the right place as well. Geographic clustering, where many companies in the same industry are located in the same area[1]. For example, Detroit became preeminent in auto production. Likewise, Hollywood is preeminent in movie production. Furthermore, the clustering in Hollywood continues as tech companies from Silicon Valley seek to be near to content developers.

In the digital age when everything is online and there is a lot of air travel and English spoken, one would think that clustering no longer matters. However, what do you do if you need 100 software engineers or specialized equipment or an ecosystem of suppliers, tomorrow? On the other hand, if you are a software engineer, where do you go if you are looking for the hot new companies? Can you capture all the nuances of team building over videoconferencing? Would Eastman Kodak have fared better in digital photography had they been in Silicon Valley and not in upstate New York? Eastman Kodak largely believed that digital photography was just a substitute for film photography. But had they been in Silicon Valley, perhaps they could have

---

[1] Among many other sources about clustering, http://martinprosperity.org/content/venture-capitals-leading-industrial-clusters/

understood earlier that digital photography is very different from merely taking pictures to put into a scrapbook.

One venture capitalist in Asia imposed a condition that some of his invested companies must move from Asia to California. That was in order to be close to a supply of engineers and be face-to-face with key customers.

As certain clusters get more expensive and crowded, other clusters could absorb some of the overflow. Los Angeles, for example, is absorbing some overflow from Silicon Valley. Nonetheless, clustering persists. Human beings live in a physical world. We like connecting with other people face-to-face. Ideas can emerge from small groups. But to get big, clustering is necessary. Though not every business needs it, in order to scale up your business, you may have to move.

Ideas Need Deals

Ideas go nowhere without deals. Deals are needed to assemble the resources to exploit the idea. Suppliers, investors, inventors, partners, employees and customers must come together at the right time to make things happen. To commit people and resources, there must be agreements to get commitment. Timing, thus good luck, is crucial since all these participants and agreements must converge at the same time. Some of these agreements are straightforward, like purchasing inventory from your supply chain. But in other cases, in order to acquire a needed resource, the transactions are more complex, like fundraising, a joint venture or a reseller agreement.

The entrepreneur must have an awareness of the nature of the required deals and key negotiation terms. We'll address many of these deal points in subsequent chapters but, for now, keep in mind that an idea goes nowhere without deals.

A Final Word from Henry Ford

"I invented nothing new. I simply assembled into a car the discoveries of other men behind whom were centuries of work. Had I worked 50 or 10 or even 5 years before, I would have failed.

So it is with every new thing. Progress happens when all the factors that make for it are ready and then it is inevitable. **To teach that a comparatively few men are responsible for the greatest forward steps of mankind is the worst sort of nonsense.**"

Henry Ford understood the importance of timing.

Takeaways

- There are multiple ways to start a business without an original idea.

- If you need an idea, there are many ways to get one.

- For an idea to succeed, the idea must grow in the right place and at the right time. These are necessary so that all parts of the ecosystem come together. Therefore, timing (hence, luck) is important - but be ready when good fortune comes your way.

- Despite all this, the recognition of a good idea and its timing is elusive, even for the best of us. There is an outstanding, successful venture capital firm named Bessemer Venture Partners (bvp.com) with offices in Silicon Valley, Boston, New York, India and Israel. BVP traces its lineage back over a century to Andrew Carnegie's steel empire. It is arguably America's oldest venture capital firm.

   Though BVP has a decades long history of successful investing, the firm has overlooked some major opportunities. But it has the modesty and confidence to admit those over-sights and publish them on its website. It passed on Apple, Google, Intel, FedEx, Facebook and many other familiar names. Search online for 'bvp antiportfolio'.
   If really smart people like BVP can't evaluate ideas correctly all the time, don't be surprised if you can't either.

SELF STUDY

Questions

1. When is a sustainable advantage NOT needed? What types of companies or industries don't need sustainable advantages?

2. Why is the acquisition of a small company a particular effective way for MBA students to become entrepreneurs?

3. Running a coffee shop doesn't seem like a hard problem. There are a lot of coffee shops worldwide. So why did Starbucks get to be so big?

4. Here's a list of ideas. What would be your quick appraisal of each?

   - Sushi in Moscow.

   An American considers starting a luxury restaurant in Moscow for sushi. Locals couldn't or wouldn't start such a restaurant. But a guy named Alan did.

- La Lacquerie.

A mobile service for manicures and pedicures for Silicon Valley. Install 4 or 5 chairs in a recreational vehicle and park it on company parking lots, like at Google. People can get their nails done at lunch time or shortly before or after.

- In-N-Out hamburger chain knockoff in Shanghai.

Would the popular chain of hamburger stands in Southern California work in Shanghai, where there are lots of American hamburger restaurants already?

For each of these, answer the following:

- Who is your competition?
- What's the market?
- What are the fatal flaws? How would you mitigate them?
- Would you have an MVP? If so, what hypotheses would you be testing?

Answers

1. Project oriented companies, like movie production. Companies following fads.

2. MBAs are training in DCF, NPV and other valuation techniques for ongoing businesses.

   They are familiar with marketing techniques to improve the marketing strategies of small companies that never used advertising and digital media for promotion.

   They often have coursework in post M&A integration.

   They learned fundraising techniques from institutional investors

3. Hard to say. We leave this to your consideration. But it starts with ambition, a vision and the ability to raise capital from investors who share that vision.

4. Case discussions

Sushi restaurant in Moscow.

Competition	No sushi competition in Moscow
Major Flaw	Procuring fish, how to get fish when hundreds of miles away from the nearest ocean. Hiring sushi chefs
Market	Asian tourists and expats. Moscovites with international food tastes. Both segments paid premium
MVP	None. Just did it pursuant to cursory market analysis
What happened	Business started with major investment from local investors. It carried on for a couple of years then folded.

La Lacquerie, a Mobile Manucurist

Competition	Brick and mortar nail salons
Major Flaw	Hiring technicians. Major turnover and need to pay premium rates. Low wage labor is hard to come by in Silicon Valley. Each technician could see more clients per day at brick and mortar salons.
Market	Silicon Valley office workers
MVP	None. You either have an Airstream or you don't
What happened	Business sold to a competitor, a traditional nail salon

In-N-Out Hamburger Chain Knock Off in Shanghai

Competition	American and Australian hamburger restaurants in Shanghai. Many American chains for other fast foods. Chinese street food.
Major Flaw	Are there enough Americans who follow the Southern California brand?
Market	American expats and tourists. Local Chinese concerned about food safety and the appeal of a California life style
MVP	None. Relatively low cost rollout and limited menu in any case.
What happened	Big hit. Market evolved to local Chinese who were more interested in food safety.

(People who never take risks, end up working for those who do)

Most risks of starting a business are obvious. For example, the product doesn't work, there are no buyers, the entrepreneur can't execute operationally. However, in this chapter we highlight some less obvious, but no less fatal, risks and possible mitigations. We will group risks into these categories.

- Product
- Market
- Sales
- Competitive
- Financial risk

PRODUCT RISK

Even though a product works as intended, there still can be risks associated the product. Key among these product risks are:

- Commoditization
- Requirement for users to change behavior
- Inability to scale up production
- Uncooperative supply chain
- Lack of a complete product

Commoditization

Commoditization risk means that your product is being replicated by others. Two common responses to commoditization are lower prices or higher quality. Although small companies have less overhead than bigger competitors, they do not have economies of scale. Thus, lowering prices may not be a long-term solution. Better quality can reduce product risk. But better quality usually increases cost. Even if you can provide a higher quality product, making the market aware of your superior quality may take more time and money than you can afford.

Usually, the best antidote to commoditization is a product roadmap. Products must evolve. If not, they become a stationary target, a sitting duck. Entrepreneurs are often too enamored with their product and they fall into the trap of believing a single product can make a company. A product is not a company. A company is a mechanism for making products. Excepting, for example, a cure for cancer, it is rare that a company can succeed with a single product. "Even if you are on the right track, if you just sit there you'll be run over" (Will Rogers).

Requirement for users to change behavior

Remember buyer inertia. If buyers have to change the way they do things to accommodate your product, you have created a market barrier. It's not a good idea to retrain an existing, happy customer without a compelling reason. Mainstream markets don't like being retrained.

Inability to Scale Up Production

While it is possible to make a few high quality widgets under the close supervision of the founder, making thousands of widgets dependably on budget and on time is a different skill altogether. Scaling up involves procedures, controls, discipline and a dependable supply chain. Since the founding team can't do it all themselves, there is a reliance on new hires, equipment and outsourcers which are often outside the scope of, and unfamiliar to, the founders.

An innovative product without the ability to scale merely provides an idea for a fast-follower to take over the market.

Uncooperative Supply Chain

A problem related to scaling up is the inability to get inputs in sufficient quality and quantity to make your business viable. You may have a great recipe for baking bread, but if you can't get the right flour in the quantity or quality needed, your fancy bread recipe won't help you.

A company invented a new type of battery using an exotic material called single wall carbon nanotubes that promised to power automobiles for long distances. The batteries worked fine in the lab but the company could not acquire the nanotubes in sufficient quality and quantity to support profitable businesses, despite the promises of suppliers. The innovative concepts and lab results didn't matter. The supply chain did.

Lack of a Complete Product

When you buy an iPhone, Apple tells you exactly what's in the box. You get a phone, earbuds, cable and a power adapter. We'll call that the "basic product". A "complete product" includes those accessories that make a complete user experience. For example accessories would include extra cables, a protective cover, a mount for your car, and a screen protector. Accessories could be made by you or another company. You know you have arrived when other companies sell accessories to augment your basic product, like Belkin does for Apple.

Or, take the example of an all-electric car. Suppose it is relatively easy to make a basic all-electric car. However, making a complete product would include maintenance, parts, extended warrantees and financing/leasing. These latter product elements are often where long-term profits lie.

Sometimes ancillary products, like accessories, are more profitable than the basic product. For example, gross margin percentage for a specialty cable for an iPhone is considerably more than the iPhone itself. Better margins or not, the basic product will not provide a complete user experience. Consumers want something more and you should consider providing it before the aftermarket does.

MARKET RISK

Entrepreneurs often risk overestimating revenue potential and underestimating sales productivity and expense. Here are some approaches to address this problem.

Measurement of market potential

The term for the potential market size is "total available market" or "total accessible market", both abbreviated as TAM. Market TAMs are normally time-limited by year in order to provide an annual estimate of potential revenue.

How big should the TAM be in order to justify a market entry? Of course, the TAM for a neighborhood restaurant is smaller than for a biotech company. But that doesn't make the restaurant a bad idea. The advisability of entering a market is a function of both the TAM and the investment required to enter the market. If there is a small TAM, that is fine. It only means the investment required to attack that smaller market must also be small.

How is one to measure TAM? The most direct way is to estimate the number of potential customers and multiply by price each customer will pay. In order to estimate the number of customers, you characterize them, segment them into groups and count them. That's the easier part. The harder part is pricing.

Pricing

After you have a very rough estimate on number of potential customers, you need to estimate how much each customer will pay. You don't know the TAM unless you know the price. Anyone can sell anything for a penny. But if you want to stay in business, you need to have a price that yields a profit. It's okay to have introductory pricing but eventually you need to price sustainably. Only then do you know your TAM.

Pricing is a task that entrepreneurs have very little experience with. When you have a new product, there is likely no comparative pricing to go on. You're either going to price it too high or too low. So how is the first-time entrepreneur to think about pricing?

There is a lot of market analysis and modeling that would go into a sophisticated pricing strategy. But the entrepreneur typically doesn't have these tools available. Thus, we would consider taking a more simplified approach. Accordingly, a pricing strategy should consider three factors. These are:

- Cost of production. Clearly you must cover your costs. So be sure you understand your cost accounting and properly allocate fixed costs.

- Competition. If there is no directly competitive product, you need to consider the pricing of equivalent products. If you price to competition, then you may go below production cost. It's OK to be above competitive prices, but you need to give the customer a reason to buy at the higher price point.

- Value pricing. A bottle of water may be priced at $1.00 at your neighborhood store. But if you are in the middle of the desert and it's 100° outside, the price of water goes up. This is value pricing. It reflects on the needs of the buyer and your value proposition at a particular time and place. Of course, all entrepreneurs want to value-price because it is unconstrained by cost or competition. But can you? Do you have a tourniquet or a vitamin?

We said that entrepreneurs rarely get pricing right. Prices are too high or too low. If the price is too high, the market tell you, but if your price is too low, what do you do about that? Raising prices could negatively impact your early purchasers who took a risk in buying your product. This is particularly for subscription services. The market and public reaction won't be good. While your brand is weak and you're relatively unknown, it's best to protect those early buyers. In order for you to raise prices, you need to introduce at least a minor enhancement to provide the cover you need to raise prices. This is yet another reason to have a roadmap.

However, overestimating market demand and underestimating sales is not the end of market risk. A more subtle risk is losing customers over the product lifecycle as the market changes. We now take a look at those changes and examine how they affect the company's growth.

Market Evolution

To get an understanding of the market evolution problem, we refer to the following Figure 4-1. It is taken from a classic text called "Diffusion of Innovations", written by Professor Everett Rogers of Ohio State University in 1962. In the book he estimates the diffusion of innovative products through the economy. Similarly, we use the diagram to illustrate the progress a company makes through various markets, given the same product.

The point we raise here is that markets evolve even as the product ages. The things that attract early buyers, whom we call Innovators, are different from what attracts the mainstream markets, whom we call the Majority Markets. Even if the product stays the same, the buyers change. To elaborate, we'll use Prof Rogers' classification of these different markets as Innovator, Early Adopters, Early Majority, Late Majority and Laggards.

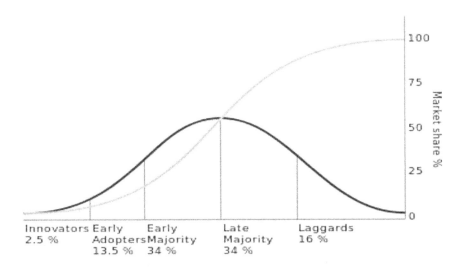

Everett Rogers, "Diffusion of Innovations", 1962

Figure 4-1. Market Evolution of a Product Lifecycle

Innovators

When a new product into the market, it initially attracts buyers who want the newest thing. Rogers called these the Innovators. Using the iPod (2001) as an example, the Innovator Market refers to those people who camp out overnight at the Apple Store to get their hands on the first iPod.

Innovators have psychological needs to be early buyers and are attracted to new things. This segment has the following characteristics,

- They are attracted to a unique look and feel. They appreciate speed, elegance and unique functionality.

- They are price insensitive. They will pay more for being first and are not interested in a bargain, yet.

- They want to be perceived as leaders and in-the-know.

- They want to be admired for having the latest thing.

This is a small market segment, but it is crucial because these buyers pave the way for the Early Adopters and provide important feedback to the company about the later markets.

Early Adopters

After the Innovator market has purchased the new product, the company moves on to the Early Adopters in order to find more buyers. Early Adopters are not as daring as the Innovators but they're not as conservative as the mainstream Majority markets either. These buyers are more pragmatic then Innovators.

What do Early Adopters want?

- They want a solution to a problem. For example, the value proposition of an iPhone is that it obviates the need for separate devices for a separate camera, cell phone, data storage unit and music player. It saves space, money and headaches versus a variety of single purpose products.

- Business-to business (B2B) buyers want a competitive advantage. By being a relatively early buyer of a new product, they may achieve cost or feature improvements over their business competitors who may be wedded to their supply chains. For example, a manufacturer of automobile tires may use a new form of synthetic material which gives longer life or a more comfortable ride than the competition. On the other hand, this tire manufacturer wants to see some real-world use beforehand since they are pragmatic.

- Early Adopters want to see approval from Innovators. They pay attention to word-of-mouth references and recommendations.

- Price is important but not crucial.

- They are willing to be educated but can be harder to please than Innovators.

Majority Markets

For the sake of brevity, we'll group Prof Rogers' Early and Late Majority Markets into a single Majority Market.

In order to scale up to great heights, the company must move past the Innovator and Early Adopter markets and penetrate the Majority market. That's where the money is.

Majority market takes a wait and see attitude. There's considerable buyer's inertia. They want to see what the Innovators and Early Adopters think. They are largely satisfied with the products they have and have no particular reason to change absent some compelling value proposition. The problem for the entrepreneur is that while the Majority market matures, the entrepreneur may run out of cash.

What does do the Majority Market want?

- Ease of use. Broad functionality is fine if users have to change their behavior or run into complex user interfaces, they'll wait.

- References from Early Adopters.

- Customer support. If something breaks or must be returned, they want a company that will fix things or offer refunds.

- Simplicity. They don't like be educated.

- Competition. They like choice.

- Low total cost of ownership, including low or zero switching cost. They are value oriented.

- They care about brand and want to deal with a reputable seller.

- They are often older and thus have been burned by bad products. They are skeptical of outlandish claims. They don't get psychological value in being early.

The entrepreneur should note that as the new product progresses into the Majority market, marketing costs go up. There are more target buyers in more geographic locations with more diversified incumbent products and possibly more competitors to deal with.

Laggards

Finally, there are the Laggards. These are people who may never buy a smartphone. They may be perfectly satisfied with a flip phone or even a land line. Laggards are not necessarily elderly. They simply see no need to adopt new products. Their needs don't change and transition costs may not be justified.

However, as we pointed out earlier in the discussion of Ideas and Declining Markets, there could be opportunity catering to Laggards. It's not a major growth market but it can be stable.

Laggards are loyal. Buyers of vinyl records or automobile carburetors for vintage automobiles are examples. As the number of vinyl record sellers dwindles, the supply/demand situation could change in favor of the supplier since the buyers can be relatively steadfast even as the number of suppliers drops.

The point of this discussion of market evolution is that each market segment has different needs even though the product stays the same. The product/market fit that worked at the beginning may not work later on. If the company is inattentive to the changes in these segments, it risks not being able to sell into them.

The entrepreneur should not be lulled into thinking that the marketing and pricing policies that worked early in the life of the product will work as the product lifecycle matures.

THOUGHTS ON SALES

Selling is a new experience for most entrepreneurs. The thought of asking strangers for money is distasteful, or otherwise difficult, for many entrepreneurs, especially those in high tech. The budding entrepreneur must simply get over this psychological hurdle and start thinking about sales. There are a number of questions about sales the entrepreneur must consider early on.

Indirect or Direct Sales?

One way to deal with an aversion to selling is to use indirect sales channels, or distribution channels. Direct sales means you or your employees sell the product. Indirect sales involves the use of other companies to sell, and possibly service, your product on your behalf.

Although the use of indirect sales avoids the need for face-to-face sales, the entrepreneur starts with direct sales. Indirect channels are unlikely carry products of a startup with no track record. They have products they sell already, so why should they devote time an inventory to an untested product? In addition, it's important for the entrepreneur to obtain firsthand information about the market reaction to their product. If they go through a channel, information from the customers may be filtered.

Once there is direct sales success, there are good reasons to consider distribution channels. Here's a list of functions that the channel can provide:

- Generate sales leads
- Provide pre-sale and proposal support
- Provide customer credit and collection functions
- Provide installation and training of customers
- Stock inventory & spare parts
- Provide post sale service and customer support
- Build local brand image and provide local public relations
- Provide marketing research feedback
- Provide language translation in foreign markets
- Process refunds and exchanges

Each of these services cost money. The entrepreneur must decide which of these services, if any, they want to engage and at what cost.

Reasons to Use Indirect Channels

- Have a trained, instant sales organization with some scale
- Can cover a lot of geography quickly. Also, if customers are thinly distributed, an indirect channel may be necessary to cover a wide geographic area
- Are useful if you can't recruit or train an internal sales force quickly
- May be more cost effective since you only pay for performance
- May be required in certain industries, e.g. medical supply to hospitals
- Are more likely to be successful your product is relatively simple or does not require a lot of pre-sales support

- Can be assigned by territory, segment or application, thereby providing flexibility in your distribution strategy.

Disadvantages of Indirect Channels

Before using an indirect channel, here are some things to consider.

- They can be hard to manage. They are independent businesses with their own priorities, for example:
    - What if they want to resell a competitor's product?
    - How do you set diligence terms and territory?
    - Minimum sales requirement?
    - What do you do if they don't perform?
    - Remember, your reputation rides with them.

- Since they can be hard to manage, you will need a business development function in your company to manage the channel. Duties of business development involve selection and performance management of the channel.

- Potential conflict with direct sales. Occasionally your direct sales team and your indirect channel could conflict when selling to the same customer. You need a mechanism to resolve channel conflict.

- You are shielded from the customer because the channel has the direct interface with your end customer. Startups need to be close to the customer to get feedback.

- It can be hard to find and recruit good channel partners who aren't already selling a competitive product.

- Some channel partners may be poorly managed or undercapitalized so make sure you do your due diligence. Remember, your reputation rides with them.

Comparison of Direct and Indirect Sales Channels

Direct Sales	Indirect Sales (VARs, Resellers, OEMs, Integrators)
Need cash now. The entrepreneur can start selling immediately	Sales are dependent on recruiting and training the channel.
Direct sales requires recruitment and training of sales staff. This is slow to scale.	Quicker to scale, more sales people, larger geography.
Necessary for consultative sales	Better for commodity products
Customer support and enhancements are internally developed.	Resellers can add features of their own, thereby providing the Complete Product
Faster, direct customer feedback.	Harder to obtain customer input. Customer feedback is filtered by the channel
Harder to sell internationally.	Easier to sell internationally. Resellers often have sales organizations established overseas.
Greater control of sales force and message.	Can lose messaging.
Requires sales management skills.	Requires business development and channel management skills.

Table 4-1 Comparison of direct sales with indirect sales.

Questions To Ask Before Deciding Direct or Indirect Channel Partners

- How much time or cash do you have to recruit and train a sales force? Building a sales team takes time and money. Do you have enough of both? If not, you may need to work with channel partners.

- How easy is it to sell the product? The more complex the product, the more likely a direct sales approach is needed.

- How difficult is the product to install and learn? Is product customization required? The more complex the product, the more likely a direct sales approach is needed.

- How many different services will you need from the channel partner and how much will they charge?

- Are prospects geographically dispersed? The more dispersed the sales opportunities, the more the need to work with channel partners. You can't be everywhere at once.

- Do you need the channel partner to add value? For example, to add features, packaging, customer financing, inventory management?

- If the channel partner adds value, whose name will be on the final product going to the customer? Will it be your brand, or the channel partner's?

- How much post-sale service/support will your customers require?

- Will the channel partner work on consignment? Will the channel partner take title to inventory?

- How long is the sales cycle? The longer the sales cycle, the more likely you will need to use internal sales.

- What territory does the channel partner require? Are there exclusivity requirements?

- How do you set objectives for the channel partner and monitor their performance?

Channel partners provide scaling, international coverage, support and other services but they are separate companies with their own priorities. The relationship requires careful monitoring. The entrepreneur should not think that outsourcing sales means an end to sales management.

How do you pay your sales people?

When you're selling directly, consideration must be given to the compensation plan for your sales force. You can create a very entrepreneurial salesforce my incentivizing them purely on revenue maximization. However, the risk here is they may say, or do, anything to make a sale. This could put at risk the reputation of the company or create sales for which the product is not well-suited.

In some cases, companies incentivize the sales force to promote their image or brand. This could happen at the expense of some sales. For example, in pharmaceutical or insurance businesses the sales team must be careful about the claims are making.

Another complicated sales compensation problem is how to pay salespeople when the product has a very long sales cycle. Enterprise software or real estate development are two such cases. How do you incentivize a sales team when the sales process can take months? The strategic question is do you want to incentivize the sales force given the potentially conflicting objectives of revenue maximization and branding while operating in an environment of long sales cycles.

How to handle international sales?

Startups are often tempted to try to sell internationally too soon. International sales can greatly expand market potential but, unless you're selling completely online, selling internationally is very expensive. There are issues with hiring local sales people or sending your salespeople overseas. You will almost certainly need to work with channel partners when you sell internationally. Channel partners have the contacts, and ability to get leads. Their services are costly and the quality of their services must be managed. Be careful about the timing of international sales despite its allure.

Do you really need a VP of Sales?

Start-up companies sometimes consider hiring a vice president of sales early on. However, customers often feel that they are taking a risk by buying from a new company especially if the product is very innovative or expensive. They will often ask to see the person in charge before making a purchase. That means the founder should be the chief sales person early on. Besides, how can the founder recognize the right salesperson if he/she hasn't tried to sell the product personally? The founder also benefits from getting direct feedback from prospective customer. Wait on hiring the vice president of sales until you know there is something to sell and you know how customers are reacting to your product.

Are you spending too much on sales?

How much will sales cost, as a percent of revenue? Depending on industry, you can expect them to cost between 15 to 25 percent of total revenue. Not only do you have to provide a compensation package to attract competent sales people, there is also the extra cost of sales administration. Sales administration involves setting quotas, defining territories and arbitrating disputes among sales people regarding sales credit. If you have indirect channels, the sales coordination involves the management of the channel partner and resolving overlaps with your direct channel.

Excessive sales cost is often a result of poor calibration of <u>customer acquisition costs (CAC)</u> and <u>customer lifetime value (CLV)</u>. CAC is the cost to acquire new customer, calculated by adding the total marketing and sales costs, including sales administration, divided by the number of new customers. For example, if your annual marketing costs are $100,000, your sales expenses are $200,000 and you sign up 500 customers then your CAC is $600.

Customer lifetime value (CLV) is a measure how much revenue you derive from each customer over the total period time in which you have that customer. So, if you have a subscription service, you add up the periodic revenues until the customer goes away. If the customer makes a one-time purchase, as for an automobile, then you take that purchase amount and add ancillary services.

If you divide CAC by CLV you have a metric that should be closely watched. If this ratio as 0.25 or higher, you may have a problem – at least a quarter of your lifetime customer revenue is eaten away by sales and marketing. That doesn't leave much room for production or profit. This ratio over a long period of time should converge to your industry norm. If it's not, you'll either need to reduce your CAC or increase your CLV to get the ratio closer to your industry best practice.

Summary of sales questions for the entrepreneur

The entrepreneur is faced with a number of important sales questions, which is something new for most entrepreneurs.

- What is the beachhead market? Who is the first customer? How do you move on from the beachhead?
- What is the sales process? How do you get leads? What is the role of proposals, demonstrations, face-to-face meetings? How do you shorten the sales process?
- When should you use indirect channels and which of their functions should you use?
- How do you resolve channel conflicts between direct and indirect sales channels? What if two sales people try to sell to the same customer? What if a channel partner tries to sell to the same customer as a direct sales person?
- What are your sales costs? Does the revenue generated by each customer justify the cost to obtain the customer?
- How do you measure the productivity of your sales channels, both direct and indirect?
- How to you recruit, train, compensate and retain sales people?

Products don't sell themselves. You need to go out and buyers.
Remember, it's all talk until there is a sale.

COMPETITIVE RISK

Most people have a basic understanding of competitive analysis but our experience is that there is generally insufficient rigor paid by entrepreneurs in analyzing competition. We recommend constructing a competitive matrix.

A well-documented 2-dimensional display of your product, pricing and other factors will make a good impression on potential investors. It shows you've done your homework and understand the competitive landscape in detail. You will also get an indication of where your strengths and weaknesses lie.

	Your company	Big competitor or Foreign	Small competitor or Domestic
Product features			
Ease of use			
Price			
Financial stability			
Management experience			
Partners			

Table 4-1 A Competitive Matrix.

When constructing a competitive matrix, the competitors that you analyze should be different from each other. For example, you may include one big competitor and a smaller competitor. Or have a foreign competitor and domestic competitor, or include competitors who take a different technical approach from you. The point of this orthogonality is to cover a wide range of competitors on a single page.

The rows of the competitive matrix, should include factors other than the product features and price. Other salient features to compare can be financial stability, management experience and partnering. These can change your view as to whether or not you enjoy a competitive advantage.

When you prepare a competitive matrix, populate the cells with numbers or other verifiable entries. For example, when comparing pricing, put in numbers rather than descriptors such as expensive or inexpensive. Or if you are comparing ease-of-use, indicate how many steps it would take to accomplish a specific task rather than saying simply, easy or difficult.

The best impression is made when your matrix is filled with real data rather than subjective judgments.

FINANCIAL RISK

Ultimately, the reason companies die is that they run out of cash. Cash management is key to survival. The following diagram illustrates some key cash management events in the early life of a startup.

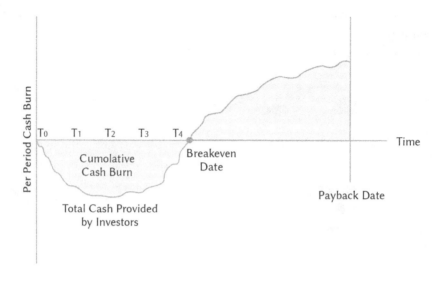

Figure 4-2. Key early stage financing events

In Figure 4-2, the Y-axis denotes the amount of cash burned per unit time, e.g. per month. The company starts life at time To. At time T1 the company is burning a little bit of cash each month and at T2 it is burning more cash each month. Then the company bottoms out and things start to look better so that at T3, the company is burning less cash. At T4 the company is almost at breakeven. The <u>Breakeven Date</u> is that date when revenues equal cost.

The amount of cash you burned from To to the Breakeven Date is the cumulative cash burn which must be financed by investors. After the Breakeven Date, profits can accumulate until the <u>Payback Date</u>. At the Payback Date, the area under the curve between the Breakeven Date and the Payback Date equals the cumulative cash burn. So, in theory, it would be possible to payback the investors.

The question for entrepreneurs is when to raise money and how much money to raise. Does the entrepreneur try to raise money at T1 or T2? Or should the entrepreneur try to squeeze by on initial capital from To to get to T3?

Breakeven is a good milestone. But that does not end your cash problems. You may need more cash to solve scaling and roadmap problems. Therefore, even if you are at breakeven, you still may be fundraising until you are <u>fully-funded</u>. Being fully-funded means the company doesn't need more investment capital since it has sufficient cash to fund growth and product development.

What happens when you almost run out of cash?

Running out of cash kills the company. But <u>almost</u> running out of cash creates some subtle, near fatal, problems as well.

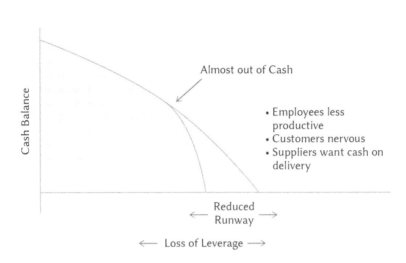

Figure 4-3. Almost running out of cash reduces runway

In Figure 4-3, the Y-axis is cash balance and on the X-axis is time. At time, To, you have some initial cash. As time progresses, cash dwindles. This continues to a point where you could be ALMOST out of cash. At that time, one of 3 bad things can happen. The first is employees may become less productive. They know the company is in trouble so they start looking for jobs while on the job. The second is customers become nervous. They may stop purchasing from you. This is especially true for B2B businesses. If you sell to other businesses then you are part of their supply chain. If they perceive that your part in the supply chain is no longer reliable, then they look elsewhere, even if they like your product. The third bad thing is that suppliers we'll start demanding cash on delivery. You're less likely to get 60 or 90-day payment terms. They want their cash now, accelerating your cash flow problems.

The point here is bad things happen when you're ALMOST out of cash. Entrepreneurs should not think that <u>at their current cash burn rate</u>, they can live for another 6 months, that they actually will live for 6 months. They may have less runway because their cash burn rate could accelerate. Your cash situation deteriorates faster than it otherwise would have and your runway is shortened. Losing leverage with customers, suppliers and investors is deadly. Maintain enough cash in order maintain leverage and bargaining position. Leverage is more important than a few percentage points of dilution.

- There is product risk even if your product works.

- Be mindful of how markets evolve, even if your product doesn't evolve.

- Get comfortable with selling direct. You may not have access to channel partners and you will need to get first-hand information from your customers.

- Not only can you not afford to run out of cash, you should not <u>almost</u> run out of cash.

- Maintain leverage with your suppliers and partners, don't obsess over dilution.

SELF STUDY

Questions

1. Familiarize yourself with the Webvan story. The story can be learned by consulting sources online. You can start with Wikipedia and follow some of the references there or other resources online. Better yet, find other sources for online grocery shopping. Then answer the following:
    - What were market factors that convinced the founders and investors that this was a good idea?
    - What information should Webvan have derived from an MVP? How would you design an MVP?
    - What advantages does brick and mortar grocery stores have over online groceries
    - Other than convenience, what advantages does online groceries have over brick and mortar grocery stores?

2. Why is product risk easier to mitigate than market risk? Why are entrepreneurs rightly more concerned about market risk?

3. A company has annual sales of 100,000 units. The selling price is $100.00 each, variable cost is $60.00 and the allocation of fixed overhead is $3,000,000. You have 2 pricing options.

- Increase sales by 1% by keeping the current price of $100.00
- Increase price by 1% and have the same sales as this year.

Which option would you pick and why?

4. Hospitals now incur a $1.5 billion annual cost due to surgical errors. If there were a device which could eliminate this cost, it would save the industry $1.5B in pain annual. Is $1.5 billion a reasonable estimate for the total available market (TAM) for the device? If not, what is the qualitative difference between pain ($1.5B) and TAM?

5. How is it possible to be unprofitable yet have positive cash flow? Conversely, how can you be profitable yet have poor operating cash flow?

Answers:

1. Webvan

- What were market factors that convinced the founders and investors that this was a good idea?

  The grocery industry is nearly a trillion dollar business in the USA. Investors like Big Ponds.

  Aging. There is a growing number of elderly who can't drive any more.

  Urbanization, makes large grocery stores expensive in dense urban areas.

  Growth of disposable income to pay for convenience, more access to online.

- What information should Webvan have derived from an MVP? How would you design an MVP?

  Webvan needed to learn how much shoppers would buy online and whether the 30 minute delivery time was needed.

  Should design an MVP without the capex, specifically with the warehouses. Contract with brick and mortar grocers, like Instacart does today

- What advantages do brick and mortar grocery stores have over online groceries?

  Familiarity, local brand, ability to pick produce and meat, impulse buying, no need to pay workers to pick groceries.

- Other than convenience, what advantages does online groceries have over brick and mortar grocery stores?

  Long tail inventory, availability of low volume inventory, like ethnic items, impulse buying at the checkout register, no need to pay workers to pick groceries.

2. The entrepreneur has control over product risk. It's internal. There is no control over market risk. You react to it.

3. Raising prices creates a superior profit improvement. The top line for both options is the same, but by increasing volume, variable costs go up. Whereas by simply raising prices, costs stay the same.

   The reason to go with lower prices is if there is a reduction in unit costs due to volume or if the company seeks greater market share. But the price would be lower profits.

4. If TAM = pain, then there is no value proposition for having the product or service. It would cost just as much to buy your product as it would to endure the pain.

5. Investment is a source of cash that doesn't come from profit.

   Conversely, it is possible to increase revenue and, hence, profit. But if the sales go to accounts receivable, that doesn't help your cash flow. Likewise, changes in depreciation and amortization all impact profit (both positively and negatively) but not cash flow.

Chapter 5 – Founders' Issues

"Twenty years from now you will be more disappointed by the things you didn't do than by the ones you did do."
-Mark Twain.

Having sized up ideas and risks, the decision to go ahead with starting the company is made by the founders. Having made the decision to go ahead, they face key early questions. Among these are:

- How do you create the founding team?
- What's in a founders' agreement?
- How should founders' equity be allocated?
- What initial administrative steps must be taken by the founders?
- What's the difference between a founder and an early employee?

HOW DO YOU CREATE THE FOUNDING TEAM?

There are some things you must think about when creating the founding team.

- Account for necessary skills up front.

Not all skills are necessary up front. For example, sales and accounting can be postponed. But the product skills must be in place. You must build something or at least convince people that you could build something.

- Make sure the founding team has a sense of cohesion

  A founding group of strangers is a bad start. Has the team worked together before? Is there alignment on work style and communication? How well does each individual react to stress? With strangers, you don't know how people will react when faced with the inevitable dramatic moment. You don't have to like each other but you need to trust each other.

- Make sure the founding team is a manageable size.

  One is too few. Ten is too many. Three to five would be about the maximum. There is the temptation to start with all your friends and colleagues so as not to offend those who may feel left out. If the company is very high-tech, there may be a need to have several of the inventors involved. However, starting with a large team makes consensus building more cumbersome. Quick decision-making is a key asset for startups.

FOUNDERS' AGREEMENT

Once there is a group which has worked together, understands each other and is manageable, the next step is a founders' agreement. The founders should agree on the following:

- Purpose of the business. What product is the business going to sell? What's the product roadmap? Is the intention to build a business meant to exit or will it be a lifestyle business? What's your business model? For example, if you are in the drug development business, will you license the drug or try to manufacture the drug? Similarly, if you are considering a restaurant, what about catering, packaged foods or event planning?

- Identification of founders and their initial contributions of time, money, intellectual property or other resources.

- Job descriptions. Who is the CEO? Who handles mundane chores like accounting, human resources, real estate problems and customer service? Who will raise money?

- Future work commitment. Who will work full time on the startup? Is it permissible that some founders contribute only cash or intellectual property and not work in the company? What if one of your key inventors is also an Olympic athlete and the Olympic games are next year? What concessions, if any, will you provide to that founder/athlete? (This actually happened to the author.)

- Disposition of shares upon the death or disability of a founder. If a founder/CEO is paralyzed in an auto accident and is incapacitated, what happens to his/her shares? (This also actually happened to the author.)

- Is there a vesting scheduled for each founder? Is there mandatory repurchase of shares at original cost if a founder departs before the vesting period?

- What intellectual property will the company own? For high tech companies, it's possible that one founder has key patent(s) the company needs. Will there be a license agreement between the patent holder and the company or will the patent holder exchange the patent(s) for shares? If there is a license agreement, what are the royalty terms, if any? If patents are exchanged for shares, what is their valuation?

- Financing plans. How much initial cash will each of the founders provide? Is there consensus on future fundraising needs? What role do the founders play in fundraising? There should be alignment among the founders regarding how much money will be raised, when and for what purpose. This can be an early source of conflict among founders since fundraising will cause dilution of ownership.

- Non-compete agreement. If one of the founders leaves and decides to compete against the initial startup, what are you going to do about that? There should also be a provision preventing recruitment of customers or employees by departing founders.

- Role in governance. Who among the founders will sit on the board of directors? Will there be extra compensation or equity for board participation?

- There should be agreement on initial strategies such as:

  - Product first or market first?
  - Milestone selection process?
  - Fundraising strategy?
  - Horizontal or vertical? If vertical, which one?
  - MVP or stealth mode?
  - What are the ambitions of the founders? Lifestyle? IPO?

After making initial decisions, should there be a written contract? Founders' agreements are difficult to enforce. For example, trying to enforce a clause regarding purpose of business could be difficult as circumstances change. Since startups don't have a lot of money for legal fees, drafting a founders' agreement may be overkill. However, at a minimum, founders should have an open discussion to get clarity on key issues before people quit their jobs to start a company.

HOW IS OWNERSHIP ALLOCATED AMONG FOUNDERS?

This is a very tricky problem that must be faced even before starting a company. Getting it wrong can get the company off to a bad start. Let's say three people are involved in producing a movie. One person contributes the script, another raises money and the third manages the production. Who gets what? There is an opportunity for hard feelings at the very start of the enterprise. Here are some factors to consider when allocating initial equity:

- Past contribution, such as cash, creating the idea, prior market research or product development. What are each of these worth?

- Initial contribution. What contribution will each founder make now?

- Future contribution, such as labor, cash. What contributions will each founder make in the future, and when?

- Equal share for everybody, or not?

Too much equality or too much inequality may create problems. If everyone has an equal share, then those who contribute more, either in the past or the future, will feel unfairly treated. If there is too much inequality, then those with lesser ownership will feel the same way. In addition, great inequality of ownership may lead future investors to believe that the team is not cohesive. This is the view of a major Silicon Valley VC firm. The author is aware of one case in which the ownership was so lopsided that the investor demanded the ownership be revised as a condition of investment. The investor felt the main contributor didn't have enough ownership and was not incentivized sufficiently. The equity adjustment was not made and the investment didn't happen.

In a paper entitled, "The First Deal: The Division of Founder Equity in New Ventures", Thomas Hellman and Noam Wasserman of the University of British Columbia and Harvard Business School[1], respectively, the authors note that smaller founding teams, of two or three people, divide equity equally and quickly, often within a few days. With smaller groups there is an element of altruism and resistance to small group conflict. Larger founding teams, of five or more, divide shares unequally, usually in detailed negotiations among the founders that can take longer to complete.

Founders who initially divided shares equally tend to see lower valuations in their first round of outside financing. A possible explanation is that, because they are better negotiators, they tend to get better results when negotiating with investors as well as when negotiating among each other. Moreover, when there is unequal ownership, the founders with higher stakes tend to drive harder bargains with outside investors.

One way to handle the ownership allocation problem is to defer the decision. Provide minimum ownership to everybody and then grant stock options at a later date. But this is a painful process as well – it is best to have some allocation that founders and future investors will be comfortable with.

WHAT ARE ADMINISTRATIVE STEPS THAT FOUNDERS MUST AGREE UPON?

There are some, often overlooked, administrative tasks that founders must complete.

- Picking a company name
- Finding a place to work
- Insurance
- Intellectual property management

Is Picking a Company Name *That* Important?

Picking company name seems to be a simple problem, but there are potential pitfalls. First don't get too fancy, and make it easy to spell since people will go online to look for you. A good

---

1   https://www.nber.org/papers/w16922

company name is "Cisco". It was picked on a whim, since the founders were at a bit of a loss as to the company name. Sandra Lerner and Len Bosack picked the name and created a logo that was an outline of the Golden Gate Bridge in San Francisco. What did the logo have to do with data communications? The bridge symbolized the connection of the city of San Francisco to Marin county, like Cisco's products connected computing equipment. It's easy to spell, the URL was available and there were no trademark issues.

Company names do not have to reflect the business. For example, "International Business Machines" became "IBM", formally. The nature of the IBM business changed over the decades from a company producing computer hardware to a services organization. The name became anachronistic since the old name did not reflect the new reality of the business. Changing a company name is very expensive; you have to change the logo, website links, business cards, promotional materials, stationary, signage. There may be a need to notify the IRS as well. (See https://www.irs.gov/businesses/business-name-change.) Worst of all, it confuses customers. What happens if California Pizza Kitchen starts to sell another type of food?

Finding a place to work

Your personal residence can work for a while, but after a while you may run into zoning restrictions and neighbors may start complaining. You will ultimately need space. When you go out to look for office, or warehouse space, here are some details to consider.

- Tenant improvements (TIs). There may be some light refurbishment needed before you move in, such a paint, carpeting and soundproofing. Will the landlord pay for these, or will you?

- Furniture, fixtures and equipment (FFE). This applies to items that are moveable. For example, if you want to operate a restaurant where there was a restaurant previously, what will you have to pay for the existing stoves, refrigerators, tables and other equipment? This will factor into your initial capital outlay.

- Duration of lease and option for renewal. In particular, can you sublet? Let's suppose things are going badly and you don't need all the space you contracted for. Can you save cost by leasing a part of your facility to someone else? Conversely, if things are going well, then what kind of expansion privileges do you have? Is there room in the same building you can lease, or will you need to move? If you move, you may want to sublet the space you vacate.

- Amenities and parking appropriate to your locale and expected employee pool.

Co-working facilities and incubators are transitional places to work offering flexibility and good amenities. If you need a lot of space, consider the services of brokers who can help with the acquisition of space, particularly for warehousing and manufacturing. This can be a time-consuming headache which may best be solved with professional help.

Insurance

This is another mundane detail that is best solved with professional help. There are lots of insurance policies that entrepreneurs should consider, some more obvious than others:

Obvious insurance policies include:

- Property and casualty. What if someone slips on a banana peel in your office? Or one of your sales people has an auto accident while making a sales call?

- Employee health, life and disability benefits for you and your employees.

- Workers' Compensation. If an employee is hurt on the job, this form of no-fault insurance protects you from an individual suit and is required in many jurisdictions.

Less obvious insurance policies are:

- Directors' and officers' liability (D&O). Any outsider you recruit to sit on your Board of Directors may insist on this insurance, in case he or she is named a lawsuit against the company. Absent this, it may be difficult to recruit board members.

- Key-person insurance. If a key employee, such as the CEO, dies or is disabled, this policy indemnifies the company. Some investors may require this as a condition for investment.

- Business continuation insurance. If the business is prevented from operating, due to, for example, an earthquake, this insurance provides a steady stream of cash until such time as the emergency is fixed and the operations of the company can resume.

Intellectual property (IP) decisions

In later chapters, we will describe protections accorded by patents, trade secrets, copyright and trademarks. Our purpose here is simply to point out that founders make early decisions on IP. For example:

- What are the company's trade secrets?
- What should be patented? How will you decide of an invention needs to be patented or kept as a trade secret?
- Will the company license-in or license-out IP? That is, will it be acquiring IP from others or will it monetize its IP by licensing its inventions to others? For either licensing-in or licensing-out IP, what are the terms?
- How much are you willing to pay to go through the legal process of obtaining patents?
- Do the same licensing questions regarding patents apply to copyrights, trademarks, service marks and trade dress?
- Which of the founders' personal IP will be transferred to the company and under what terms?
- Will you need a <u>material transfer agreement (MTA)</u>? An MTA is a document that protects the company in the event it provides samples to potential licensees of the company's IP.

If intellectual property is a core element of a company's value, then serious thought must be given at the outset.

The point of this discussion about administrative matters is that the company must take care of mundane issues at the start. At the beginning entrepreneurship is exciting. It keeps you up at night thinking of the possibilities. But don't forget about the routine aspects as well.

If you can't do these, learn to do them or find someone who can. Remember, the job isn't done until the paperwork is finished.

We have been talking about founders but early employees are interested parties as well at the beginning.

We mentioned that the founding team must be of manageable size. That means very soon after the start of operations, there will be employee #1. Since employee #1 is joining the company at basically the same time as the founders, she is taking roughly the same risk as the founders. Yet employee #1 does not get founder shares and has no voting rights or any control. What will induce employee #1 to join so early?

The key difference between founders and early employees is that founders must contribute something, like money, to start the company. Early employees don't. So, if the company fails, employee #1 only loses time, whereas the founders will lose their contributed capital.

On the other hand, since founders pay for their founder shares, they get capital gains treatment in the event that things go well. Generally, early employees get stock options which are treated as ordinary income.

Table 5-1 illustrates the differences between the founders and employee #1.

	Founders	Early Employees
Equity compensation	Stock	Options or restricted shares
How is equity obtained?	Purchased	Granted
Capital gains treatment	Yes	No
Voting rights, Board membership	Yes	No
Cost basis of stock	Lower	Higher than founders
Risk in case the company fails	Loss of contributed capital	Loss of time and opportunity cost

Table 5-1. Differences between Founders and Early Employees

Broadly stated, the difference between founders and early employees is that Founders get favorable tax treatment and control but risk losing initial capital. Early employees bear most of the risk of being a founders with less benefit. Hence, there is the desire by early employees to be considered as founders, which tends to expand the size of the founders group and can be the cause of some tension early on.

WHERE DO SUCCESSFUL HIGH-TECH ENTREPRENEURS COME FROM?

According to a study entitled "Entrepreneurial Spawning of Scientists and Engineers", Elfenbein, Hamilton, Zenger, Washington University, St. Louis, 2008.[2]) they come from smaller, but not tiny, prior companies.

When you work for a small company, you observe what a CEO does, good or bad. In a large company, it is rare for employees to meet top management in person. But observing a CEO provides good object lessons for the attentive, would-be entrepreneur. They see first-hand the mistakes that the CEO makes and take those lessons to their own start-up company. The study documented that 50% of high-tech entrepreneurs came from firms with 25 or fewer employees and 66% came from firms of less than 100. Furthermore, scientists and engineers who come from small companies tend to be more successful than those who come from big companies or universities.

When working in a small company, you must wear a variety of hats. In a large company, professionals work in silos. Engineers do engineering, sales people sell, and that's all. But in a small company engineers may have to sell, sales people may get involved in accounting and finance. The number of business functions (production, operations, sales, finance and the like) is the same as large companies but there are fewer people. Thus, everybody has to wear more hats. Working in a small company provides an opportunity to learn a variety of business functions and thus provides training for the engineer to go off on her own.

So, if you want to learn entrepreneurship in a high-tech environment, work for a smaller, but successful company and see what works on someone else's time and money.

WHEN AND UNDER WHAT CONDITIONS SHOULD FOUNDERS BE REPLACED?

When someone starts a company, there is the presumption that one of the founders should be the CEO and maybe be CEO for as long as that person wants to be CEO. It becomes a sort of birthright.

However, it may be that the founder is not the right person to run things for long. Or, maybe the founder wants to leave if the job is overwhelming or just not fun anymore. Some go willingly, others go reluctantly. The transition, or even the discussion of a transition, in leadership can be traumatic to the company and the persons involved.

---

2   Search for 'Entrepreneurial Spawning Elfenbein' for links to this study.

Ben Horowitz, the very successful venture capitalist with the firm of Andreesen Horowitz, speaks for many investors and entrepreneurs when he argues that founders should never be replaced because they have[3]:

- Domain knowledge
- Moral authority
- Greater commitment to the company

Accordingly, he points to a long list of entrepreneurs who started companies and ran them until they became billion-dollar, publicly traded enterprises. Jeff Bezos of Amazon and Bill Gates of Microsoft to name just two of many that he cites.

An alternative point of view goes as follows. If one partitions the life of a startup into 3 stages, we see that the role of the CEO is different for each stage. The 3 stages are

- Founders/Evangelist, when the company is brand-new, then
- Growth/Process, when the company experiences growth and
- Fiduciary/Ambassador, when the company has achieved brand name status.

Here are characteristics of each stage to show why the job of CEO changes.

Stage One: Founder/Evangelist

At this stage, the company has very little except the energy and vision of the founders. Key functions of the founder are:

- Make people believe, when there is little to go on. The founder's main role is that of an evangelist. The founder must sell employees, investors and customers on a vision.

- Makes all key decisions. Since there are so few people involved, the founders make all the decisions. In fact, that's why many become entrepreneurs; they want to be the decision maker.

- Raises money when it's the hardest. Founders raise money based largely on good storytelling and less on financial metrics.

3   On the Andreessen Horowitz website. https://a16z.com/2010/04/28/why-we-prefer-founding-ceos/

- Operates with the least amount of information. Founders are comfortable making decisions based on insufficient or conflicting information. They are comfortable with ambiguity.

- Focuses on cash management, less on profits and assets. You must make payroll and pay vendors. Cash is king, profits come later.

- Hires people they know. A strong sense of trust is needed and there is a reliance on people they already know and trust. This builds a work culture. But eventually the pool of competent friends is exhausted.

Then, as the company grows, the role of the CEO changes.

Stage Two: Growth/Process

The company is growing and requires formal processes to manage growth.

- The company needs more people. Hence the company starts hiring strangers. A vetting process is necessary as well as training, disciplining and terminating employees. This is the start of bureaucracy.

- Not only that, the company starts delegating authority to strangers. This is hard for many entrepreneurs who started the business in order to have control. They are reluctant to delegate and thereby relinquish some control.

- The company gathers and analyzes more information. Many evangelists prefer to operate on intuition. But as the enterprise grows, it needs to be more data-driven.

- Changes financial focus from cash to strategy.

- Implements process. Staff meetings, budgets, vetting and observing regulations become necessary to manage a group of people who don't know each other. Thus, more bureaucracy, more execution, and less evangelism.

When the company gets very big, things change again.

Stage Three. Fiduciary/Ambassador.

When a company gets very large, it has assets to protect, particularly its brand. There is a fiduciary responsibility to shareholders, regulators and, possibly, the public that many evangelists are not suited for. At this stage the job becomes fiduciary and ambassadorial. The job includes the following:

- Guarding the assets. Big companies have lots of assets to protect. The management cannot be cavalier on how it manages those assets, as they perhaps did in earlier stages. Shareholders are watching and want the management to protect those assets. This induces some conservatism in decision making that the State One or Stage Two CEO may find uncomfortable.

- Guarding the brand. At a sufficiently large scale, the most important asset of a company is its brand. Managing optics and behavior becomes important. The Fiduciary/Ambassador is sensitive to that.

- Managing to capacity utilization and investment targets. There is less concentration on inventiveness and more on execution and meeting financial targets. How well are the assets of the company being used?

- Courting Mainstream or Majority markets. At Stage One the company can sell to Innovators or Early Adopters. But as the company and its products mature, it must cater to the masses. This requires a different approach to sales, customer support, product development and marketing than simply introducing innovations.

- Courting Wall Street and major investors. If the company is publicly traded, the Securities and Exchange Commission (SEC) in the United States, and analogous regulatory bodies in other countries, become involved in the oversight of the company. This is an audience that the Evangelist and the Process manager didn't have to deal with.

- Managing cultural diversity. This is the key difficulty in managing a large company versus a small company. In a small company, people know each other. They know each others' work habits and performance. In a large company, there are many different work styles and cultural pockets. Managing diverse populations is a key behavioral challenge, particularly when new products, markets or outside stimuli, for example, regulation, impinge on the company.

- Jerry Yang (Yahoo), Travis Kalanick (Uber) and Adam Neumann (WeWork) are examples of excellent Evangelists and growth CEOs, who had problems adapting to the ambassadorial role.

This is why founding CEOs don't often last; the job changes.

In many instances the investor replaces the founders. When entering into delicate negotiations with the founder about his removal, they often ask "would you rather be king or would you rather be rich?" Many entrepreneurs happily step aside either knowing the job changed or because they are no longer having fun. In other instances, the founders will hang on as long as possible. Sometimes it works, sometimes it doesn't.

The case of Cisco Systems is a case in point. Cisco was founded by a smart pair of technologists at Stanford University, Len Bosack and Sandra Lerner. They built their first piece of data communications equipment in 1986. Within a year or so, the company had over $1 million in sales. Sequoia Capital invested in Cisco and immediately ousted Bosack and Lerner. The CEO job was handed to John Morgridge who stayed until 1995. In 1995 John Chambers became CEO.

By this model, Bosack and Lerner were the evangelists. They wanted to remain but the investors felt that process was needed to manage growth. Morgridge succeeded at this stage. Sandra Lerner was not happy about being forced out and said so on an interview with NPR[4]. But, interestingly, after a few years, Morgridge relinquished the CEO role to John Chambers, who was subsequently CEO for 20 years. Chambers was well suited to the ambassador role. He like being on CNBC and Bloomberg, wearing nice suits and selling. He dealt very well with Wall Street and the media.

Of all the American manufacturers of data communications equipment, Cisco has maintained its leadership role. One can argue that Cisco managed the transition from Evangelism to Growth to Ambassadorship better than any of its competitors and that explains its long-term leadership position.

ARE ENTREPRENEURS BORN OR MADE?

The reason this question comes up is that many (modest, self-effacing, introverted) people feel they don't have the genetics for entrepreneurship and therefore should not think about starting a business.

We don't think there is a gene. Entrepreneurship can be taught[5]. There have been entrepreneurs around the world for centures and millions of people around the world are entrepreneurs

---

4   https://www.npr.org/2018/09/28/652663380/cisco-systems-urban-decay-sandy-lerner

5   https://hbswk.hbs.edu/item/entrepreneurship-it-can-be-taught

today. Therefore, it's hard to say there is a rare gene for it. Founders are regular people who come to entrepreneurship by in a variety of ways.

- Some are problem solvers, some are opportunists, some are tinkerers, some are fixers of other people's ideas.

- Some entrepreneurs want to change the world. Steve Jobs famously said he wanted to make a dent in the universe.

- Many simply want to provide for their families and have a good time doing it.

- Some entrepreneurs have big company experience and want to have more control over their lives.

- Some have a hobby they want to monetize.

- Many are forced by circumstance into it. Globally, the majority of entrepreneurs have no choice. In developed economies, people may lose their jobs in an economic downturn. In developing countries, their economies don't create enough job opportunities. So they must hustle.

All these are legitimate motivations to entrepreneurship.

In any case, it doesn't matter if entrepreneurs are born or made. There are tools and processes that can be used whether or not there is an entrepreneurial gene.

The important point is that you (too) can be an entrepreneur.

TAKEAWAYS

The formation of a founding team is the key early test for entrepreneurial success.

- Founders need to make early administrative and strategic decisions, or the decisions will be made for them.

- There is a big difference between founders and early employees.

- Don't expect to stay in the founding role forever as the job of the CEO changes as the company grows.

- You can be an entrepreneur.

SELF STUDY

Questions

1. The Case of Garrett's Dilemma.

   There was a situation in which a faculty member had 2 PhD students working on a patentable invention. The 3 decided to form the company. The faculty member and one PhD student, named Bonnie, were the inventors, with their names on the patent. Garrett was the other PhD student in the same lab but was not involved with the invention and thus was not named on the patent. However, after the patent was filed, Garrett became more involved with the lab work and making the invention more cost effective. The 2 patent holders took 85% of the ownership of the newly formed company. Additionally, Garrett was willing to make a full-time commitment to the startup, whereas Bonnie needed to complete her PhD and was thus working only part time. The faculty member kept his faculty position and was only providing periodic consulting service. Is this a fair allocation for Garrett?

2. The Case of the 5% Business Plan

   There was a situation in which a student had a business idea but didn't know how to write a business plan. She recruited the assistance of a team of 5 MBA students who agreed to write a business plan as part of their classroom requirement in a business plan writing class. The business plan was well done and as a result, the founding student was able to raise a small bit of money. None of the 5 students who wrote the plan were willing to continue with the startup. They all had student loans and needed regular paying jobs. However, they felt their plan was worth of some equity. They jointly asked for 5% equity in the company, even though none of them intended to work for the company or make any further contributions. Is a business plan worth 5%?

Answers:

1. Garrett didn't think it was fair, but fairness is determined by what he would do about it. Eventually it was agreed he would be granted more shares through a stock option agreement. However, the increased number of shares didn't satisfy him and he soon left the enterprise. The enterprise later died.

2. Business plans are not worth anywhere near 5% equity. Investors who come along later would object to this amount of "dead equity". Dead equity refers to shares which cannot be put to product use, like attracting staff. A business plan, though important, is a one-time work for hire which can be paid for in cash, like any consulting fee.

Chapter 6 – Legal Considerations for Entrepreneurs – Choice of Entity

Previously we talked about administrative details in setting up a company. In doing so, there are a number of legal details be aware of during the creation of the company and shortly thereafter. Here's a short list of some legal considerations.

- Choice of entity
- Equity compensation
- Startup HR/employment issues
- Legal issues regarding raising capital
- Common legal errors
- Working with lawyers
- Intellectual property

In this chapter, we'll discuss the choice of entity. We will address the other topics in later chapters.

Choice of entity refers to the selection of a form of the legal organization of the new company. A key function of having a legal organization is to separate the founder's personal assets from the business in order to protect the founder against liabilities incurred by the business, especially bankruptcy. In addition to liability protection, the choice of entity has tax and control consequences as well.

Due to these considerations, the choice of entity can generate anxiety for first time entrepreneurs. They are concerned about being an LLC, S corporation or C Corporation without knowing what the terms mean. But this choice shouldn't generate such angst. Choice of entity is an important legal consideration, but it can be changed, so the choice of entity is not a make-or-break decision. If it is necessary to change the form of entity there is a cost in time and money. And, in any case, knowing the jargon, the forms of protection and tax consequences is useful.

Each type of entity has different setup costs, taxation, control provisions and interest to investors. Table 6-1 displays key differences among different forms of entity. The "Management" column refers to individuals or business entities that have formal legal authority over the enterprise.

Type of entity	Who has liability protection	Entity pays taxes?	Management
Sole Proprietorship	No one	No	Proprietor
General Partnership	No one	No	All the partners
Limited Partnership	General Partners – No Limited Partners - Yes	No	General Partners
Limited Liability Company (LLC)	Members	No	Managing Members
S Corporation	Shareholders	No	Board of Directors, which derives its authority from shareholders
C Corporation	Shareholders	Yes	Board of Directors, which derives its authority from shareholders

Table 6-1. Choices of Entity

SOLE PROPRIETORSHIP

If a company consists of one person and does not do any paperwork with any government agency to form a legal entity, by definition the business is a sole proprietorship. It is the DEFAULT entity for a one-person business.

If you are starting a simple lemonade stand on the corner, there's probably little need to setup a legal entity. A single person can engage in business.

But even if you are a simple lemonade stand, there may be a need to register your business with a local authority, in order to obtain a business license. You may also need a business license to open a bank account in the name of the business, rather than cycling funds through your personal bank account.

Local registration may also require the filing of a DBA, 'doing business as' name. This puts the public on notice that the name of the business is the DBA rather than you, personally.

The Sole Proprietorship, as a business entity, pays no Federal income taxes. All profits and losses are passed through to the personal income taxes of the proprietor. Hence, the Sole Proprietorship is called a pass-through entity. This can be good or bad for the proprietor depending on the profitability of the enterprise and the tax situation of the proprietor.

We emphasize there is no liability protection in sole proprietorships, meaning your house could be subject to creditors or tort claims (someone getting sick from drinking your lemonade, for example). Due to a lack of liability protection, this form of entity is not a good idea.

What if 2 people start a business and don't take legal steps to form an entity? The default form of entity when 2 or more people work together, (whether they know it or not) is a general partnership.

The Case of Alan and Jack, who were once good friends

We illustrate the problem of a general partnership by way of an example. Alan and Jack were colleagues and personal friends involved in the restaurant business. Alan owned and operated a series of restaurants over a 30-year career as a restaurant entrepreneur. Jack operated restaurants for various major international hotel chains.

A restauranteur named Philippe wanted to sell his restaurant in Santa Monica, California, eponymously named Philippe's. Philippe's had revenues of about $3 million per year but was just a breakeven proposition. That was due largely to Philippe having other restaurants in the Los Angeles area, which diverted his attention.

Word quickly circulated by word of mouth that Philippe wanted out of his lease and have someone else take over the restaurant. Alan and Jack discussed the matter with Philippe and the landlord. While negotiations were ongoing, Jack took a job running a restaurant for a luxury hotel in Asia. Alan was left alone to pursue the venture.

In a few months, Alan took over Philippe's. A few months after he did, he got a call from Jack inquiring about the restaurant. How was it doing and what was his split of profits? No written agreement was ever consummated between Alan and Jack. When Jack left for Asia, Alan assumed Jack was out of the picture. Jack asserted there was a partnership due to their long-standing relationship and his early involvement in negotiations. Alan didn't know he was in a general partnership. Jack said since he was part of the negotiation and contributed some ideas about running the restaurant, he was a partner.

Under Alan's sole management, the new restaurant did reasonably well. This made Jack unwilling to walk away from his "share" in the partnership, and he sued Alan asking for half the profits. Since there was no formal agreement, Alan's defense against Jack was that they had not *acted* like a partnership. They only had informal discussions with each other and Philippe. These, Alan said, did not to rise to the level of a business association.

After a series of depositions, the case went to trial. Alan prevailed when the judge issued a summary judgement in his favor. However, the experience took a financial and emotional toll on Alan and he retired shortly after the trial. He never spoke with Jack again after 30 years of friendship and collaboration. Alan and Jack could have saved themselves some legal expenses, and a friendship, by having a founders' agreement, regardless of form of entity.

Another point about general partnerships, is that each individual partner is responsible for the others' errors. After a series of corporate scandals, like Enron, accounting firms are no longer in this form.

The lesson here is that, while a general partnership does not require documentation, there should be a written partnership agreement. Who are the partners and how are they admitted and terminated? Who gets what? Who does what? Many of the issues to be raised in the general partnership agreement would mirror the elements of a founder's agreement for corporations which we discussed in chapter 5 on founders.

As with sole proprietorships, general partnerships pay no income tax. They are pass-through entities. All profits and losses are recorded against the personal income taxes of the partners. This can be good or bad for the partners depending on the profitability of the enterprise and their respective tax situations.

Because of the sharing of liability among partners, this is no longer a popular choice of entity, for good reason.

LIMITED PARTNERSHIP

To avoid the shared liability problems of the general partnership, there is an important variant of that form called the limited partnership.

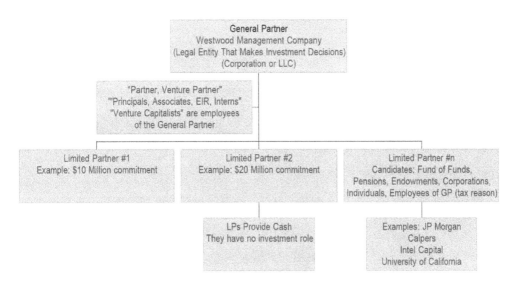

Figure 6-1. Schematic of a Limited Partnership

In a limited partnership, some partners are more equal than others. There is an entity called a general partner (GP) and others called limited partners (LPs). The GP (not to be confused with the form of entity described above) and the various LPs could be individual human beings or business entities, such as a corporation or partnership. The GP controls the Limited Partnership, makes the business decisions and thereby incurs liability. The LPs have no control over the operations of the entity and, hence, have no liability. Thus, the term limited partnership.

In Figure 6-1, we diagram the case of a limited partnership we'll call Westwood 1. Westwood 1 raised $80 million for the purpose of investing in startup companies. Westwood 1 has a general partner which is the Westwood Management Company, which makes all the investment decisions. In this case Westwood Management Company is a corporation.

Here there are 3 limited partners. LP #1 invested $10 million, and therefore holds 12.5% of the partnership. LP #2 invested $20 million and therefore holds 25%. The remaining 62.5% is owned by LP #3. You may wonder how the general partner gets paid, and we'll discuss this in chapter 10 on venture capital.

This form entity requires a contract called a limited partnership agreement (LPA) which binds the various LPs to the GP. It specifies, among many other details:

- The amount to be invested and the terms by which funds are released by each LP to the GP.
- What happens when a particular limited partner is no longer interested and staying with the limited partnership.
- How the GP is to be paid.

LPAs are complex legal documents. If you choose this form of entity, reserve time and money for legal bills.

As with sole proprietorships and general partnerships, limited partnerships are pass-through entities.

LIMITED LIABILITY COMPANY (LLC)

In the case of a limited partnership, the general partner has liability. A refinement of that form is called the limited liability company (LLC). In this form all partners have liability protection. To distinguish this form from a limited partnership, the owners of an LLC are called members, not partners or shareholders.

Since all members could have a management role, there needs to be an agreement amongst all members as to the management and operations of the company and the role of each member in the company. That agreement is called an operating agreement (OA). The OA covers many issues normally covered by corporate law. Since an LLC is not a corporation, the LLC must write the rules of engagement for itself. For example, what happens to the other members when one member wants to leave? How are new members admitted? How does a particular member acquire greater membership interest due to recent contributions? In a corporation you just buy more shares, but in an LLC there is a bit more paperwork to deal with changes in ownership. These mechanics must be documented in the OA.

The OA defines who the members are. If there are changes in membership then the OA could change. Because of that the LLC works better for enterprises whose ownership is relatively static. This is unlike the situation of the startup company which is constantly adding owners due to the need for further fundraising.

Like a limited partnership or general partnership, an LLC is a pass-through entity. Profits and losses flow through to the individual members. However, U.S. tax law gives LLCs the choice of being taxed as corporation or a partnership. Choosing to be taxed as a corporation seems odd but it protects members from being taxed individually on the profits of the LLC. This choice is not available to limited partnerships.

An LLC is often used when founders contribute something other than money, such as a movie script or a patent. This allows the contributor of the script or patent to receive a larger equity interest in the enterprise than would otherwise be available by contributing cash. For example, in the case of a movie production, the script writer or other artists.

Who gets what? With an LLC you can get be specific about ownership, regardless of cash contribution. The script writer can get 30%, other artists can get 20% and cash investors can get the remaining equity. These percentages are specified in the OA. Hence the LLC is a very flexible form of allocating ownership for project-oriented enterprises, like a movie production or real estate development, since the membership doesn't change much.

C CORPORATION

For a variety of tax and control reasons, the form of entity preferred by investors is the C Corporation, so designated in Subchapter C of the US Federal Tax Code. Search for "irs subchapter c" for official language about C Corporations.

In a C Corporation, ownership of the entity is vested in the shareholders and the shareholders have liability protection. Not all shareholders are alike and therefore the shares they purchase are not alike. Large investors seek rights over other shareholders. We call these rights preferences and shares that have these preferences are called preferred shares. Preferred shareholders have rights not accorded to common shareholders. Some preferred shareholders have rights superior, or senior, to other preferred shareholders. We will say more about preferences when we discuss fundraising.

Class and Series Rights

Shareholders in C Corporations are divided into 2 <u>classes</u>. These classes are common shareholders (typically issued to employees and founders) and preferred shareholders (typically reserved for investors). Common stock is sometimes referred to as the <u>residual class</u> because, in the case of bankruptcy, common shareholders get what is left after the creditors and preferred shareholders get their shares. As you can expect, the common shareholders get next to nothing if the C Corporation becomes bankrupt.

The class of preferred shareholders is further divided into different <u>series</u>. The first time a company raises money from an institutional investor, like a venture capital firm, the transaction is called Series A fundraise. The second time is Series B, the third time is Series C, and so on. Each series of preferred shareholders has separately negotiated rights since their respective investments come at different times, from different investors and in different amounts of money. Therefore, each series of preferred shareholder may, or may not, have preferences senior to other preferred shareholders.

We illustrate seniority by discussing provisions for membership on the board of directors.

When the founders start a company, they will issue themselves common stock and decide who is on the board of directors.

When the Series A investor comes along, the Series A will get preferred shares. One of the preferences could be a reserved seat on the board. Therefore, after Series A, there will be founders, who have common stock, and investors, who have preferred stock, both sitting on the board. By the way, if the founders issued themselves preferred stock at the very beginning, it is generally the case that their shares will be converted to common stock as a condition of the Series A.

Let's say that a year or two later, the company needs more money and finds a Series B investor. The Series B investor, as a condition for investment, may require board seats. In this case either the founders or the Series A, or both, will be asked to reduce their board membership, possibly to zero. Later, a Series C investor may make similar demands.

Unlike preferred shareholders, common shareholders generally come in one flavor. Public shareholders who buy shares on the New York Stock Exchange (NYSE) or NASDAQ, typically buy only common stock, which is more less the same thing.

Conversion of Preferred Stock to Common Equivalents

Regardless of series, the preferred shareholders will have the right to convert their preferred shares to common stock. Why would someone give up their preferences? Because the ownership of common shares determines the percentage ownership in the event that the company is liquidated, either because of a trade sale or bankruptcy. The number of preferred shares held by each series of preferred shareholders is normalized to a number of common shares by multiplying the number of preferred shares by a conversion ratio. The conversion ratio is defined in each round of financing and may differ across separate rounds of financing. If you multiply the number of preferred shares by a conversion ratio you compute the equivalent number of common shares, called common equivalents. It is common equivalents that determine the percent ownership of a company.

Double Taxation of C Corporations

Unlike sole proprietorships, partnerships and LLCs, the C Corporation pays income taxes on its annual profits. It is not a pass-through entity. Since the C Corporation pays corporate taxes, it is referred to as a double-taxation entity because the corporation pays taxes annually and individual shareholders also pay taxes on dividends, or when they sell shares.

Net Operating Losses (NOL)

Another feature of the C Corporation is the ability to accumulate net operating losses (NOL). If a company loses money in its first few years of operation, which is common for startups, then instead of passing those losses on to their shareholders, the corporation can keep the accumulated losses on its books to offset profits in later years, thereby reducing taxes when the company is profitable. The shareholder may not be interested in receiving the losses at all. For example, the shareholder may be a non-profit organization, like a pension fund or university endowment. A C Corporation is the only form of entity that can accumulate net operating losses. There are tax rules which restrict ways to use NOLs to offset profits, so seek professional tax help on their use. The ability to accumulate losses, and to use them to offset profits at a later date, makes the C Corporation a useful form of entity for startups. Some profitable companies even acquire a lossmaking company to use its NOLs to offset some their profits.

Retained Earnings

Pass-through business entities distribute profits to their owners annually. That is, the profits go out the back door to the owners, leaving less available to the company for growth. As a result, pass-through entities sometimes find it difficult to accumulate cash to grow the company.

C Corporations retain their earnings inside the company. They distribute cash to their shareholders by way of dividends.

Of course, pass-through entities can also retain their profits with the company. But if they do so, the owners still have a tax liability, without the cash being distributed from the company. For example, let's say an LLC has a profit of $1,000 and a specific member has a 20% ownership. That member owes taxes on $200 of income. If the LLC chooses to withhold the $200 from the member, that member still owes taxes on the $200 even though no cash was distributed. Of course, the LLC can distribute sufficient cash so its owners can pay their taxes but it is still not retaining the same amount of cash as if it were a C Corporation.

Where to Incorporate?

In the United States, business entities are creatures of state law, which subjects the company to the corporate law of that state.

If you have a business which manufactures product in California and has customers in California, it seems sensible to incorporate in California and most such companies do. But many companies incorporate in Delaware, even if they never set foot in that state. That's because the company, or, more likely, its investors, wish to be subject to Delaware corporate law.

What various states provide is a body of state corporate law and case history under which disagreements are adjudicated. Investors will typically insist on conversion to a C Corporation incorporated in Delaware, because Delaware provides responsive civil service, has a body of mature and well-tested corporate law and is viewed as investor friendly. For example, in California, minority shareholders have more rights than in Delaware incorporated companies, such as the ability to call special shareholder meetings. Since it is relatively easy to reincorporate in Delaware, companies are often asked to do so.

Some people have the erroneous belief that incorporating in Delaware or Nevada will enable them to escape California corporate taxes. That's not true. All companies incorporated in Delaware and doing business in California, pay California corporate taxes. Business activity determines tax liability not the state of incorporation. In fact, incorporating in Delaware can increase the burden on the company due to the requirement to pay Delaware fees (Delaware has no corporate taxes but they do have modest incorporation fees) as well as California corporate taxes.

Conversion from a C Corporation Can Be Tricky

We mentioned before that converting between choices of entity is possible. However, if a company starts life as a C Corporation and subsequently wants to convert to an entity that that does not pay taxes, the accounting becomes tricky. For example, if the C Corporation acquires certain assets which increased in value, and then converts to an LLC, how is it to apportion the capital gains on those assets to the various members of the LLC? How to allocate the capital gains, when shareholders have come and gone? This requires really good bookkeeping and expensive accountants to untangle this.

Because of the difficulty in converting from a C Corporation, we suggest that the startup begin as a pass-through entity, and then convert to a C Corporation as necessary. If you never raise money from an angel investor or venture capitalist, you may not need to make the conversion.

S CORPORATION

The S corporation is much simpler then a C Corporation. There are no preferred shareholders, only common shareholders and hence, no shareholder preferences. There is a limit on number of shareholders. A quick search using "shareholder limits of an S corporation" should provide a quick answer.

Some people imagine that they avoid the limit on the number shareholders by banding together in a partnership, or corporation, to buy shares in an S corporation. That will not work because each shareholder of an S Corporation must be a human being, in particular, an American human being, or a resident alien. If you are in the USA on a work (or other non-immigrant) visa, you are not allowed to own stock in an S-Corporation. Check the latest laws and regulation on these restrictions since Congress and regulators make changes from time to time. Most of what you need to know about S Corporations are found on the IRS website; https://www.irs.gov/businesses/small-businesses-self-employed/s-corporations

S corporation shareholders enjoy liability protection, like members of LLCs. The S corporation is a pass-through entity and involves relatively little paperwork to execute.

Investors could convert you to a C Corporation

Investors want their preferences and usually prefer Delaware corporate law. Therefore, if you are not already a C Corporation, investors will convert you to one. And if you're not already incorporated in Delaware, don't be surprised if you're asked to re-incorporate there.

THE PROBLEM OF "PIERCING THE CORPORATE VEIL"

A key reason to form a business entity is to secure liability protection. Owners of business entities, whether partners, members, or shareholders want to shield their personal assets from potential misfortunes of the business, such as bankruptcy or someone slipping on a banana peel.

Nevertheless, owners can lose liability protection due to some forms of bad behavior, which is called 'piercing the corporate veil'. This can happen if you do any of the following:

- Commit fraud.
- Co-mingle business and personal funds. This often happens in an S-Corporation. Take care to act like a separate entity. That means separate bank accounts and arms-length transactions with the owners.
- Fail to observe business formalities (annual meetings, minutes, separate address, banking account), which gives the appearance of co-mingling.
- Have thin capitalization. This occurs when there is very little equity and a lot of debt. Thin capitalization is a problem if someone slips on a banana peel and has a claim. If the company cannot take care of its liabilities since there are no assets, plaintiffs can sue the shareholders.

Be extremely careful, any of these could expose your personal assets.

FORM THE BUSINESS ENTITY EARLY IN THE LIFE OF THE COMPANY.

Entrepreneurs should formally incorporate their startup as a legal entity relatively early because:

- You want every founder to assign all rights (for example, patents) to the entity. The longer you wait, the greater the risk that one or more of the founders will not be willing to do this.

- Once you start dealing with third parties, you'll want them to sign a agreements (for example, a confidentiality agreement) and you'll want them to sign those agreements with your entity rather than with you personally.

- You want to have clarity on who the founders are.

- The longer you wait, the more difficult it is to establish a valuation for founders' equity.

- You want to have personal liability protection as early as possible.

Now that you have a business entity, you can (finally) start to raise money and hire employees.

TAKEAWAYS

- You have a legal business entity even if you haven't filed legal paperwork.

- Legal entities differ according to liability protection, taxes, handling of profits, and governing law by state.

- The decision of choice of entity may be made for you by investors. Investors prefer C Corporations to get preferences.

- The choice of entity is reversible, but each has restrictions and consequences. If you want to take advantage of net operating losses or will be raising significant amounts of capital, you are well advised to start as a C Corporation. If your business has more modest aims and won't be raising a lot of capital, then an LLC or S Corporation make sense to avoid the double taxation.

Chapter 7 – Equity Compensation

"The main ingredient of stardom is the rest of the team"
- John Wooden

Early-stage companies typically don't have enough cash to pay market rates for staff but still need to attract competent people. How can you pay people if you don't have sufficient money? Why would early employees, who take similar financial risks as founders, work for a below market salary? By compensating them with equity. Rewarding employees with equity in lieu of cash essentially makes them early-stage investors, and they can expect some of the same rewards.

Equity compensation can involve awarding;

- unrestricted shares,
- restricted shares,
- restricted stock units (RSUs),
- incentive stock options (ISOs) and
- non-qualified stock options (NQ)

UNRESTRICTED SHARES

Granting unrestricted shares means the company grants shares which the employee can sell immediately. That is, there are no restrictions against selling the shares, hence the name. If the company is private, there is no established marketplace to sell the shares. The employee must make other arrangements to sell the shares, if permitted by the company.

Due to their potential liquidity, unrestricted shares are a proxy for cash, so the employee is subject to ordinary income tax when the shares are granted.

If the stock is public, it has a fair market value (FMV) which is the public share price. If the stock is private, a valuation is determined by means of a valuation process called a 409A valuation or by reference to a recent, prior transaction of preferred shares that was priced.

The IRS keeps tabs on these things, especially if there is a liquidity event shortly after the unrestricted stock is granted. For example, if the employees were granted unrestricted shares at

$1.00 on a Monday, and on Tuesday the company goes public at $20.00 per share, the IRS won't accept that the FMV on Monday was only $1.00. The IRS will ask that taxes be paid on the difference between what it estimates the FMV was on Monday and $1.00 per share.

Because private companies don't have ready markets for unrestricted shares and there is an immediate tax liability for employees, companies rarely grant unrestricted shares.

RESTRICTED SHARES

In contrast, <u>restricted shares</u> cannot be sold, even if the company is publicly traded. When you receive restricted shares they are earmarked for you, but you cannot sell them until they are vested. <u>Vesting</u> is a process by which the employee can take possession of restricted shares piecemeal over a period of time. For example, if you are granted 5,000 shares that vest annually over 5 years, it means you would take possession of 1,000 shares after one year, then an additional 1,000 shares after another year and so on. Only after the employee has remained at the company for 5 years is the employee said to be <u>fully vested</u>. Granting of restricted stock is designed to incentivize the employee to remain with the company until the end of the vesting period.

As the shares vest they become the property of the employee and become unrestricted shares. Therefore the shares are subject to ordinary taxes on the FMV at the time they vest. We emphasize the FMV at the time they vest, not the earlier time when they are granted, presumably at a lower valuation. As they vest, the employee pays taxes at ordinary income rates.

As an example, let's suppose you are granted 5,000 shares with a FMV of $1.00 per share. After one year, 1,000 shares are vested and the FMV has increased to $5.00 per share. You now owe taxes on $4,000 of income, computed as the $5,000 in the FMV less the cost basis of $1,000. If the stock is public, you can sell some of the shares to pay the taxes. If the company is private, you still must pay the taxes, regardless of whether you can sell the stock.

This seems rather harsh on the employee. To alleviate this situation, the tax code provides a provision called the 83(b) election, which allows the employee to pay the taxes on all the restricted shares up front, even though the shares can't be sold. In this example, you would elect to pay taxes on $5,000 <u>at the time of the grant</u> ($1.00 Exercise price times 5,000 shares).

By paying taxes when the stock is granted, you receive several benefits. There is no further tax liability as the stock vests, and taxes are paid upfront when there was the lowest FMV. Moreover, if the shares are sold after they vest, capital gains tax rates apply, not ordinary income rates.

This sounds great for the employee. No taxes paid in the intermediate years and at the end there is a preferential tax treatment. So, what is downside of exercising your 83(b) election? The risk is that the company goes bankrupt *after* you paid the taxes, and *before* you could sell any shares.

The tax code requires that you must exercise an 83(b) election, and pay the income tax, shortly after you receive the restricted shares. This is to prevent you from simply waiting until the day before the company goes public to exercise at, in this example, $1.00 and then selling at the public share price. Essentially, you must take the same risk as everybody else when the company is in its infancy in order to get the preferential tax treatment offered by 83(b). Search for "83(b) exercise time limit" to get the most recent time limit to exercise your 83(b) election. At the time of this writing, you must elect 83(b) within 30 days of receiving the grant.

If you believe in the company and stay employed during the vesting period, then exercising 83(b) election makes sense. If you are worried about paying your tax liability upfront, then why are you joining the company in first place?

RESTRICTED STOCK UNITS (RSU)

RSUs are similar to restricted stock but with a bit more flexibility. RSUs can be paid out in stock or cash. The basis of the compensation can be time-based or event-based. Time-based RSU's are subject to a vesting schedule, whereas event-based RSU's are paid based on an event that the employee or the company accomplishes.

There is no cash outlay for an RSU and the gains are subject to ordinary income. There may be vesting for stock-based RSUs but not for event-based. Although RSUs have a great deal of flexibility they can be more complicated to administer. One particular concern is how to determine when an event was actually accomplished.

	RSU	83(b) restricted shares
Paid out as	Stock or cash	Stock
Basis of compensation	Time or event (individual or company)	Time
Cash outlay upon award	None	Yes, taxes immediately on FMV of shares
Subsequent tax liability	Ordinary income	Capital gains treatment
Vesting	Stock, may or may not No, for event based	Yes
Flexibility	A lot, since can be event based	A lot but not as much as RSUs

Table 7-1. Comparison of Restricted Stock and Restricted Stock Units (RSUs)

A stock option agreement gives the employee the right to buy a given number of shares at the exercise price or strike price within a predetermined period of time. The exercise price is the FMV of the common stock established early in the life of the company when the FMV is low, and is fixed for the duration of the share option agreement.

The act of obtaining shares is called an exercise. This means the employee pays the exercise price multiplied by the number options and obtains shares in exchange. For example, if the exercise price is $1.00 per share and the employee has the right to purchase 5,000 upon full-vesting, the employee pays $5,000 and receives 5,000 shares.

In this example, if the FMV at the time of exercise is $20 a share, the employee pays ordinary income taxes on $19 per share multiplied by 5,000 shares. The employee must therefore add $95,000 to her taxable income. The tax liability holds even if the employee does not sell any shares. The mere act of exercise precipitates the taxable event.

There is no tax liability upon receipt of the option (unless the option price is mistakenly below FMV). So, stock options impose the smallest cash outlay on employees upfront. No cash up front; no taxes up front; just promises given. Therefore, stock options provide the greatest leverage for employees.

The key concepts of stock options are illustrated in Figure 7-2.

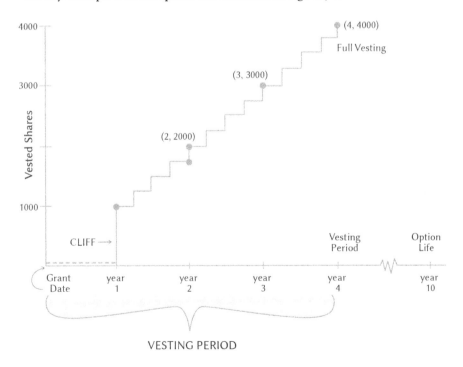

Figure 7-2. Stock Options Vesting and Terminology

This figure indicates the case of an employee who is granted 4,000 options with an exercise price $1 per share. The options fully vest over four years and vest quarterly. The exercise price of the stock options is the FMV of the company's shares on the <u>Grant Date</u>, when employee was granted the stock options. The Grant Date is early in the life of the company, when the FMV of the shares is minimal.

After one year the employee can exercise 1,000 share options. After two years 2,000 options, and so on. Since the options vest quarterly, the employee can exercise 1,500 options after 18 months. Only after the employee has been with the company for four years can the employee exercise all 4,000 share options.

In this particular case notice that there is no quarterly vesting during the first year of the vesting period. The employee would get nothing if he or she leaves the company within a year. Upon completion of one year the employee gets the full first year of options vested, hence the term <u>cliff</u>. This is to incent the employee to stay a minimum of one year to qualify for any options.

There is another important concept called <u>acceleration</u>. Let's say there is a miracle and your company is sold *before* all your options vest. The company could be acquired by another before four years or even before the cliff is reached. What happens to your unvested options?

Acceleration is a clause that provides for full vesting upon purchase. If the company is purchased 11 months after you were hired, you can exercise your 4,000 options if there is acceleration. Read your option agreement, or employment agreement, to be sure it has an acceleration clause.

On the other hand, some key employees may not be given acceleration. The acquiring company could be fearful that key employees could leave upon purchase. In some cases, certain key employees may be asked to waive their right to acceleration as a condition of the purchase.

Exercise Upon Termination

Employees who voluntarily leave the company may be required to exercise their vested but unexercised options. The options must be exercised in a relative short period of time, for example, 90 days. This can be a surprise to some employees who feel they can keep the stock options in their former company and get new options from a new company. Mandatory exercise done to control the distribution of shares. Since they are required to exercise, they may get a big tax bill simply by changing jobs.

So before you leave your comfortable position with unexercised options, you should consider the cash and tax effect of an exercise, and whether or not you intend to sell the stock after exercise.

Key Terminology of Stock Options

- Exercise price. The price at which you can buy stock, regardless of market price, when you convert your options into shares
- Vesting period. The number of months/quarters/years after which options are no longer subject to forfeiture.
- Option life. The number of years in which you can exercise your options. You are not required to exercise your options when you are fully vested. However, at the end of the option life, you must exercise your options or else they will expire and you will lose you right to buy shares at the exercise price.
- Cliff. The amount of time and the number of shares you receive upon first vesting.
- Fair market value (FMV). The stock price as determined by a third party, either valuation or purchase price.
- Grant date. The date you receive the stock options
- Exercise date. The date you convert the options into stock.

NON-QUALIFIED STOCK OPTIONS (NQ) OR INCENTIVE STOCK OPTIONS (ISOS)?

The above discussion on stock options described a form of options called Non-Qualified Stock Options (NQ). They are called non-qualified since they don't qualify for capital gains treatment.

In fact, there are two kinds of stock options, Incentive Stock Options (ISOs) and Non-Qualified (NQ) stock options.

ISOs qualify for capital gains treatment to the employee. To qualify for capital gains treatment, the employee must satisfy holding period requirements. However, ISOs are granted less frequently since there's no compensation deduction for company and there are limits as to how many ISOs can be granted.

Therefore, employees most often get non-qualified (NQ) stock options. There is ordinary income to the recipient and a compensation deduction to the company, when they are exercised. Therefore, NQ options are preferred by employers.

The tax treatment of nonqualified stock options is depicted in Figure 7-3.

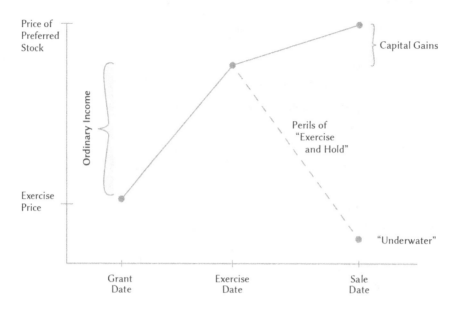

Figure 7-3. Tax Treatment of Stock Options

In this example, the employee is granted options for 4,000 shares at the grant date with a low exercise price of $1.00 per share. Over time the prospects of the company improve, the FMV of the stock rises until such point as the employee exercises the stock options. Let's say the employee exercises the options at $10.00 per share at the exercise date.

Exercising options means the employee pays the company $4,000, computed as 4,000 shares @ $1.00 per share, and receives 4,000 shares. The shares are valued at $10.00, so the employee now owns $40,000 worth of stock and paid only $4,000. That's a good thing. However, upon exercise, there's a tax liability to the employee of $36,000 of ordinary income. That is, the tax liability is the $40,000 value of the shares, less the cost basis of $4,000.

Sometimes the employee chooses to hold on to the stock, rather than sell. We call this exer-cise and hold. If there is further appreciation of the stock price and the employee completes the minimum holding period, then gains after the exercise are taxed at the capital gains rate. That's good for the employee because of the preferential tax rate.

If, however, the stock price drops after exercise, then the employee still has a tax liability based on the $36,000 of ordinary income but may not have the cash to pay the taxes. That's bad for the employee. For example, if the stock price drops to $2.00, he can only sell his shares for $8,000, which may not be enough to cover the taxes on $36,000 of income.

Our advice on exercise and hold is simply, "Don't do it". Good practice is that, upon exercise, the employee should sell enough shares to at least pay the taxes. It might be a good idea to pay off your mortgage as well. You can let the rest ride, but at that point, you're simply playing the public stock market.

Another unfortunate situation for the employee is when the FMV of the stock drops below the exercise price *before* the options are exercised. That means between the grant date and the exercise date, something bad has happened and the FMV of the stock has fallen below the exercise price. For example, suppose the FMV of the illiquid stock drops to $0.50 per share and the employee has not exercised. In that case the options have no value since it would be cheaper to buy the stock at $0.50 rather than by exercising the options at $1.00. If this happens, the options are said to be "underwater". The term "underwater" means the market price of the stock is under the Exercise Price.

HOW TO DETERMINE THE EXERCISE PRICE

The exercise price is set to FMV at the time the options are granted. That begs the question of what is the FMV for a startup company that is not traded. The FMV is set by the board of directors, generally upon a formal valuation process, called a 409A valuation. The valuation process is necessary so that the company can defend itself against claims that the FMV was set below market. Valuations are performed by banks and consultants. If the IRS decides that the FMV was set below market value, then the difference between the exercise price and the FMV is taxable to the option holder. The company will also be penalized if it issues options below FMV. The exercise price must be adjusted periodically, perhaps once a year, to reflect progress the company is making.

In lieu of a formal valuation, which can be expensive, a recent financing event could provide a valuation. After all, the most recent investors would have conducted an arms-length valuation when they invested. When there is a recent preferred stock investment, common stock exercise price can be estimated by using a gearing ratio. Gearing Ratio provides a short cut to common stock valuation. As a rule of thumb, the common stock is worth somewhere between 20% and 33% of the price of a recent preferred stock pricing. For example, if a VC recent bought preferred stock at $6.00 per share, the common stock could be priced at $1.50 to $2.00. At $1.20 you are pushing the envelope. At $0.60 for the common stock (1:10 gearing ratio), you are out of bounds. The use of gearing ratio only works if there is a financing event within the past 12 months.

In any case, it's best to get a formal valuation.

Typical Treatment of Stock Options Upon Termination

Employee should examine their option agreement to see what happens to the stock options in the case of termination:

Event	Typical Plan Provision
Involuntary termination **without** cause	• Vested options can be exercised up to 3 months following termination • Unvested options are forfeited
Involuntary termination **with** cause	• Unexercised options (vested and unvested) are forfeited
Voluntary termination	• Vesting options can be exercised up to 3 months following termination • Unvested options are forfeited
Retirement, death, disability	• Vested options can be exercised up to 12 months • Accelerated vesting on unvested options

These are sample terms. Read your option agreement to get the final word.

Warrants versus Options

Warrants are similar to options in that they provide the opportunity to buy shares at a set price within a specific period of time. However, unlike options, they are not issued to a specific person. As such they are tradable and there can be a market for warrants. For example, if a bank advances a loan to a company, the bank may require that warrants are issued to the lender. Warrants give the lender a <u>sweetener</u>, or added benefit, in addition to loan repayment. The lender can in turn sell the warrants to another party or exercise them if the price of the shares increase.

Warrants therefore have a very different motive than options.

	Warrants	Options
Flexibility	Issued ad-hoc	Option plan
Transferable	Yes	No; intended to incentivize an individual
Holder	Any entity (person, corporation, LLC,..)	An employee
Exercise	Usually shorter than an option	10 years is common

- There are a variety of ways to provide equity compensation to employees.

- The company and employee should consider when offering or accepting equity compensation.

  - The cash position of employee and company.
  - The FMV at the time of the offer. If the FMV is very high, then that puts a burden on the employee to pay the taxes in the event the 83(b) election is taken. In this case, RSUs may make more sense.
  - The probability that the company grows, or at least survives, until the share options vest.
  - Leverage for employee.
  - The type of incentive you want to provide to employee. The employer may prefer event-based compensation, in which case RSUs are a better choice.
  - Compensation deduction for the company.

- The employee must fully understand the terms of the equity compensation agreement, especially the clauses on number of shares, vesting, acceleration, termination and exercise price. The compensation agreement can be part of the employment contract or a separate options agreement.

- Stock options have made millionaires out of a lot of people due to their leverage, so it is very useful to understand the terms.

SELF STUDY

Case

This is an actual case of an engineer named David who has been offered a job and received the following letter from the CEO. The company has a various equity compensation agreements it can offer David and is asking David which he would prefer.

"I (the CEO) am working on the draft and should have something to you shortly. Which of the scenario's would you prefer so that I can have Steve (our counsel) put it in the employment agreement?"

With respect to the stock purchase, a lot of this is going to be driven by what works best for you, tax-wise. 5% of the company on a fully diluted basis is 319,549 shares. You are getting a valuation that is $0.21 per share, and thus the aggregate purchase price/value of 319,549 shares would be $67,105.

The most favorable tax outcomes for you (David) will be a purchase of common stock or a grant of common stock, because, after paying any income tax due at the time of the issuance you will just have capital gains relating to any gain in value. If the FMV is $0.21 per share and common stock is sold to you at FMV then you would have to come up with $67,105 to purchase the shares. On the other hand, if common stock is granted, you have received $67,105 in income and he will owe income tax on that amount.

An option will provide for a less favorable tax outcome for him because the most likely outcome will be income tax on the spread between the FMV at the time of grant and the exercise price. If the option is $0.21 per share and the FMV at the time of exercise is $2.00, you would owe income tax on $1.79 per share, but an option has NO tax consequence at the time of the award. The best combination of outcome for the company is to buy in, because it is $67,105 more into the company than in the case of a grant. The best outcome for David is probably a grant of restricted stock, assuming he can pay the income tax on $67,105 in value awarded to him, because he will not face any income tax relating to the gain in value, he will just have capital gain.

Question #1. What are the three choices the company is offering to David?

Question #2. What fourth scenario could the company offer to David?

Question #3. From the company's point of view, which would be the preferred choice?

Question #4. How should David select from these choices? What are the key factors he should consider? What would be your process in deciding?

Answers

1. Stock options, grant of unrestricted stock, purchase of common stock.

2. Restricted stock with 83(b)

3. Purchase of common stock. It provides cash to the company.

4. After enumerating these 4 options, construct a scorecard to compare the options. Here is a sample.

	Weight	Purchase of common	Grant of Unrestricted shares	Grant of Stock options	Grant of restricted shares with 83(b)
Immediate cash required	?	$67,105	0	0	0
Capital gains if price increases	?	Yes	Yes	No	Yes
Immediate tax consequence	?	None	Tax on FMV of granted shares	None	Tax on FMV of granted shares
Subject to vesting	?	No	No	Yes	Yes
Leverage; upside	?	Increase in FMV	Increase in FMV	Highest; no commitment up front	Increase in FMV
Signal to company	?	Highest; cash commitment to company	Medium	Lowest commitment to company	A little more commitment than unrestricted
Early termination consequences	?	Keeps stock	Keeps stock	Lose unvested	Lose unvested
	1.0				

Chapter 8 – Employment and Other Legal Matters

"Nobody likes lawyers, . . . until they need one."

We continue our discussion of legal issues for start-ups by addressing employment and fund-raising issues. The topics we discuss are highlighted below.

- Choice of Entity
- Equity Compensation
- **Startup HR/Employment Issues**
- **Legal issues regarding raising capital**
- **Common legal errors**
- **Mediation and Arbitration**
- **Working with lawyers**
- Intellectual Property

STARTUP HR/EMPLOYMENT ISSUES

The employee/employer relationship is usually governed by an <u>employment agreement</u> between the employee and the company which defines:

- Duties, compensation, and benefits.

- Non-Disclosure Agreement

- Stock option agreement, including the number of options, exercise price, vesting period, option life, cliff, and acceleration provisions.

- Patent assignment; any invention made by the employee while working for the company will become the property of the company.

- After termination the employee still could have responsibilities to the company:

- Non-competition clause; the employee cannot compete with, or work for another company that competes against the company. There may be consideration granted to the departing employee for agreeing to a non-compete clause.

- Non-solicitation of customers or employees; the employee cannot recruit customers or workers

- Honoring trade secrets.

If the company doesn't want to go through the time and expense of executing an employment agreement with each employee, the state in which the company operates will have default provisions. In the United States, the employer-employee relationship is governed by state law in the absence of an employment agreement.

State laws typically provide for <u>at-will</u> employment. That means the employee can quit at any time with, or without, notice. Also, the company can terminate an employee with, or without, cause, provided that the cause does not include discrimination on the basis of race, age, sex, religion, sexual orientation or other protected classes. Certain exceptions may exist allowing for some discrimination. Stay apprised of state law in which you operate.

Employee or consultant?

Companies are tempted to classify workers as consultants rather than employees. By having consultants instead of employees, the company avoids payroll taxes, Social Security contributions, and benefits. Having consultants can also be a means to discriminate. While it is illegal to fire employees, because of race, gender, age, or sexual orientation, you don't need to fire consultants; you can simply let them go by not retaining them.

There are a number of tests to determine whether a worker is actually an employee or consultant. For an employee, these are:

- Company specifies location, extent, time, how work is done and otherwise exercises control over the worker.
- Company supplies tools.
- Company reimburses expenses.

In the world of the gig economy, this distinction is contentious. You may need to check with legal counsel to be sure your classification is correct.

Hourly or salaried?

The company can get into trouble by classifying hourly workers as salaried workers, which avoids overtime and some labor laws.

There are a number tests to determine whether a worker is salaried or not. Among these are job duties, working hours and the amount of salary. Salaries need to be at least a multiple of full-time hourly wages based on a 40-hour week.

Rules can become tricky in the case of remote workers, who are governed by the labor laws of the state in which they live, not the company's location.

Again, you should check with legal counsel to be sure your classification of hourly or salaried is correct.

Interns, paid or unpaid?

The use of interns, particularly unpaid interns, can be abusive. There must be a benefit to the intern, such as teaching or mentoring. If the intern is unpaid, the company may need to show there is more benefit to the intern than the company. If the intern is simply performing unpaid labor, and not getting any educational benefit, the intern could sue for backpay.

Two other points to consider about interns are:

- What if the intern invents something? Will the company claim the invention and will the intern give up the invention if the intern is unpaid and without an employment agreement?

- What about trade secret protection? The company should want some assurance that the intern will honor trade secrets learned on the job. This could also mean an employment agreement should be in place.

Expatriates (expats) from your company working overseas

If you have production or sales overseas, the company has the basic question of whether or not to send your employees overseas (expatriates or expats) or to hire local people in country.

Overseas employees are subject to labor laws of the country in which they're working. That means provisions for non-compete, employee solicitation, customer solicitation, trade secret rules and termination rules may be different. Provisions for employee/consultant, hourly/salary and unpaid interns may also be different in foreign countries.

In some countries you may need to create a local business legal entity to employ people overseas; a branch office may not be sufficient. Finally, expats may need work permits or visas to work overseas.

{Reintegration upon return to U.S.}

Although not a legal question, there is a need for reintegration of the expat into the domestic work force upon return to the home country. Will the expat return to the same job or a new job? Was someone else filling that job when the expat was away? Statistics show that returning workers have a higher rate of attrition. Proper planning is needed to ensure that the returning expat remains with the company, and it retains their valuable overseas experience.

Hiring foreigners to work in your company in the United States

Most employers are familiar with the H1-B visa. Lessor known are other temporary and permanent work visas to work in the United States. A sample of the many visas are:

Work Visa Type	Qualifications
E-3	Professionals who are Australian nationals, with at least a Masters' Degree.
J-1	Temporary exchange for foreigners supporting cultural exchange. English language skills and evidence of financial independence.
O-1	Extraordinary ability. Athletes, artists, scientists, business leaders who can demonstrate international recognition.
R-1	Religious workers
NAFTA Work Visa	Canadians and Mexicans in qualifying professional fields who possess graduate level education and can show they have been offered jobs in the U.S.
EB-5	Investors in commercial enterprises. As of 2019, the minimum capital required to qualify was $500,000.
H-2B	Non-agricultural temporary jobs, like hospitality, recreation.
Q	Cultural exchange

Table 8-1. A Sample of Visas to Work in the United States.

There are many others at the U.S. Department of Homeland Security website. Legislation changes eligibility; for the latest updates, refer to https://www.uscis.gov/working-united-states/working-us.

Employment Checklist Upon Hiring

- Present an offer letter which includes job description, compensation, equity compensation (if any), and a declaration that employment is at-will.
- Have the candidate sign an invention disclosure agreement.
- Have the candidate sign a non-disclosure and non-solicitation agreement.

Employment Checklist Upon Termination

- Obtain office keys and company-issued computer or phone. These may contain sensitive data.
- Schedule an exit interview. Have the candidate sign an acknowledgement of trade secrets.
- Issue a final paycheck, including payment for accrued vacation.
- Make it clear what benefits will be continued for what period of time.
- The company and the employee should separate on the best terms possible. You never know when paths may cross again.

LEGAL CONSTRAINTS ON RAISING CAPITAL

At the heart of U.S. federal legislation regarding raising capital is to protect the uninformed investing public (so called "widows and orphans") from unscrupulous promoters of stock. History is filled with swindles exploiting the lack of investment sophistication by the general public.

Federal legislation from the time of the Great Depression required that investors be accredited in order to make investments. Definitions of who is an accredited investor vary from time to time, but they basically involve means testing. That is, the prospective investor must meet income and wealth standards to be deemed accredited. Furthermore, the rules prevent general solicitation, which means promoting stock in the popular press.

When the company offers to sell shares to any individual, the individual buying the shares is asked to sign a form that declares their accredited status.

The United States Securities and Exchange Commission (www.sec.gov) oversees the rules of accreditation. Search for "sec accredited investor" or https://www.sec.gov/fast-answers/answers-accredhtm.html to get the latest rules.

What about friends and family?

Under SEC Regulations, as many as 35 non-accredited investors are allowed. Quite a few of your friends and family can fit under this exemption.

Crowdfunding

Crowdfunding is an increasingly popular way for start-up companies to raise equity, and Federal Regulation CF now permits this. There are limits on the amount of money the company can raise and the amount of money a single individual can invest. These limits are adjusted from time to time so the company and the investors must check in with the SEC to determine what limits apply in a particular case. Search for "sec regulation CF" for the latest rules.

Initial Coin Offerings and Security Token Offerings

Raising equity capital through an initial coin offering (ICO) has met with resistance from the SEC who view ICOs as securities and therefore regulated as shares. More recently, the SEC has permitted offerings of security token offerings (STOs). You can search for "difference between ICO and STO" to get some unofficial articles providing background information.

The regulatory framework is defined in SEC Regulation A+. The difference in federal regulation between ICOs and STOs involves whether or not the item being sold is a security or not. This is a complex legal discussion with a legal history going back to 1946 when the United States Supreme Court ruled in the case of SEC vs. Howey. For our purposes, suffice it to say that companies willing to live within the constraints of an STO will have an easier time getting SEC approval then those companies raising capital via ICOs.

MEDIATION

Not all legal disputes need to be resolved by going to court. You can create bad public relations and demoralize your staff during long, drawn-out legal proceedings. Even if you win, the time and expense could mean you ultimately lose.

Mediation and arbitration offer alternative, less expensive and less time-consuming alternatives. See aaamediation.org for details and mediators.

Mediation involves simply talking over your disagreement with an independent, trained mediator who will issue a non-binding opinion. The mediator cannot impose any decision on the parties. Arbitration, on the other hand, is typically binding. Here are some pros and cons of mediation.

Pro	Con
Confidential	Could spend time without obtaining a success conclusion
Less adversarial. Preserves continuing relationship. Less formal.	No binding agreement
Can be done in conjunction with arbitration or court proceedings	May set floor for settlement later on
Can graduate to arbitration	Doesn't work if either party is operating in bad faith.

Table 8-2. Pros and Cons of Mediation

ARBITRATION

If the parties cannot come to an agreement after facilitated mediation and they need a decision, then the next step could be binding arbitration.

In arbitration, both parties present their case to an independent arbitrator who will vigorously question both parties. After the cases are presented, the arbitrator will make a decision. One of the two parties wins. No compromises will be offered by the arbitrator.

Here is a list of arbitrators and venues.

- Worldwide Intellectual Property Organization (WIPO; wipo.int). WIPO focuses on international IP disputes, involving patent, trademarks and copyright.

- International Chamber of Commerce. (iccwbo.org)

- International Centre for Dispute Resulution (www.icdr.org)

- Country specific venues, like the American Arbitration Association (adr.org or aaamediation.org) or the Japan Commercial Arbitration Association (JCAA; www. jcaa.or.jp/e/). Most industrialized countries have an arbitration venue.

Arbitrators are paid depending on the *amount* in dispute. Usually, the losing parties pays costs.

Generally, when two sides enter into a contract, they will agree upfront to binding arbitration, even before any dispute arises. For example, when drafting a license agreement, the following clauses could be inserted into the license;

- what issues are subject to arbitration,

- venue and institution,
- pre-arbitration steps, like mediation,
- scope of discovery, time limits and
- single arbitrator or a panel of three, for example.

WIPO and AAA offer model arbitration clauses on their websites.

https://www.wipo.int/amc-apps/clause-generator/

https://adr.org/clauses

Here are some pros and cons of arbitration:

Pro	Cons
Confidential	You could lose and pay arbitration fees for both parties.
Limited discovery. Some information, like patent information, can be specified off limits.	If you feel you have a strong case, litigate. If the dispute is international and you have a home court advantage, litigate.
Final with no appeal. Good if you win.	Final with no appeal. Bad if you lose.
Faster and cheaper than litigation	No dispositive motions (Motion to Dismiss, summary judgement) prior to merits hearing.
	If you have money and the counter party doesn't, you may want to go to court.

Table 8-3. Pros and Cons of Arbitration

Careful consideration should be given to mediation and arbitration. This is particularly true for small companies that don't have the time or money to go through expensive legal proceedings.

Here is a short list of common errors made by entrepreneurs, all of which are entirely avoidable and unnecessary.

Error	Why this happens	Consequences
Forming entity too late	Too busy	• Liability incurred before the company is formed • undervaluation of equity causing tax problems • early participants claim to be founders when maybe they are not (see the case of Alan and Jack in chapter 6)
Failing to act like a company	Using the company for personal use	Owners lose liability protection, the corporate veil is pierced
Undervaluation of options	Maximize profits on stock options	Tax consequences if options don't reflect FMV
Failing to protect trade secrets and trademarks	Don't know how or just an oversight	Loss of intellectual property
Infringing on other's IP	Don't know or willful infringement	Lawsuit against you
Misclassifying employees as contractors	Don't want to pay payroll taxes or benefits	Back taxes, penalties, interest, employee issues
Hiring former competitors and using their trade secrets	Aggressive hiring or inadvertent	Lawsuit against you
Not considering mediation or arbitration to resolve disputes	They don't know about options	Going to court unnecessarily and spending more time and money than necessary

Error	Why this happens	Consequences
Selecting the wrong form of entity	They all seem the same	Legal and accounting expenses to fix things, but not too serious a problem
Failing to understand term sheet provisions	Too complicated	Entrepreneurs not able to calculate their personal stake
Failing to implement an 83(b) election	Too complicated or the company may fail	Tax consequences
Selling shares to unaccredited investors	Don't know better	Potential Right of Rescission claims
Ignoring employment visas	Desire for labor	Immigration enforcement
Employment issues for your expat workers going overseas	Work rules overseas are complex and different	Severance, possible loss of IP, confidentiality issues
Raising capital through unregistered brokers or "finders"	Others did it	Potential rescission, fines, shareholder lawsuits

Table 8-4. Common Errors to Avoid

WORKING WITH LAWYERS

Many of these problems can be averted by engaging legal counsel before problems occur. When working with lawyers consider the following before engaging.

- Is the initial meeting free of charge? Ask.

- Find someone with startup experience in your field.

- Ask what to expect, given your company's stage. Will there be further legal work? What information do they need from you?

- Money is not an embarrassing question. Ask for an estimate. What work can you do so the lawyers don't have to?

- Who will do the work? Partner or associate? Get references.

- Note that you may engage different lawyers or firms depending on legal services required. For example, intellectual property firms generally specialize. You may need one of these and another firm to handle transactions and labor matters.

- Lawyers have experience and will give good advice. But the entrepreneur is the final arbiter of business decisions.

TAKEAWAYS

- There are many ways startup companies can get into legal trouble, in ways that are not obvious to entrepreneurs who haven't done it before.

- Save yourself time, money and reputation by doing things the right way.

- Mediation and arbitration can be alternatives to legal proceedings.

("... In preparing for battle, battle plans are useless but planning is indispensable"
– General Dwight Eisenhower, 34th President of the U.S.)

The formal business plan is a much-maligned step in starting a business. While we don't necessarily advise entrepreneurs to write a formal, 20-page business plan, we do recommend that they go through the thought process. Investors rarely read business plans. They are bombarded with thousands of inquiries, executive summaries, pitch decks, let alone business plans, every year. An investment firm of a few people could not possibly read all the business plans they could receive. So, they don't.

But absent a business plan how is the entrepreneur to convince key stakeholders that all the elements of starting the business have been considered? A business plan goes beyond product/market fit. It extends to supply chain, operations, staffing, financing, ongoing sales and marketing, intellectual property strategy and other contributors to success or failure. You need to demonstrate to others, and to convince yourself, that you have thought through the major issues even if it's only on the back of an envelope.

Having said this, a formal business plan is a good idea in most, though not all, cases. A written plan forces discipline into the planning process. Besides, for some forms of entrepreneurship, like spinoffs, it is required.

WHAT IS A BUSINESS PLAN?

A business plan is a statement of intentions, resources, environment, credentials and actions to move the <u>enterprise</u> forward. A business plan is a

- checklist of assumptions,
- retrospective tool, to review performance.
- fundraising device, to convince others to invest in you.
- supporting document for a prospectus, to satisfy regulatory and financial reporting requirements, and
- framework for thinking about the enterprise.

We use the term "<u>enterprise</u>" here since a business plan applies to;

- startup companies for fundraising,
- established companies for annual planning,
- non-profit entities for fundraising and reporting,
- government entities for operational planning, and
- spinoffs and acquisitions, or purchase of businesses or assets, for justification.

WHAT IS THE PURPOSE OF A BUSINESS PLAN?

A business plan should provide a <u>convincing</u> scenario for <u>success,</u> it must have a point of view and be persuasive. It's not just analysis; it specifies action. It says what success looks like, and how to get there. Accordingly, it should:

- Set management objectives
- State assumptions
- Specify who does what over the plan period, thereby assuring operational coordination
- Communicate with employees, partners, board, advisors, consultants, bankers, government regulators
- Provide support for a private placement memorandum (PPM) or annual review

It is useful to obtain funding, recruit employees, recruit business partners, justify an allocation of internal resources, communicate with investors, satisfy regulators and provide assurance that people know what they are supposed to be doing.

BUSINESS PLAN BASICS

You'll find hundreds of thousands of business plans online. Here are some common threads.

- Start with an Executive Summary, which should state your purpose. Why is your audience reading this document or watching this presentation? What are you asking for?

- Present your plan in 20 to 30 pages of text, with illustrations, diagrams, charts and other visual aids. This page count includes the title page and executive summary but excludes the appendix.

- Include supporting information in the appendix, which could be print or digital.

- Include contact information.

- Mark as "confidential" when appropriate.

- Packaging is important. Appearance matters. Pay attention to grammar, punctuation, spelling, sequencing, parallelism, and tone. Make it look interesting. Include visual aids such as charts, flowcharts, matrices, diagrams, etc.

You are trying to be persuasive and therefore you must have facts and tell a story.

IT ALL STARTS WITH RESEARCH

A business plan should be persuasive and to be persuasive you must have facts. Fact finding is divided here into secondary and primary research.

Secondary Research

Secondary research means going online or finding printed material which has already been prepared by someone else. While curation of secondary research can lead to useful insights, secondary research provides information someone else already knows. Your competitors also have access to secondary research. Therefore, it's hard to get a competitive advantage simply by relying only on secondary research.

Apart from providing novel insights of the existing information, the main value in secondary research is its role in preparing you for primary research. Secondary research helps to:

- Identify hypotheses to test
- Provide background information in preparation for primary research.
- Identify sources of primary information, such as conferences, trade shows, and persons to interview.
- Provide questions and help in the preparation of questionnaires

Secondary research must precede primary research. Summarize and document key findings and maintain good citations in case you need to refer to the documentation again.

Primary Research

To learn something no one knows, it's necessary to conduct some primary research. Primary research includes

- Focus groups
- Conducting experiments, including test marketing or minimum viable product introduction
- First hand observation
- Interviewing

Hypothesis Testing

Primary research starts with a set of hypotheses, much like scientific research. A <u>hypothesis</u> as a declarative statement that is either true or false. For example, "Consumers will purchase one day old sushi at half price". That hypothesis is either true or false and can be validated or refuted in focus groups, by observation, by test marketing or by interviewing.

The purpose of having a set of hypotheses is to focus your research. Focus your research on validating or refuting hypotheses. Otherwise you run the risk of collecting extraneous data.

Hypotheses that are refuted are not signs of failure. They help you identify things you should not do when developing a business. In the above case, the idea was to acquire leftover sushi from restaurants and resell online.

Since hypothesis was false, the entrepreneur knew not to acquire leftover sushi for resale. As hypotheses get refuted, develop new ones based on what you've learned. This is progress. Eventually you get to a hypothesis of the form "There are xxx buyers of our green widget and will pay $yyy each." and will be validated.

In the case above, once the first hypothesis was refuted, another came to mind. That was "customers will accept sushi made from unsold fish that morning at the wholesale fish market". Unsold fish is sold at a discount at wholesale market since it couldn't be sold the next day. The entrepreneur validated this hypothesis. The idea was to buy unsold whole fish in the morning and prepare sushi for sale the same day at discounted prices. This is now a real business in Tokyo.

Other possible hypotheses:

"Online grocery customers require 30 minute delivery". True or False? Webvan could have benefited from testing this hypothesis. See the exercises in Chapter 4, Risks.

"If we increase prices by x% we will lose y% of customers"

"Drivers of electric vehicles will sense range anxiety after driving 200 miles without a recharge".

Interviewing

Apart from test marketing or minimum viable product, primary research often involves interviewing. Here are some suggestions for interview techniques.

1. Don't surprise the interviewee with your questions. If possible, send four or five questions in advance to the interviewee. It may be that the interviewee is not in a position to provide good answers. Having questions in advances gives them an opportunity to find a more appropriate person to add to the conversation. Or you may need to adjust the questions to accommodate interviewee. This is why advanced preparation makes for better interview.

2. During the interview it is possible, even advantageous, that the interview will go off script. If the interviewee has something interesting to say that you did not consider, let them talk. If, however, the interviewee is rambling on, then you need to politely get them back on track. The point is that the list of interview questions may not be ironclad. Its function is to give both parties a general roadmap on the point of discussion. But you should have a clear idea what you want to get out of the interview.

3. Best practice is to have 2 interviewees participate. Not 1, not 3. Both participate in the Q&A. However, one should have the primary responsibility of notetaking.

4. Notes be taken in handwritten form rather than typed on a laptop. The clicking can be distracting. More importantly, it may be necessary to make drawings during the interview. Organization charts, flowcharts, product schematics and the like are often the most useful results of an interview. Have paper and pencil (not pen) in hand.

5. Interviewees are more guarded if they know they are being recorded. Therefore, sessions should not be recorded. (Of course, if you do record, we must obtain

permission preferably in written form. There may be some jurisdictions which prohibit anonymous recordings.)

6. At the end of the interview, here are key questions to ask.

   - Is there any question we should've asked but did not?
   - Is there anything you want to add to any of the questions we asked?
   - Is there anyone else we should talk to?
   - If so, can you provide an introduction or can we use your name as reference?

7. Immediately after the interview is over, the interviewers should review the handwritten notes to make sure they are in agreement with what transpired. Transcribe notes into digital form as soon as possible and add to your primary research database while it's still fresh.

Research should not go on forever. At some point the entrepreneur needs to start writing the business plan with incomplete information. To determine whether the entrepreneur has enough information to proceed, we suggest writing an executive summary, described in the next section. If the entrepreneur cannot write a satisfactory executive summary, then maybe more research is indicated. However, if the summary makes sense and is only lacking details, then maybe it's time to write the business plan.

EXECUTIVE SUMMARY

The storytelling part of a business plan should be no more than 20 to 30 pages, single-spaced in a reasonable sized font. However, this is too much reading for investors. At best they may read the executive summary, which must tell the entire story and induce the reader to look at the rest of the business plan. It is a one or two page summary of everything that follows in the plan. It must stand alone, as many readers will make the decision whether to proceed or not based only the executive summary. Key elements are:

- Be two pages maximum. It may be a double-sided handout.
- It's an abbreviated form of the complete plan
- Refers each chapter of the business plan; describe the product market, operations, competitive situation, headcount and financials
- Include your request or purpose

- The purpose of the summary is to persuade the reader to read the rest of the plan, or take some other step, like call for a meeting

Executive summaries are often used as the first written introduction of the company to the potential investor. For example, when submitting documentation to an angel investor website, you can upload your executive summary. It often makes the first impression.

It is natural that the executive summary written at the beginning will need to be re-written completely when the business plan is completed. This is natural. In fact, if the executive summary does not change, the entrepreneur was possibly not open to new information developed in the writing process. It is interesting for the writer to compare the initial executive summary, which was originally a statement of intention, with the re-written executive summary, which summarizes the way things turned out.

BUSINESS PLAN CONTENTS

The storytelling part of the business plan is still relatively short, about twenty pages. Anything longer than that and people stop reading. The plan should be easy and fun to read, while addressing all the key concerns unique to your business. This is a challenge since it's easier to write a lot than to write a little.

Here is a generic table of contents.

- Executive Summary

- Company Backgrounder: Provide the basic identifying facts about your company. Location, history, where and when incorporated. If you are in a highly specialized field, you should provide some background of your field in layman's terms. A company backgrounder is not needed for a startup company.

- Products or Services: Explain the problem you are solving and how your product solves it. Describe the functionality and how it's built.

- Market Assessment: Characterize and quantify buyers.

- Marketing Strategy: How do you convince buyers? Go-to-market strategy.

- Competitive Analysis: Identify your direct and indirect competitors, and describe how you compete.

- Operations: Describe how you service customers

- Management/Staffing plan

- Financials: Provide summaries of your P&L and cash flows, including underlying assumptions. Describe funding needs, and milestones.

- Appendix. This can be lengthy. It could contain questionnaires, survey results, patents, resumes, blueprints and other backup data that does not fit in the body of the plan or in storytelling mode.

There is no one "right" structure - experiment to find a structure that best suits your enterprise, purpose and audience. Here some example tables of contents.

ERNST & YOUNG EXAMPLE

The accounting firm of Ernst & Young published a popular and inexpensive text to writing business plans. Search online for "Ernst and Young Business Plan Guide". Their model table of contents is as follows. This structure is appropriate for a mature company. There is emphasis on company background and management, highlighted.

- Executive summary
- **<u>Company description</u>**
- Products and services
- Marketing plan
- Operational plan
- **<u>Management and organization</u>**
- Milestones
- **<u>Structure and capitalization</u>**
- Financials
- Attachments
  Resumes, detailed financials, product line profitability, confidentiality agreements, patents, licenses

BIOTECH (KOLCHINSKY) EXAMPLE

Another example is from a biotech company called Evelexa. Search for "Kolchinsky biotech startup" or go directly to www.ctsi.ucla.edu/researcherresources/files/view/docs/EGBS4_ Kolchinsky.pdf

Biotech companies rely heavily on technology and intellectual property and many exit by trade sale. Therefore, there are chapter headings on technology, intellectual property and exit strategy that would not be applicable in the Ernst & Young case.

- Executive Summary
- Summary/Mission
- Opportunity
- **Technology**
- Business Model
- Competition
- **Intellectual Property**
- **Exit Strategy and Comparables**
- People
- Financials
- Appendix

As you can see, business plan structures can vary considerably. Pick the topics that are appropriate to your enterprise and needs.

WRITING THE BUSINESS PLAN

Assuming you've done your research,

1. Start with forecasting revenues. Define the product and its features, the TAM and market strategy. Identify your sales assumptions and pricing. Create the sales plan (channels, compensation, and sales costs). What's the TAM? How many customers will buy? How many units will you sell?

2. Now you know your expected revenues, but do you believe it? If you don't believe it, or don't like it, then you need to reconsider your product and target market and go back to step 1. If the revenue story looks plausible, continue to the next step.

3. Determine startup costs and capital expense (Capex) plan. Identify your cost assumptions and supply chain dependencies. Document the operations plan and expenses (Opex). This is driven by headcount, facilities, information technology costs and other recurring costs.

4. Now you know your expected costs, but you believe them? If not, go back to step 3. If you can't make your Capex and Opex work, then go back to step 1. If costs look okay, then continue to the next step.

5. Create financial statements. See if the numbers add up.

6. If the numbers don't add up, loop back to Step 1. Rethink your product and market definitions. If the finances look okay, continue to the next step.

7. Edit, condense and format your plan. Move details to the Appendix.

8. From your business plan, compose the elevator pitch, final executive summary and slide presentation.

9. Rehearse your elevator pitch and slide presentation to get comfortable making verbal presentations. Get feedback on your performance. You will need to make this presentation multiple times.

TIPS ON WRITING PLANS

- Start with a **detailed** Table of Contents. It's OK to have a 3-page outline for a 20 page plan.

- Balance the attention given to each section. Writers generally write most about what they know best. If a technologist is writing a plan, often too many pages are spent on technology. Allocate balanced page count to all topics specified in your table of contents. Balanced allocation is enabled by a detailed outline.

- Have a research plan. Specify secondary research sources, trade shows, conferences, interviewees, focus groups, industry luminaries, and so on.

- Include many (dozens of) primary research contacts.

- Use charts, graphics, matrices and other visual aids. The written report should not be pure text.

- Include a competitive matrix.

- Include a sensitivity analysis of financials in the appendix.

- Remember what your high school teacher taught you about storytelling, parallelism, development, clarity and grammar. Use a spellchecker.

- Include citations, references, footnotes. Build credibility with your choice and range of source materials.

- See the SEC handbook (www.sec.gov/pdf/handbook.pdf) for some writing tips.

- Observe these mechanics

  - Number your pages (both the plan and presentation).
  - Use a consistent font.
  - Don't repeat yourself (except for executive summary).
  - Include contact information.
  - Include a date and version.
  - Include a bibliography
  - Number your copies.
  - Use copyright and confidentiality notices.

THINGS YOU SHOULD NOT SAY

- "This is a conservative financial forecast". Better use "This forecast is based on the following facts . . ."

- "This is based on conservative estimates". The audience will decide for themselves what is conservative.

- "Our product will revolutionize your business". The audience will decide for themselves.

- "I can't give details (since I'm afraid you'll steal my idea)". Then why is the audience supposed to believe you?

- "We have no competition". Status quo is competition but if no one else is interested in your market, why is that?

- "Unparalleled in the industry". Hype.

- "Unique and unlimited opportunity". Hype.

- "No one has thought of this before". Maybe you haven't looked hard enough.

- "Superb returns with limited capital investment". Show financials.

- "Cancer is a serious disease". Obviously.

- "Streaming is a growing phenomenon". Obviously.

- In general, forget the hyperbole. Hyperboles impair credibility and waste time. The audience will decide for themselves. Lay out the facts and cite sources. Saying obvious things doesn't help your credibility.

WHY BUSINESS PLANS FAIL

- A weak operations plan;

- A weak sales plan; see "Thoughts on Sales" in the prior chapter on Risks.

- Erroneous, or unsubstantiated, assumptions about either revenues or costs or both. When the financials don't look good, entrepreneurs tend not to go back to the beginning to rethink the product.

- Too long. Make it punchy. Put details in your Appendix.

- Too much emphasis on product, and not enough on market, sales and operations.

- Too technical. Business plans, especially those authored by scientists and engineers are often packed with technical details and scientific jargon. Describe the technology only to show how it (1) solves the problem, (2) can be protected through patents or other means; and (3) can be implemented on a reasonable budget. All else goes to the appendix.

- Amateurish financials. "Conservative assumptions", unrealistic assumptions, and top-down rather than bottom-up financial analysis. Include income statements, balance sheet, cash flows and important schedules, such as fixed assets. Show sources and use of capital.

- Lack of recognition of competition or substitutions. The competition section of your plan is an opportunity to showcase your strengths.

- Lack of focus. Trying to be all things to all people. Paranoia about leaving some market out. Decide on a focus.

- Forgetting Cash. Revenues are not cash, gross margins are not cash, profits are not cash. Only cash is cash. Include a credible cash flow statement.

- Insufficient consideration of risks. Identify your vulnerabilities and address them. Let the reader know you have thought about their potential concerns.

- The plan should be persuasive and fun to read. If it doesn't tell a story, it won't be read.

- Appearance matters. If it doesn't look good, it won't be read. Use visual aids.

- Unbalanced allocation of text.

- Overtweaking. You can spend too many hours tweaking your plan in the pursuit of perfection. Often this time would be better spent working on content. If the reaction to your plan is negative, get feedback. Don't keep mulling the plan over by yourself.

- Insufficient rehearsal and outside review. Rehearse for timing, Q&A and poise. Have backup slides. Get critiques from people who have no vested interest but are knowledgeable about some aspect of the business or business planning.

- While it isn't necessary to write a formal business plan, the entrepreneur should use the plan as a checklist. It is used to convince all parties, including the entrepreneur, that all significant issues have been addressed.

- A business plan is communicated in a variety of ways. Elevator pitch, formal presentation, executive summary and full business plan. Prepare for each.

- Pick a format for the full plan that works for your enterprise and your purpose. One size does not fit all.

- Packaging matters. The plan should look good and you should sound informed, confident and poised.

Chapter 10 – Funding Sources

"I don't know anybody with money. Can you introduce me to some investors?"
Common question from students

In this chapter, we discuss funding sources during the early stages of a company's life, when the company is at the very earliest and most fragile.

In rough chronological order, money can come from any of the following sources.

- You (in a process we call "bootstrapping")
- Friends and Family
- Crowdfunding
- Accelerators/Incubators
- Government
- Angels
- Venture Capital
- Strategic Investors

This is where the money is. The next chapter will present thoughts on how to get it.

BOOTSTRAPPING

The first investor in your startup is You. You invest your money and maybe other resources into the embryonic beginnings of your startup. This process of using your own resources rather than external help is called bootstrapping. The problem with bootstrapping is that you are in constant fear running out of cash. However, a key advantage of bootstrapping is that you don't spend time raising money when fundraising is the most difficult and time-consuming. If you can get by, you can devote all your attention working on the company rather than raising money.

There are multiple forms and techniques to consider when bootstrapping.

- Savings, credit cards, second mortgages, spouse (your first venture capitalist)

- Consulting. This is usually just a transitional step but can be useful since builds your network, provides industry insight and market information.

- Custom product development. This is work done under contract to someone else. As a startup strategy, this works if you can retain some rights to the customized products you develop. Often clients will let you do so, in exchange for a discount. Then you could resell product developed on someone else's money.

- Moonlighting. Keep your current job but work on your startup at nights and weekends.

- Customer financing (my favorite). That means getting money from potential customers even before you built your product.

When in bootstrapping mode, the entrepreneur must work out operational problems before too much growth. Selling too much, too soon can create cash flow problems or cause you to turn away early customers which in turn can lead to future sales problems. In the digital space, scaling is less of a problem. But if you rely on a supply chain, or inventory financing, or labor, then you must be careful to match your expenses to the revenue opportunity.

Bootstrapping is necessary to improve your optics with potential investors. If you expect to raise money from strangers, you need to show them you have sacrificed to start the business, colloquially known has having "skin in the game". An investor doesn't want to be the first dollar in a deal if the entrepreneur has put in nothing. A common question a prospective investor will ask is "how much money have you put in so far?". "None" is the wrong answer.

FRIENDS AND FAMILY

After you and your spouse/significant-other have invested in the company, you may need more money. At this stage you may go to other people who already know you. That would be friends and family.

When raising money from friends and family, the first thing to consider is whether it's gift, a loan or equity.

If it's a gift, the giver does not expect repayment. But that doesn't mean you won't have issues. For example, if it's a gift from parents, consider the problem of equitable treatment of siblings. You are getting $10,000 from Mom and Dad. What should your brother get, even though he is 10 years younger? This can be of particular problem if the business doesn't do well. In the US, there is also the issue of gift tax, if the money is expressly a gift.

If friends and family money is a loan, then customary elements of a loan must be at least discussed, if not documented. What's the collateral? Maturity date? What happens in case of default? What's the repayment plan? Should repayment begin only after there is revenue or operating profit? Loans from friends and family should probably have a written loan agreement. This can be a touchy matter. It's hard to ask Grandma for a signature on a loan document. You may want to forego this formality but consider what happens if the company fails.

If money from friends and family comes in as equity, then ownership and shareholder rights must be specified. Does your Grandma or Uncle Joe want to have voting rights or sit on the board of directors? What about information rights? Make sure the shareholders understand their rights.

In the case of loans or equity, what if the lender or investor dies? How do you handle estate problems? How are the shares disposed of?

The problem with friends and family financing is that it causes drama. You don't need more drama in starting a business. Is the relationship more important than the money? You might end up losing one or both. Nonetheless, a majority of startups use friends and family financing because they must. To minimize drama, there should be understanding if the money is a gift or loan or equity. Have a clear discussion. Paper the deal if it's not a gift, at least on the back of a napkin.

CROWDFUNDING

Kickstarter, IndieGoGo, GoFundMe and a host of other web sites enable entrepreneurs to sell either product or equity in their company on their respective e-commerce platforms. Crowdfunding websites differ in focus, services offered and pricing but some key elements are common.

Crowdfunding to Sell Product

Crowdfunding began as a site where entrepreneurs could sell product, even before the product was shipping. This was a form of customer financing, which is why we like crowdfunding. Non-dilutive money is raised which could be used to complete product development. Buyers advance money to the company, receive some consideration (perks) and patiently wait for the goods to show up. The vast majority of crowdfunding campaigns are well intended with good results for both the company and the buyer. However, history tells that, occasionally, they don't. If the goods don't show up, there is no recourse for the 'buyer'.

Companies desiring to raise a significant amount of money must mount a marketing campaign on the website to attract buyers. This is marketing and it's not free. There are hundreds of products for sale on a crowdfunding website at any given time. If your product is not on the first few pages of the crowdfunding site, then you are unlikely to sell much. A quick look at the first page of key sites (kickstarter.com, indiegogo.com) shows you must produce a persuasive, convincing video, develop pricing and offer incentives. Even so, the vast majority of campaigns fail to reach their intended targeted amount of financing.

Crowdfunding to Raise Equity

In addition to product, it is possible to sell shares on crowdfunding sites. Crowdfunding for equity was enabled by the JOBS Act of 2012 and later amended December 2015 to liberalize equity crowdfunding. There are SEC rules regarding crowdfunding. Search online for "sec regulation crowdfunding".

There are two advantages of using crowdfunding for equity. First, it removes geographic limits on who can buy your stock. You can raise money from anybody in the world. The second is that it allows the entrepreneur to bypass the investment community. A common question entrepreneurs ask is "Can you introduce me to some investors?". With crowdfunding they don't need to know investors personally.

For potential investors, the advantage of crowdfunding is access to deal flow they didn't have before. Investors can see more deals that were previously visible only to well-known investors. By removing these constraints on both the entrepreneurs and investors, crowdfunding is said to democratize fundraising.

However, if you raise equity by crowdfunding, you may have lots of shareholders, perhaps dozens or even hundreds. This can pose a few legal problems. For example, if the company is an S Corp, then the limit on the number of shareholders could be exceeded or some shareholders may not be Americans. Or if the company is an LLC, there may be changes required in the Operating Agreement to reflect new members.

More importantly, future investors may object to dealing with a lot of other shareholders. If the startup ends up with dozens of shareholders, it may be tricky to call a shareholders' meeting or obtain majority consent for certain actions. The term for this is 'dirty cap table', which professional investors prefer to avoid.

Crowdfunding Early Success

Whether product or equity is sold, the company must mount an early marketing campaign to get people to take the offer. Campaigns on crowdfunding sites don't last forever. They're typically limited to 1 or 2 months. You must show success on day one. That means the video and marketing materials must be well-prepared. The campaign must begin before the campaign is launched in order to have interest early on. You must tell all your friends and family to buy something on day one.

If your product or equity is not showing traction within a few days, the website will move you down in priority so that you will get buried by other campaigns that come along after you. There're so many products for sale on so many websites that if you don't get off to a great start you'll get lost in the noise.

If you search online for "how to launch crowdfunding", you'll see a number of folks who at least purport to coach you on launching successful campaigns.

The various crowdfunding website have information on fees, tips on setting targets and tips on running successful campaigns.

INCUBATORS AND ACCELERATORS

Incubators and accelerators are shared work places where startup companies interact with each other and share common resources, such as WiFi, packaged delivery, speaker programs and mentorship. Some incubators or accelerators offer equity investment, some don't. Incubators, by our definition, are long-term programs typically sponsored by civic organizations who are promoting economic development in a targeted area or for specific populations. Accelerators are short-term programs generally lasting from 3 months to 6 months that target companies which demonstrate the likelihood of attracting further institutional financing.

	Incubators	Accelerators
Sponsor	Local government Chambers of Commerce Development authorities	Private investors, VCs, universities promoting campus related companies
Term	Can be months or years	Months. Since companies will be vacating soon, there is greater pressure to perform than in incubators.
Invest cash	Usually no	Yes, occasionally
Equity taken	Usually no	Yes, occasionally
Mentoring	Not much, maybe guest speakers	Yes, usually a lot

Table 10-1. Incubators vs Accelerators

Civic incubators tend to attract higher tech companies due to the longer gestation period required. For example, the Los Angeles Business Technology Center (labtc.org) has many high-tech tenants due to its proximity to CalTech and the Jet Propulsion Laboratory.

Important accelerators such as TechStars and YCombinator offer intensive mentoring and equity investment to their tenants. YCombinator, in particular, has many successful alumni companies such as Airbnb, Dropbox and Instacart.

The networking, mentoring, facilities and maybe cash infusion, make incubators and accelerators worth considering, although entry into better incubators and accelerators is highly competitive.

GOVERNMENT FINANCING

In addition to providing shared workspaces, governments around the world provide financing and support services for startups. Government entities which provide support range from municipal up to national governments. For example, Business Finland (https://www.businessfinland.fi/en/) takes a direct role in financing startups in Finland as Vinnova (https://www.vinnova.se/en/) does for Sweden. The government of Singapore invests through government agencies, such as their National Research Foundation (https://www.nrf.gov.sg/funding-grants/early-stage-venture-fund).

In the United States, federal support is offered through programs called the Small Business Innovation Research (SBIR), Small Business Technology Transfer (**STTR**) and other programs which provide grants or contracts. In addition, the Small Business Administration (https://www.sba.gov) provides a loan guarantee program for businesses that are not necessarily technical in nature.

Some data sources for SBIR and STTR are:

https://www.sbir.gov
https://www.sbir.gov/about/about-sttr
http://www.nsf.gov/eng/iip/sbir/
http://grants.nih.gov/grants/funding/sbir.htm
http://www.acq.osd.mil/osbp/sbir/

SBIR and STTR are aimed at technology startups. If you don't have a tech startup, money can be obtained through the Small Business Administration (SBA).

The qualifications and details on obtaining funding are on the various websites. But for our purposes here we make the following points about government funding.

Federal Government funding has 4 advantages.

- You don't have to pay the money back. Many programs are grants. Others may be contractual but even in those cases the government won't ask for the money back unless there's fraud.

- When the government provides financing, they take no equity in the company. This is non-dilutive financing.

- If you invent something using government funds, the government allows you to keep the intellectual property.

- Perhaps most importantly, if you can obtain government funding for high-tech projects, you have earned some investment credibility. Someone in the government thought you're onto something. Future investors may take that into consideration.

On the other hand, getting government money is problematic.

- Since there are these advantages, government funding is highly competitive.

- The government offers relatively small amounts of cash. It's rare that a recipient of SBIR and STTR are grants can get more than $1,000,000.

- For SBIR and STTR, use of cash is mostly restricted to technical or product development. There is no allowance for sales or business development.

Nonetheless, these grants and contracts are popular among high-tech entrepreneurs, and rightly so.

ANGELS

Angel investors are high net worth individuals who dip into their own pockets to invest in complete strangers, often in fields they know little about. Angel investors certainly want to make a profit, but they are also motivated by a desire to help young people get businesses is off the ground and to help their communities. Angel investing keeps recently retired investors and executives active. They appear to have a lot of fun doing so. Here are some of their characteristics.

- High net worth, accredited investors.
- Operate individually or in groups
- Invest up to $100k of their own money in each deal
- Have experience, normally with a management background
- Want to "stay in the game". They are tired of playing too much golf

- Invest <u>before</u> the venture capitalists, when valuations are lowest

Angels operate individually or in groups. If they operate individually, they're hard to find by entrepreneurs. Individual angels normally seek opportunities among their trusted friends and advisers.

Angels in groups tend to have better results than those operating alone. A group of angels can collaborate to mentor the startup and are easier to find since they have a web presence and thus have good deal flow. Examples of well-established angel groups in California include:

- <u>www.bandangels.com</u>
- <u>www.techcoastangels.com</u>
- <u>www.pasadenaangels.com</u>

Go to AngelList at <u>angel.co</u> for further information. Search online for 'angel groups' for lists of angel organizations in your area.

The process of obtaining funding from angels is roughly as follows:

- First, a startup company seeking funding from an angel group submits an application on the angel group website. Most angel websites have a simple dropbox for this.

- A screening committee reviews the applications and invites a few to make a personal presentation. Only a fraction of companies will be invited to present. The odds of the startup company are improved if the entrepreneur is already known to one or more angels already or if the deal is referred buy another angel group.

- The startup company will present to the angel group. The group will consist of 20 to 50 people at a single sitting. In most cases, the startup company will have to 20 to 30 minutes, including Q&A. Inexperienced presenters often make the mistake talking too long thereby leaving too little time for Q&A.

- The company is asked to leave the room and the next company will present.

- There will be about four presentations. After all presentations are made, entire group of angels will debate the merits of each deal.

- If no one in the room is interested in a deal, the startup company is so informed shortly thereafter.

- If a particular deal draws the interest of one or more angels, one of the angels will lead a due diligence investigation. The investigation will take a few weeks to complete. If the company satisfies the angels, then the angels will collectively make a single offer, in the form of a term sheet.

- If there is agreement between the startup company and the interested angels, then legal documents are drawn up and the company is funded.

This is a simple process which is familiar around the world. The activities of angel groups in a specific geographical area contribute strongly to the clustering effect of entrepreneurship.

However, since Angels write personal checks, the amount a company can receive is relatively small, usually less than $1 million. If you need more money, you may need to go to venture capitalists.

VENTURE CAPITALISTS (VCs)

Venture capitalism is the first form of <u>institutional financing</u> the company is likely to encounter. Whereas Angels invest their own cash, institutional investors raise money from other investors, such as pension funds to invest on their behalf. If you will, this is a form of outsourcing, whereby the pension fund, for example, is outsourcing early stage investing to the venture capitalist. Some points about venture capitalists are:

- They are usually stage focused. Some VCs invest in early stage early companies while others prefer to invest in late stage, more mature startup companies. If you are an early stage company, there's no reason to pitch to a late stage investor.

- They are usually industry focused. Industry focus means the firm specializes in a particular domain such as healthcare or information technology. Some new VC funds will say they are industry agnostic. This suggests they have no particular domain experience.

- VCs always purchase preferred shares. You won't see them buying common shares.

- VCs share information and deals among each other. Syndication is common.

Search for 'venture capital information sources' to find links to VC news and sources. The National Venture Capital Association (NVCA.org) is a good place to start.

In the United States, VCs are usually organized as limited partnerships.

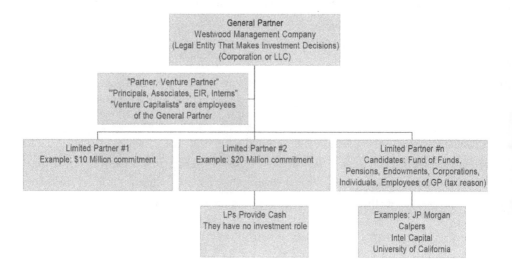

Figure 10-1. Structure of a VC Partnership

All investment decisions are made by the General Partner (GP). The GP is a legal entity such as a corporation or LLC. Using that form of entity, the individuals making investment decisions are shielded from liability. When an individual person says he or she is a 'venture capitalist' that means that person is employed by, or part owner of, the GP.

The various limited partners (LPs) are typically large financial institutions, such as investment banks or not-for-profit institutions, such as pension funds or university endowments. The LPs invest in the fund but are otherwise passive. They make no investment decisions. Due to their passivity, they have no liability. LPs can invest different amounts and the distribution of profits is shared pro-rata.

{Not for profits LPs }

Not for profit LPs such as university endowment funds have no interest in receiving losses incurred by the portfolio companies since they pay no taxes. This means VC firms cannot invest in pass thru entities, such as LLCs. Otherwise, portfolio company losses will pass to the VC who in turn passes the losses to the not-for-profit LP. The value of the losses vanishes since the not-for-profit LP pays no taxes. Therefore, VC firms must invest C Corporations.

It is the job of the GP to raise funds from LPs in the same way that entrepreneurs raise money from VCs. The GP must exhibit domain expertise and a value to the LP. When the GP and LPs come to an agreement, there is a complex contract, called a <u>Limited Partner Agreement (LPA)</u> which binds the parties. The LPA will specify the maximum amount of capital the partnership will raise. After the GP has invested in an array of portfolio companies, it will patiently wait until each company has either succeeded or failed. Proceeds from the successful companies are distributed to the LPs. Due to the requirement to redistribute funds to the LPs in a timely manner, each LP fund has a finite lifespan, usually on the order of 10 years. At the end of the lifespan, the fund is terminated.

When a particular VC fund invests a large part of its capital, it will try to raise another fund rather than simply wait for the portfolio companies to exit. The second fund is a separate legal entity from the first fund. Sometimes the second fund raises money from the same LPs, sometimes not. Successful GPs are able to raise successive generations of funds, called <u>vintages</u>. Each vintage is a separate entity with separate amounts and different LPs.

We mentioned before that LPs provide the capital for the VC fund. But the LPs do not write a check up front. They <u>commit</u> the funds, meaning they earmark the money for future disbursement to the GP. Hence the term <u>committed capital</u>. LPs disburse funds as requested by the GP. When the GP finds a deal and needs the cash to fund the deal, the GP will issue a <u>capital call</u> which is a request to the LPs to wire funds to the GP. The LPs will have just a few days to wire the funds. After the funds are received, the GP will fund the deal.

If the fund has cash available due to a prior liquidity event, there may be no need to issue a capital call. The GP will simply use money from prior exits. This is called <u>recycling liquidity</u>. In this happy circumstance, the LPs get credit for making capital call without having to wire additional funds.

It is possible an individual LP will decide not to honor a capital call. Perhaps the LP is running into financial difficulties. Or perhaps the LP decides it's no longer interested in venture capital at all. What happens then? See your Limited Partnership Agreement. This is the sort of contingency that makes LPAs complex agreements.

We depict the lifecycle of a deal from capital call to exit as follows:

Flow of VC Investment & Capital Return

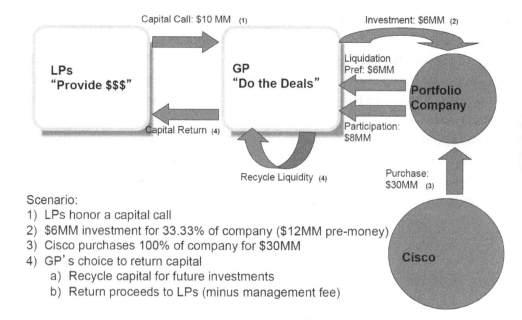

Scenario:
1) LPs honor a capital call
2) $6MM investment for 33.33% of company ($12MM pre-money)
3) Cisco purchases 100% of company for $30MM
4) GP's choice to return capital
   a) Recycle capital for future investments
   b) Return proceeds to LPs (minus management fee)

Figure 10-2. Flow of VC Investment and Capital Return

In this depiction, the GP invests $6 million dollars into a portfolio company and receives a one third interest in the company. In order to fund the deal, the GP issues a capital call, in this case for $10 million. The LPs wire their pro rata share of the $10 million. The GPs retain $4 million for expenses and subsequent deals.

Let's assume that over the next few years, the company makes progress with the $6 million. It subsequently receives a buyout offer from Cisco for $30 million. Since the investor owns one third of the company and the company is sold for $30 million, does the investor receive $10 million? The answer is no, due to provisions in the investment called Liquidation Preference and Participating Preferred. The VC will get $14 million in a calculation we describe later on when we discuss Term Sheet, Series A.

How does the General Partner Make Money? Why are Individual Venture Capitalists So Rich?

GPs make money by a form of profit sharing, called <u>Carried Interest</u>, or <u>Carry</u>. We illustrate by this example of a Carried Interest Calculation.

- Assume the VC fund raises $100 million in committed capital

- Assume exits of $150 million in 10 years

- Assume 80/20 distribution. This means the GP gets 20% of the amounts received over the committed capital. The distribution is specified in the LPA.

- Using these figures, the carried interest to the GPs is $10 million calculated as 20% of ($150 million - $100 million)

- Proceeds to LPs is $140 million calculated as $100 million committed capital plus 80% of ($150 million - $100 million)

- The $10 million that goes to the GP is shared among the partners or owners of the GP. Other employees of the GP such as analysts or associates generally do not share in the carried interest. They get a salary. It's a good salary but it's not profit sharing. It's good to be a partner in the GP.

The percentage of carried interest is negotiated between the GP and the LPs and stated in the LPA. Particularly strong GPs can get more than 20% carried interest. New venture funds may get less.

VCs can also collect management fees of 2 to 3% per year on committed funds. If a particular GP is operating several vintages at once, it can be collecting fees for multiple funds at once. This is called 'fee stacking' and can be a contentious negotiating point between the GP and various LPs.

Finally, individual VCs can make direct investments into the fund, just as the LPs do. This may be necessary so that individuals can receive capital gains treatment upon receipt of carried interest.

How to become a Venture Capitalist.

Individuals who think they want to become venture capitalists are really thinking about how to become a partner in a VC firm. It is only at the partner level that real money is made due to participation in carried interest. The question, then, is how to become a partner?

A seemingly obvious path is to the start in a VC firm as an associate or analyst and eventually get promoted to the partner level. However, it is rare for new entrants into venture capital to become partners this manner. What is needed at the partner level is deal flow. Can the analyst or associate produce deals? Do they know entrepreneurs who can get funded? Generally, the deals that analysts and associates are aware of is the same as the partners in the firm.

A more successful route to partnership is to succeed outside the VC community and move laterally to the partnership level. One can start a company that has a successful exit or have a successful career in an industry that's of interest to the VC firm. In both cases, access to fresh deals is what's of interest.

The ability to perform due diligence and analyze companies is a fungible set of skills. That's what MBAs from top schools do. The cultivation of deal flow and having a network of entrepreneurs are the assets of greatest interest.

PRIVATE EQUITY DIFFERS FROM VENTURE CAPITAL

We view venture capital investment as a proper subset of private equity (PE) investment. What they have in common is that both invest in privately held companies. This commonality can give rise to the view that private equity investing is the same as venture capital investing. However, the table below indicates key differences between the two.

Private Equity Investors	Venture Capital
Invest in any industry.	Invest usually in high growth, high tech
Will fund with debt and equity. Can do leveraged deals.	Will fund with equity only. No leverage.
Prefer funding large deals	Invests in smaller deals
Prefer funding later stage, more mature companies	Invests in early stage deals

Investment banking background needed. Emphasis on financial skills	Emphasis on operating skills. Entrepreneurial experience desired
Objective is to turnaround, recapitalize, or flip companies.	Objective is growth with large multiples, over a longer term
Quick liquidity	Long time to liquidity
Larger amounts invested with smaller multiplex on exit	Smaller amounts invested with huge multiples on exit

Table 10-3. Private Equity vs Venture Capital

Our view is that private equity investors have different objectives and skill sets from successful VCs. The VC must be adept at operations and longer term growth. Exits take several years. The PE investors are financial engineers, intent on quick turnaround. This is the opposite of what is needed in supporting small early stage companies. Therefore, our view is that private equity investors rarely make for successful venture capital investors.

STRATEGIC INVESTORS

Strategic investors are large corporations that invest in startup companies.

They fund deals through either a closely held, corporate owned VC fund or from operating funds of a business unit.

They have financial motivation just like any VC fund. But in addition, they are motivated to advance a strategic corporate interest as well as make an investment profit. Therefore, the objectives of the strategic investor or different from a VC. This provides advantages and disadvantages to the entrepreneur of having a strategic investor.

Advantages	Disadvantages
Industry knowledge. Can help with sales, product development and staffing. Possible access to lab space and intellectual property.	Usually won't lead the round
Patient money. Won't insist on quick exits.	Risk of captive product development
Possible customer, supplier and mentor.	Risk of sales to competitors precluded
Possible higher valuation since there are operational as well as financial motives	Some financial investors advise against strategic investment until very late stages of financing
Confers credibility to the startup when looking for financial investors	
Path to liquidity. Once invested, the strategic partner is in a position to acquire the entire company.	

Table 10-4. Pros and cons of strategic investment

Industry dynamics which tend to favor strategic investment.

- Thought leaders are important. Having an investment from a leader could be crucial to operational success or finding additional investors

- A possibility of a buyout by the strategic investor who desires vertical integration.

- Possibility of a long-term client relationship with the strategic investor if the public investment climate is not friendly to exits. Having a strong strategic investor can be protective in difficult times.

The Case of Trillium Digital Systems

The case of Trillium Digital Systems illustrates the end to end process from bootstrapping to strategic investor exit.

Jeff Lawrence was a solo entrepreneur when he started a company called Trillium in 1988. Soon he was joined by an immigrant from the then Soviet Union named Larisa Chistyakov. Jeff and Larisa were mostly hustling for programming jobs from computer companies in Los Angeles. Their business was custom software development projects on a fixed price basis. They had to go fixed price because that's what customers wanted. Customers did not want exposure paying an open-ended hourly rates.

Their specialty was data communication software. This was before the popularization the Internet protocols. In the 1980s, hardware manufacturers had proprietary software to communicate with other computers of the same manufacturer. The job of Trillium was to provide software so that different hardware companies could communicate with each other. For example, IBM to Data General or Hewlett Packard to Quotron. Since they were writing these programs for a fixed price, they bore the risk of underestimating the time it took to complete the project. Many projects they wrote for were basically for minimum wage.

Another problem Trillium had to deal with was change orders. Customers sometimes altered their requirements after they began work. Keeping these change orders to a minimum was a major challenge for new entrepreneurs who were working for a fixed price. However, they kept to their fixed-price business model rather than charging hourly rates as they were trying to build the business and reputation.

An important insight they derived after completing some projects was that they could retain the rights to these programs for resale to other customers. Since initial customers we're not in the business selling data communications software, they agreed to allow for resale by Trillium.

This is how they were able to make a product company from a custom development company. This business model had advantage of customers paying for product development. Another advantage of fixed-price software development is that it allows for greater profit than hourly rates. Using hourly rates, your profits are limited by the number of hours you can bill. With fixed price, if you're able to estimate accurately, then your profit potential is greater than hourly rates while still providing comfort to the client on the maximum they would pay. Indeed, for most large-scale systems projects, bidding is fixed price with contractual provisions on managing change orders.

Trillium's business grew and in due course they needed outside financing to expand operations. One of the two investors was Intel Capital, a strategic investor. Intel's motive to invest was to get information as to whether to enter the communications business either as a software or semiconductor vendor. Being an investor in Trillium gave them eyes and ears into the communications business. Intel invested $4 million in 1999.

In 2000, Trillium was able to consider an <u>initial public offering</u> (IPO). Intel Capital stepped in to preempt the IPO by offering to buy the entire company. In a mere 12 years after they started the company, Jeff and Larisa sold the company for $300 million to Intel.

The takeaways from this case are how to transform the consulting business into product business, the advantage of offering fixed-price contracts, why strategic investors use venture capital to assess their entry into other fields, and, finally, that strategic investors can provide exits for their portfolio companies.

We've discussed a number of sources of early stage capital, from bootstrapping to institutional capital. Now you know where the money is. The questions is how do you get it?

TAKEAWAYS

- There are many sources of cash for startup companies. Some may be unfamiliar. When consider sources of capital, consider these:

  - Amount of money being raised. The more you need, the higher the probability you need to go to institutional investors.

  - Time to raise money. The more urgent the need, the higher the probability you go to people who know you already or crowdfunding.

  - Probability of a close. Investors were unfamiliar with your subject matter are less likely to find your company. Venture capitalist see a lot of deals. The percentage of deals funded buy VCs is relatively small.

- Dilution. Some investors require more ownership than others. Government money usually comes with no ownership requirement at all.

- Relationship desired with the investor. Some investors provide greater value then others. Look for investors who can provide mentorship and ongoing support, such as sourcing suppliers.

- Control. How much of it do investors want? Are you willing to provide preferences to institutional investors?

- Our objective here is to present some of the terminology of fundraising and thereby assist the entrepreneur in selecting investors.

SELF STUDY

Question #1

Of the following, which should the entrepreneur be most concerned about?

a) Growth
b) Profit
c) Cash Position

Question #2

Why is customer financing an excellent form of early stage financing? Pick one or more.

a) Market validation
b) Early revenue
c) Mentoring
d) Availability of large pools of capital

Question #3

Crowdfunding can be used to sell equity thereby bypassing angels and VCs. But the sale of equity poses a problem for future investors. What is that problem?

ANSWERS

#1 (c)

#2 (a) and (b)

#3 The entrepreneur ends up with dozens or hundreds of investors. That makes it more difficult to obtain consents. Also it can an create legal problems for pass through entities.

(Now you know where the money is. How do you get it?)

Previously we discussed where the money is. Now we'll discuss how to get it. Topics covered here are:

- Chronology of fundraising
- Packaging
- Due diligence
- Why investors say "No"
- Legal documentation

CHRONOLOGY OF FUNDRAISING

The chronology of fundraising for a particular startup is roughly as follows:

1. Somehow you get your business plan or executive summary or pitch deck in front of potential investors. This is often the hardest part.
2. Initial meetings, emails and phone conversations.
3. Due diligence by the potential investor.
4. Investor presentation.
5. Further due diligence.
6. An investor syndicate is formed.
7. Potential investors offer a non-binding term sheet.
8. Closing documents, also known as definitive documents.
9. Funding.

Steps 1 and 2 can be very time-consuming, especially if you don't know anyone in the investment community. How do you meet investors? Unless you know people, or have an introduction, this frustrating step takes time, often weeks, or even months, depending on the availability of investors near you. Clustering matters. This partly explains the popularity of crowdfunding.

To get through this step, you will need to network and work your acquaintances for referrals. Networking events are the most time efficient of these, since that is where you will find investors who want to expand their list of potential entrepreneurs. Find out where people congregate, polish your elevator pitch, and start meeting people.

After some initial contacts, the potential investor will initiate a due diligence process. This means doing some preliminary research on you, the business idea, markets, the supply chain, whatever.

If the investors like with they see and hear, we reach step 4, the investor presentation, or the pitch. Investors will allocate more or less time to hear your pitch, depending on their process and how interested they are. Typically, you will present to angels for less than half an hour. It is likely that a VC will allocate more time, since there is probably more money involved. The investor presentation is a crucial step and few entrepreneurs actually make it this far.

If the potential investors like your pitch, they'll continue with their due diligence. After the presentation due diligence will be more rigorous.

Eventually, the investors may decide they want to invest. There will be a lead investor who will have the responsibility for offering the valuation of your company, presenting a term sheet and recruiting other investors into the investment group, which is called the syndicate. Sometimes there'll only be one member of the syndicate but generally it's to the benefit of both the entrepreneur and investor to have multiple investors and therefore multiple looks at the deal.

The investor syndicate then makes a non-binding offer called the term sheet. The term sheet is a memo of understanding or a letter of intent. Both parties can sign the document but we emphasize it is non-binding meaning either party can back out. It's rare and unfortunate that parties back out of a signed term sheet but it's possible due to findings uncovered during due diligence, or one party just changing its mind.

The term sheet serves as the basis for binding legal contracts drafted by lawyers for the company and investors. Drafting contracts takes weeks and costs thousands of dollars. The company will receive money only after the completion of legal documentation.

Our rule of thumb is that it takes about six months to raise serious money from people you don't know. If you know investors personally, then you reduce the time it takes for steps 1 and 2. In any case, don't wait until you are six months away from completely running out of cash before starting your search for funding.

PACKAGING

In order to raise money, you need a good story and good packaging. The components of good packaging are these:

- Elevator pitch.
- Executive summary, which was discussed earlier in the chapter on business plans.
- Presentation, using PowerPoint or similar presentation software.
- Presentation skills. Be sure to rehearse and inspire confidence.
- Business plan. May not be necessary for the investor but it should be completed at least for your edification.

Elevator pitch

When trying to get to know potential investors (step 1 above), the entrepreneur will often attend networking events, trade shows, or conferences. In each of these venues, it is necessary for the entrepreneur to have a good elevator pitch.

The elevator pitch provides a key test of how well you can deliver your message. It is delivered in person, informally, and frequently ad hoc. Imagine yourself at a meet up, finding yourself next to a potential investor. You may have wine in one hand and cheese in the other. You have one minute, what are you going to say? A good elevator pitch conveys the following points in 60 to 90 seconds;

- a tagline - something catchy,
- a statement of the problem,
- how big the problem that you are solving (what's the TAM?),
- your product, and how it solves the problem,
- your current status,
- your credentials,
- your sustainable advantage, and
- a request - for money, a follow-up meeting, a partnership, etc.

Samples of good and bad elevator pitches can be found online, for example, on YouTube. You should always be prepared to deliver your elevator pitch since you never know when you might meet a potential investor.

Presentation

If you're invited to make a presentation, you have cleared a major hurdle. Only a few percent of entrepreneurs get this far. Presentation to investors is a big deal, so get it right. The mechanics of a presentation include:

- 10 – 15 overheads.
- Specify the money requested.
- Say what will you do with the money; identify milestones.
- Have email and phone contacts on presentation.
- Bring samples, visual aids.
- Bring more than one person, show there is a team.
- Have hard copies ready. They make take notes.
- You have one hour (or less), including Q&A.

Presentation decks, with lots of detail, tend to focus the audience's attention on the deck and not on *you*. The audience is so busy reading your presentation, they may not be listening to you. In the Guy Kawasaki school of presentation, good PowerPoint has 10 slides, delivered in 20 minutes with 30 point font. (https://guykawasaki.com/the_102030_rule/). Other similar pitch decks can be found at https://attach.io/startup-pitch-decks/?ref=producthunt

The risk of having a presentation with few details is that a week or so after your presentation, the investor may want to take a look at some details and they are not in the deck. You may need something else to leave behind. Sometimes the amount of detail will be dictated by the investor. Either way, your voice, or your deck, must convey a good story in a convincing manner.

Usually your investor presentation will be delivered without interruption. After the presentation you can expect vigorous Q&A. Here are some routine investor questions you can expect from potential investors who are not familiar with your business domain.

- "What's the TAM?"
- "What is your value proposition? Why would anyone buy your product?"
- "Who is your competition? How do you win?"
- "What incentives will you provide to your first customers, like price concessions or special services? How much will these incentives cost?"
- "What progress have you made to date (*traction*)?"
- "How do people pay you? What is your business model?"
- "Have you accounted for bad debt and accounts receivable problems in your cash flow statement?"
- "What is your customer and employee churn rate?" How quickly do they turn over?"
- "What makes you qualified to do this?"
- "What are your milestones? What are you going to do with the money?"
- "How do you know that xyz is true?" (Fill in the blanks with revenue or cost assumptions.)

- "How much research did you do? What are your sources?"
- "How do your conclusions follow from your assertions?" (Does it make sense?)
- "Who is on your team? Have you worked together before?"
- "What intellectual property protection do you have? What are your patents or trade secrets?"
- "Why hasn't this been done before?"
- "I don't get it!" (Where is the storytelling?)

These questions and observations are generic. They can be asked by anyone who doesn't know what you're talking about. But once you get through questions like these, expect detailed technical, legal, market, operational or financial questions from domain experts. You need to have answers. The more serious the investor is, there more you'll need to answer detailed questions. Anticipate as many as possible.

Presentation skills

Don't be boring during your presentation. Maybe you've given your investor pitch dozens of times before. But a particular investor is seeing it for the first time. You need the same vitality and engagement at the 100th presentation as you gave at the first.

If you are presenting to an audience that may not be familiar with your subject matter, then all they know about your deal will be your persona. You have to make sure you come across well. If the audience is familiar with the subject matter, you still have to come cross well. To do that you need to rehearse your presentation. There are four reasons to rehearse.

- Content. Get the story right.

- Timing. You'll be given your timing in advance, say 10 minutes to present with another 15 minutes of Q&A. If you're given 10 mins to present, be sure you tell your story in ten minutes. Not nine. Not eleven.

- Q&A. There will be questions from your audience. Anticipate key questions and have backup slides. If you get a question you cannot answer, don't bluff. Experienced investors can sense bluffing. Simply say you will get back to them at a later point with the complete answer.

- Show poise, maturity, confidence, and enthusiasm. Inspire confidence in you, not just the business idea. You are selling yourself, not just your knowledge. Treat it like an audition.

Both inexperienced and experienced entrepreneurs alike will be nervous. Schedule initial practice presentations with people you really don't expect to invest, or colleagues who constitute a friendly audience, who will give you honest, critical, sometimes painful, feedback. We suggest you record yourself so you can see how you come across. Use every presentation as a learning experience. With enough repetition you'll feel more comfortable.

DUE DILIGENCE

Before and after the presentation the investors will consult secondary and primary sources to check out you and your story. Here's a list of sources they could contact:

- Off sheet references. You'll be asked to provide references. Of course, references you provide will be favorable. Therefore, occasionally references you provide could be used as a "do not call" list. Diligence could be conducted by calling people in a similar position to your references.
- Your customers, prospects and competitors.
- Police background checks.
- Past and current investors.
- Professional services support, such as lawyers and accountants with whom you done business.
- Former colleagues.

Information uncovered in this process may be sensitive. Even so, do not expect investors to sign a nondisclosure agreement (NDA). For many entrepreneurs, this may be a major concern. Investors see so many proposals a year, it is impractical for them to sign an NDA for every deal they investigate. It exposes them to too much liability.

If there is information that you are uncomfortable with divulging, then say so. Put a fence around details that you cannot provide and say why. For example, you are well advised to avoid providing details of a trade secret.

As part of the diligence process, the investor may want to collect printed evidence including:

- Legal documents (Articles of Incorporation, stock purchase agreement, patent filings, for example).
- Financials (audited, unaudited, working papers).
- Personnel records (non-compete, NDAs, payroll records, patent assignments...).
- Corporate agreements (sales, subcontracts, partnerships).
- Banking agreements (loans, liens...).

- Government permits and certifications, building inspections.
- Intellectual property filings. Patents, list of trade secrets.
- Legal action pending or in process.
- Ownership, current capitalization (cap) table.

Work with your accountant, your staff, and your lawyer to have these documents ready.

Why investors say "No"

Despite having a good presentation and surviving all the checking, investors may still say "No", even if they like you, the team, the domain and the proposal. Why is that?

- Inflated Valuation. If the investor feels the entrepreneur has an inflated view of the value the company, they could take this as a sign of inexperience, or be fearful the relationship could get off to a bad beginning.

- Fund is out of money, or is reserving funds for "dry powder" in subsequent rounds of existing portfolio companies. If that's the case, why did they invite you? Perhaps to get information for when they do have more capital.

- Over-invested in this field. Perhaps there is a conflict with an existing portfolio company.

- Other investors pass. Peer pressure can have a major impact on investors, especially inexperienced investors.

- The investment doesn't fit the investor's mission or doesn't an have sufficient emotional appeal.

- External, macroeconomic factors such as a plunging stock market, or high interest rates.

Usually it's not personal. Don't take it personally.

Bill Reichert, a Silicon Valley investor with a good sense of humor, made these observations about entrepreneurs and investors. At various times he has presented his 'Top 10 Lies

Entrepreneurs Tell Investors'[1] and [2]. These lies change a bit from presentation to presentation, so I've taken what I think are his best.

- "Our projections are conservative."
- "(big marketing consultant) says our market will be $56 billion."
- "(big customer) will sign our contract next week."
- "Key employees will join us as soon as we get funded."
- "No one else is doing what we do"
- "We have first mover advantage"
- "(big competitor) is too slow to be a threat."
- "Our sales cycle is 3 to 6 months"
- "Patents make our business defensible."
- "I'll be happy to hand over the reins to a new CEO"

On the other hand, his 'Top 10 Lies VCs Tell Entrepreneurs'[3]:

- "We can make a quick decision"
- "I liked your company but my partners didn't."
- "If you get a lead, we will follow."
- "Show us some traction and will invest."
- "We have lots of dry powder."
- "we are investing in your team."
- "This is a vanilla term sheet."
- "We can open doors for you at major companies."
- "We like early stage investing."
- "Good Work !"

Howard Schultz was rejected over 200 times when trying to fund Starbucks initially. Make the best of each presentation. Upon rejection, get feedback. Here are some tips to get value from a presentation that did not sell.

- Identify comparable companies in the investor portfolio and ask the investor how they got comfortable with that company.
- Share a milestone that you have in mind and ask if reaching that milestone might allay their fears.

---

1   https://www.garage.com/files/LiesEntre.pdf

2   https://www.youtube.com/watch?v=ReE44CymfF4

3   https://www.garage.com/bill-reichert-top-10-lies-vcs-tell-entrepreneurs/

- Get suggestions regarding other funds or angels, talent or advisers that you can talk to.
- Get business development leads.
- Get introductions to related companies in their portfolio.

LEGAL DOCUMENTATION

Let's assume the investor syndicate said they would like to proceed and offer you a term sheet. Even after you get a term sheet, you're not there yet. The term sheet is just a letter of intent. To get money, lawyers for the investors and the company will jointly will draft definitive, binding legal documents for signature. Some of these documents are:

- Articles of Incorporation
- Stock Purchase Agreement
- Shareholder Rights Agreement
- Voting Rights Agreement
- Co-Sale Agreement
- Option Agreement
- Employee Agreement
- Vesting agreement for the founders
- Side letters, such as representations and warranties

We'll define some of these terms in later chapters on term sheets.

For now, let's just say these documents need a lot of "lawyering" and it really adds up. A simple 5-page term sheet is the basis for hundreds of pages of legal documents. There may be contentious issues which arise due to a misunderstanding or omission of term sheet provisions. Therefore, some points may need to be renegotiated, or at least a clarified in legal terms. The process of going from term sheet to documents takes about a month and costs thousands of dollars.

SOME FURTHER TIPS ON FUNDRAISING

- Throughout the process, have good manners. The investors will remember you for your next deal. The investment community is rather small so if word gets out about your poor behavior, that won't help you the next time you try to raise money.

- Don't ask for non-disclosure agreements.

- Do not cold call investors. Get an introduction. This can be done through other entrepreneurs you know, or your lawyer, banker, accountant, former classmates and teachers.

- Don't haggle on valuation or control. There is a fine line between haggling and negotiations; between having conviction and being stubborn.

- Always remember, you are asking complete strangers for money. How would you react if a stranger asks you for thousands of dollars?

TAKEAWAYS

- Have good packaging.

- Understand the chronology so that you won't be confused as to why it takes so long or why people are behaving as they do.

- Even with the good story and good packaging, investors may still say 'No'. They may have good reason. Don't take it personally. There may be another time for you to meet.

- Fundraising is . . .

  - Grueling. It can take months and dozens of presentations. It's not for everybody and it will test your commitment.
  - A learning process. Learn from those who say "No". You learn about yourself and how much you want to do this business.

SELF STUDY

Questions

1. Entrepreneurs don't raise debt financing. So, why would an increase in interest rates negatively impact their ability to raise equity financing?

2. Bill Reichert said one lie that VCs make to entrepreneurs is "If you get a lead, we will follow". Why is this a euphemism for rejection?

3. Despite increased dilution, why would an entrepreneur take the maximum amount of capital in an early round, rather than taking a minimum amount, which would preserve ownership?

Answers

1. An increasing interest rates may make other investments more attractive for the limited partners. High interest rates are associated with lower stock market prices. This makes the IPO market less attractive. Higher interest rates also tend to reduce economic activity which means sales for the portfolio companies could be negatively impacted.

2. Without a lead investor, no one is taking responsibility for pursuing the deal on the investor side. There is no one offering a valuation of the company or negotiating other key terms. Companies seeking funding must find a lead investor to take responsibility on behalf of all investors, offer a term sheet and recruit a syndicate.

3. • Can spend more time working on company rather than fundraising.
   • Increases odds of hitting next milestone
   • Can aim for more aggressive milestones
   • Reduces the number of rounds of financing

Chapter 12 – Term Sheet, Series A

"Things turn out best for the people who make the best of the way things turn out."
- John Wooden

This chapter explains key provisions of a <u>Series A term sheet</u>. The Series A term sheet memorializes deal terms for the first round of equity financing. Typically, this is the first investment made by an institutional investor, such as a venture capitalist. However, other investors, such as family offices or angels, may offer term sheets with similar provisions.

The key elements of the sample deal presented below are as follows:

- The investors collectively are providing $6 million dollars in cash in return for a 33.33% interest in Coldwater Circuits. Since Coldwater Circuits is issuing fresh shares to the investors, it is called the <u>Issuer</u>.

- The investors are also requiring an <u>unallocated option pool</u> for future employees which will consume 20% of the company shares. Since the investors are purchasing 33.33% of the company and there is an unallocated option pool of 20% of the company, this leaves 46.67% ownership to the Founders. The reason to carve out this pool of shares for future employees will be discussed as we walk through the term sheet.

- The investors are getting preferred rights, or preferences, that are not available to the Founders, employees or other shareholders of common stock. Investors are buying preferred shares.

  Key among these Preferred rights is the right to one or more seats on the Board of Directors. In this case the Series A investors are entitled to two seats on the board. Even though they have only a one third ownership in the company, they have two out of the five board seats and, in this case, have input on the fifth board seat.

Arguably the two most important provisions of the term sheet are (1) ownership percentage as reflected in the cap table, and (2) control as demonstrated, in part, by seats on the board. There are other important control provisions which we will explain as we go to the term sheet.

This term sheet is a minimally redacted term sheet taken from an actual transaction. It is annotated with explanatory comments in footnotes.

COLDWATER CIRCUITS

Series A Convertible Preferred[1] Stock Financing
___Month____ _Day__. 20xx

This Term Sheet summarizes the principal terms with respect to the proposed investment by Fund2000 Ventures. This Term Sheet is not intended to be and does not constitute a legally binding obligation of the parties[2], except as provided in the last paragraph herein. No legally binding obligations on the parties will be created, implied or inferred until documents in final form are executed and delivered by all parties., together with the other investors in the Series A Stock, the "Investors") in Coldwater Circuits.

General Terms

Amount of Investment:	$6,000,000
	Purchase price equal to $1.20 per share of Series A Stock (as defined below).
Shares:	Series A Convertible Preferred Stock (the "Series A Stock") of Coldwater Circuits, a California corporation (the "Company").

Investors:		
	Fund2000 Ventures[3]	$ 2,500,000
	Co-investors	$ 3,500,000
	Total	$ 6,000,000

Valuation:	Pre-money: $12,000,000
	Post-money: $18,000,000[4]

---

1   "Series A" refers to this document as the first instance of an institutional fundraising event. "Convertible" refers to the ability/requirement that these preferred shares be converted to common shares under the provisions of the Conversion clause.

2   Term Sheets are letters of intent. Both parties can walk away after signature, with certain exceptions.

3   Fund2000 is the Lead Investor. The Lead has particular responsibilities for the investment. Note that the Lead Investor need not be the largest contributor of capital. The co-investors at the time of this term sheet are not named, but will be recruited by the Lead Investor to round out the syndicate.

4   A $6M investment with a post-money valuation means the investor is purchasing 33.33% of the company. The pre-money valuation is simply the post-money valuation minus the investment.

Post closing Capitalization

Set forth below is the pro forma capitalization of the Company on a fully diluted basis, including without limitation all shares of common stock, convertible preferred stock and other convertible securities, warrants and all outstanding options and shares of common stock available for the grant of options.

Capitalization Table (Cap Table)[5]

Shareholder	Common Shares	Series A Preferred Shares	Common Equivalents	Percent Ownership
Series A Investors		5,000,000	5,000,000	33.33
Founders	7,000,000		7,000,000	46.67
Unallocated Option Pool[6]	3,000,000		3,000,000	20.00
Total	10,000,000	5,000,000	15,000,000	100.00

Stock Option Plan	20% of the fully-diluted shares outstanding post-financing will be reserved for issuance to employees (other than the Founders), directors and consultants pursuant to the Company's stock option plan. Such shares will be subject to four year vesting[7] - 25% one year from the date of award and quarterly thereafter with full vesting 48 months from the date of award.
Founders Vesting[8]	Current outstanding Common Stock held by Warren Buffett, and Abe Lincoln (Founders) will vest according to the Stock Option Plan. If Founders' employment is terminated with cause (as such term will be defined in such Founder's respective employment agreement), there is a repurchase option on unvested shares at cost. If a Founder's employment is terminated without cause all unvested stock would accelerate and become immediately vested.

---

5   The cap table illustrates two key provisions. First, who are the shareholders and second, what percent of the company does each shareholder own.

6   The option pool consists of shares reserved it for future employees. The company owns the shares, not the founders. The reason for this pool is to protect the investors percentage interest as subsequent employees are hired and receive stock options as part of their compensation package. As employees are hired they will get their options from the option pool and may ultimately deplete all 3 million shares. When the option pool is depleted and there is a need to hire more employees, then the investor percentage interest will drop below 33.33%, but not until then.

7   20% of the total shares of the company are carved out for employees. These shares are subject to a 4 year vest with a 1 year cliff.

8   The Founders are subject to vesting, even though they started the company.

Terms of Series A Preferred Stock

Liquidation Preference:[9]	On any liquidation of the Company, holders of Series A Stock to receive their investment, plus accrued and unpaid dividends, which liquidation rights shall be senior to the rights of holders of all other classes or series of capital stock of the Company.
Liquidation event	Any transaction resulting in the sale of 50% or more of the voting power or assets of the Company, including any merger, consolidation or similar transaction in which control of the Company is transferred, will be deemed a liquidation[10], triggering the liquidation preference on the Series A Stock
Dividends	Series A Stock to be granted a preferential non-cumulative[11] dividend at a rate of 7% per share per annum, when, as and if declared by the Board, and participation in all other dividends or distributions paid on any other classes or series of capital stock of the Company on an as-converted basis.

Participating Preferred[12]	Upon exercise of liquidation preference, holders of Series A stock share with the holders of the Common in the remaining assets on an as-if-converted basis.[13]

---

9   Liquidation Preference" means the investor gets money back before any other shareholders when the company is liquidated.

10   This defines when the Liquidation Preference is triggered, which could be either bankruptcy, which is obviously a bad outcome, or sale of the company, a good outcome.

11   Non-cumulative means that dividends do not accrue if unpaid for prior years. Cumulative dividends that are not paid in a given year, may be carried over and paid in the subsequent year.

12   The inclusion of Participating Preferred is sometimes called double dipping. Double dipping refers to the investors getting BOTH their investment back plus a pro-rata share of the company. A case of double dipping was shown in Chapter 10 in Figure 10-2.

   If venture capital money is particularly plentiful, it is possible for entrepreneur to resist this clause. In this case, the investor gets EITHER the investment back OR their pro-rata share of the company, but not both. On the other hand, if venture capital is scarce, investors will want their cake and eat it too and require Participating Preferred.

13   Remaining Assets is the amount of money left after the liquidation preference and dividends are taken by the investors. The Participating Preferred clause enables investors claim their pro-rata share of the Remaining Assets in addition to their liquidation preference. We will show example computations in Tables 12-1 through 12-3.

Conversion	Holders of Preferred A will have the right to convert the Preferred A, at the option of the holder, at any time, into shares of Common[14]. Series A Stock plus accrued and unpaid dividends convertible at any time (at the option of the holder) into Common Stock at a onetoone ratio. Mandatory conversion of Series A Stock in connection with the consummation of an underwritten initial public offering of Common Stock with aggregate gross proceeds to the Company and any selling stockholders of at least $20,000,000 and a per share offering price of at least 2.5 times the Series A Stock purchase price. Series A Stock also convertible on the vote of the holders of 66-2/3% of the outstanding shares, voting separately as a class.

Voting Rights	Series A Stock to vote with Common Stock on an asconverted basis, except as provided herein or by law.
Anti-dilution	Proportional adjustments for any stock split, stock dividend, dividend of other securities or of assets of the Company, reclassification, reorganization, exchange, substitution, merger, consolidation, sale of assets, recapitalization or other similar event. On the issuance of capital stock below the purchase price per share of the Series A Stock, as adjusted, the conversion ratio of Series A Stock shall be adjusted based on a standard weighted average share price formula, subject to an exception for the options to purchase common stock described in "Post-Closing Capitalization" above.[15]

---

14 Common Equivalents in the cap table table is computed as the number of Preferred Shares multiplied by a conversion ratio. It is Common Equivalents that determines percentage ownership. Normally the conversion ratio is 1 to 1, meaning 1 share of Preferred stock converts to 1 share of common. However, the conversion ratio can change, as when an anti-dilution clause is invoked.

15 Anti-dilution is a mechanism whereby the investor can get more shares in the event the price per share drops. This is done by adjusting the conversion ratio.

Board of Directors	The Board of Directors of the Company shall consist of five directors as follows: (a) two directors selected by the Series A Stock; (b) two directors selected by the Common Stock, and (c) one outside director with industry experience selected by the Common Stock and the Preferred Stock voting as a single class[16].
	All outside directors to receive reimbursement for direct, reasonable outofpocket expenses incurred in connection with attendance at meetings of the Board of Directors. The Board of Directors of the Company shall establish a compensation committee[17] and an audit committee, each consisting of three members and including one of the outside directors.
Drag Along[18]:	Holders of Preferred A and the Founders and all current and future holders of greater than 1% of Common Equivalent shares shall be required to enter into an agreement with the Investors that provide that such stockholders will vote their shares in favor of a merger or sale transaction approved by the Board of Directors and at least a majority of the Investors.
Subsequent Stock Sales	Holders of Series A Stock will receive right of first offer on their pro rata share of all subsequent equity issuances, except for issuances that are normally excluded from such right of first offer, including without limitation issuances under Boardapproved employee stock option plans and issuances that are made (for non-capital raising purposes) in connection with the Company's acquisition of another corporation, or all or a portion of its assets by merger, purchase of assets or other corporate reorganization. The right of first offer will not apply to and will terminate on the closing of the Company's initial public offering; provided, that if any other stockholder of the Company is afforded the opportunity to purchase primary shares of the Company to be issued in such public offering, then Investors shall also have such right, determined on a pro rata basis based upon Investors' percentage ownership in the Company relative to the ownership of the other stockholders participating therein.

Restrictions on Common Stock Transfers[19]	No transfers allowed prior to vesting other than transfers to certain Permitted Transferees for estate planning purposes.
	Right of first refusal on proposed transfer of vested shares (first in favor of the Company, and second in favor of the holders of the Series A Stock in accordance with their pro rata share of the Company's outstanding capital stock) until initial public offering.

---

16 Preferred Shareholders enjoy entitlement to seats on the Board of Directors, unlike common shareholders. In this case, the fifth member of the Board would usually require unanimous consent of the other 4, but this must be spelled out explicitly in the definitive documents.

17 The Compensation committee is a subcommittee of the Board which oversees salary, equity and benefits compensation. The Audit committee oversees the company audits.

18 Drag Along says that minority shareholders cannot hold up the sale of the company even if they disagree with the terms of sale.

19 Founders and employees cannot freely transfer or sell their common shares to others. This enables the company to keep control of the ownership of the company. The identification of Permitted Transferees will be specified in definitive legal documents. But these would normally include the estate of the founders and employees.

Pay to Play[20]	If the Company issues shares of its capital stock in a future financing for a consideration per share less than the applicable Preferred A conversion price in effect immediately prior to such issuance (a "Dilutive Issuance"), and a Preferred A holder has the right to purchase its pro rata share of such Dilutive Issuance and does not, then the Preferred A shares held by such Preferred A holder shall be converted to common shares.
Registration Rights[21]	The Company and the Investors shall enter into a Registration Rights Agreement, which agreement shall contain usual and customary terms and conditions, including without limitation, the following:

(1) Investors holding 35% or more of the Registrable Securities shall be entitled to two demand registrations of Common Stock held thereby (the "Registrable Securities"), exercisable any time after six months from completion of an initial public offering;

(2) Unlimited piggyback rights, subject to pro rata cutbacks, in the underwriter's discretion, to a minimum of 25% of the offering (except in the Company's initial public offering, where such cutback can be complete);

(3) The Company has the right to defer the filing of a registration statement required in connection with any requested registration for a period of not more than 90 days after receipt of the request by the Investors; provided, that the Company may not utilize this right more than once in any 12month period;

(4) No registration rights superior to those held by the Investors may be granted to any subsequent investors in the Company without the approval of Investors holding at least 66-2/3% of the Registrable Securities |

---

20 The Pay to Play clause provide a strong incentive for the Series A investor to participate in the Series B round when the company is losing value. If the Series A does not participate in the Series B round, they could possibly lose their preferences and be converted to common. This is the penalty for not participating in Series B. Series A may negotiate less onerous conditions such as the loss of specific preferences, like anti-delusion or Board seats.

21 A registration rights entitles certain Series A shareholders to force the company to file for an IPO. In this case, there must be at least 35% of the shareholders who want to do this. If a shareholder wants to with the company's or another investor registration request, then the shareholder can exercise piggyback registration rights.

Protective Provisions[22]	Consent of the holders of at least 66-2/3% of the Series A Stock will be required for: (1) Issuance by the Company of securities with equal or superior rights to the Series A Stock; (2) Merger, consolidation, sale of assets or stock or liquidation or other similar capital event with respect to the Company; (3) Repurchases of, or dividends or distributions to, Common Stock or Series A Stock, except with respect to repurchases, at cost and pursuant to the terms of pre-existing agreements with such individuals, of shares of the capital stock of the Company held by Company directors, officers or employees, not to exceed an aggregate of $25,000 in any 12 month period; (4) Amendments to the Company's Certificate of Incorporation or Bylaws that would have an adverse effect on the rights and obligations of the holders of the Series A Stock, and including without limitation, any change in the size of the Board of Directors and any change in the authorized number of shares of Series A Stock or to the rights, preferences and privileges thereof; (5) The sale by any direct or indirect subsidiary or other entity owned by the Company of any equity security or similar interest or any right to acquire an equity security or similar interest in such entity; and (6) Any material change in the Company's business as presently conducted. Notwithstanding the above Protective Provisions, Investor agrees in advance that consent of holders of Series A Preferred Stock is not required for subsequent capital raising transactions involving network transport or equipment providers..
Key Person Insurance:	$3,000,000 on each Founder, with the company as the beneficiary.
Information Rights	Holders of Series A Stock will receive unaudited quarterly financial statements for the first six months from the Series A Stock closing, and unaudited monthly financial statements thereafter, and will also receive a year to date analysis, as appropriate, as well as audited annual financial statements and annual budgets. Other information will be provided upon reasonable request.
Use of Proceeds	Working capital and general corporate overhead[23].

---

22 Protective provisions prohibit these actions which could be taken by the company or the Board of Directors without two-thirds approval of the Series A investors.

23 This Use of Proceeds clause means that no money from this round of funding can cash out prior investors, like friends and family.

Redemption[24]	If the Series A preferred stock has not been converted to common stock by 5 years after funding, the holders have the option to compel the Company to redeem the Series A preferred stock in 3 nearly equal annual installments, beginning one year after. The redemption amount shall be equal to the original investment plus any accrued and unpaid dividends.
Conditions to Closing	(1) Completion of a due diligence investigation[25] of the Company by the Investors and their advisors, the results of which are satisfactory to the Investors, in their sole and absolute discretion; (2) Execution of Stock Purchase Agreement, Registration Rights Agreement, Investor Rights Agreement and related side agreements; (3) All employees and consultants would enter into a inventions and proprietary information agreement. (4) Receipt of opinion of counsel reasonably acceptable to Investors[26]
Non-compete	Each Founder will enter into a one-year noncompetition and two year non-solicitation agreement with the Company in a form reasonably acceptable to the Investors.
Legal Fees	Company will bear its own legal fees and will pay the reasonable fees and expenses of Hood, Winkum and Slyde LLC, counsel to Investors[27], in an amount up to $25,000 and contingent upon the closing of the transactions contemplated by this Term Sheet.
Exclusivity	For a period of thirty days from the date of this Term Sheet, none of the officers, directors or employees of the Company will solicit, encourage or communicate with any other potential investors with respect to any investment in the Company.

24   If there is no IPO or sale of the company, these investors could try to get their money back starting in 5 years, if the company has the cash. This generally doesn't happen. As long as things are progressing, they'll wait for the payoff.

25   Even after the term sheet is signed, the investors will continue their due diligence investigation. If they uncover something they don't like, this gives them the opportunity to back out of the deal.

26   This opinion of counsel is sometimes called a representation and warrantee letter. Sample list of representations and warrantees are:

- The company is not subject to lawsuits, regulatory or tax claims.
- The investors have a proper list of shareholders
- Intellectual property valid
- Customer contracts in force
- There is consent of 3rd parties to the deal, such as banks, landlords or creditors
- Financial statements are complete and accurate
- There will be no changes to key personnel
- There will be no changes in business activities before closing
- There will be no changes in assets before closing. In particular, the cash balance will be intact. This is sometimes called an anti-looting clause.

27   The company will pay legal fees for both the company's lawyers and the lawyers for the investor. Legal fees are incurred by converting this term sheet into binding or definitive documents, such as those listed under "Conditions to Closing".

This term sheet is non-binding[28] and subject to negotiation of mutually satisfactory definitive documentation and to the satisfaction of each closing condition set forth above; provided, that the parties agree that the provisions of the foregoing paragraph on "Exclusivity" represents the parties' legally binding agreement, enforceable in accordance with its terms. The enforceability of those provisions is not conditioned on further negotiations or the successful outcome of any further negotiations.

The Company: Coldwater Circuits

                                        By:_____

The Investor: Fund2000 Ventures I, L.P.

                                        By: Fund2000 Management Partners, LLC
                                             Its General Partner

                                        By:_____

---

28 Either side can back out of the deal, due to the Conditions to Closing clause or either side just changing their mind. The Exclusivity Clause has some teeth, but not much. It any case, it is bad form to back out of the term sheet and carries with it reputational risk.

The Liquidation Preference and Participating Preferred clauses are of particular interest when the company is sold. These clauses largely govern the distribution of cash upon liquidation of the company.

Example 1.

Consider the case of Coldwater Circuits discussed previously. The key points of the deal are:

- $6,000,000 raised
- 1X Liquidation Preference
- 7% non-cumulative dividends
- Assume all the Unallocated Option Pool is distributed to new hires, so there is nothing left in the pool.

These result in the following cap table:

Capitalization Table (Cap Table)

Shareholder	Common Shares	Series A Preferred Shares	Common Equivalents	Percent Ownership
Series A Investors		5,000,000	5,000,000	33.33
Founders	7,000,000		7,000,000	46.67
Employees	3,000,000		3,000,000	20.00
Total	10,000,000	5,000,000	15,000,000	100.00

Given this cap table, the founder would like to know how much money he gets when the company is sold. For example, assume the company is sold for $20,000,000 exactly 2 years after the Series A round as described above. Also, assume all 20% of the employee stock options are issued.

What are the proceeds to the founders? The computation is as follows:

Event	Amount	Comment
Sale price of Coldwater	20,000,000	Given
Less, liquidation preference for Series A	6,000,000	Amount invested by Series A. They get their investment first.

Less, 1 year of dividends	420,000	7% dividend rate applied to $6,000,000 invested. Note only 1 year of dividends are paid since the dividends are non-cumulative even though the sale occurs 2 years later.
Remaining Assets	13,580,000	To be distributed to all shareholders on a pro-rata basis.
Percent ownership of Founders	46.67%	From the cap table
Proceeds to the founders	$6,337,786	46.67% of $13,580,000

Table 12-1 Distribution of Cash Upon Liquidation

Example 2

Let's assume that instead of depleting all the unallocated options, only 1,000,000 options are granted to employees and 2,000,000 are still left unallocated. The fully diluted cap table is as follows.

Capitalization Table (Cap Table)

Shareholder	Common Shares	Series A Preferred Shares	Common Equivalents	Percent Ownership
Series A Investors		5,000,000	5,000,000	33.33
Founders	7,000,000		7,000,000	46.67
Employees	1,000,000		1,000,000	6.67
Unallocated Option Pool	2,000,000		2,000,000	13.33
Total	10,000,000	5,000,000	15,000,000	100.00

Assume the company is purchased for $20,000,000 exactly 2 years after the Series A round as described above. How much money will the Founders get?

Table 12-2 illustrates the calculation.

Event	Amount	Comment
Sale price of Coldwater	20,000,000	Given
Less, liquidation preference for Series A	6,000,000	Amount invested by Series A. They get their investment first.
Less, 1 year of dividends	420,000	7% dividend rate applied to $6M invested. Note only 1 year of dividends are paid since the dividends are non-cumulative.
Remaining Assets	13,580,000	To be distributed to all shareholders on a pro-rata basis.

		Since 2M shares are left unallocated, they are
Percent ownership of Founders	53.85%	not counted in the ownership of the company. Total share count is 13M shares, not 15M.
Proceeds to the Founders	$7,312,830	53.85%% of $13,580,000

Table 12-2 Distribution of Cash Upon Liquidation with Unallocated Options

The key observation is that the 2 million unallocated shares are taken out of the total number of shares. The Unallocated Shares are not returned to the founders.

Example 3: Zone of Indifference

In some instances, the Participating Preferred clause may put a cap on proceeds to the investor. This would reflect strong bargaining power of the founder. Search online for 'participation cap' for details. The term sheet language could read:

Participating Preferred	Upon exercise of liquidation preference, holders of Series A stock share with the holders of the Common in the remaining assets on an as-if-converted basis up to a 3x cap[29].

So, while the optics for the Founder appear favorable, this clause introduces a situation in which the interests of the ounder and investor are not aligned.

First, we note that upon the sale of a company, the Investor always has the CHOICE of

(1) taking liquidation preference + dividends + participation, OR

(2) taking percentage ownership of the company.

Of course, the investor will take the greater of the 2 numbers.

Capped participation refers to the limit on the sum of liquidation preference + dividends + participation that the investor can claim with option (1). This offers some relief to the founders but can cause a conflict of interest between the founder and investor in a limited number of cases.

As an example of capping, consider the case with the following.

* $6M investment for 33.33% ownership.
* 1X liquidation preference

---

29 The sum of liquidation preference plus dividends payable plus participation, cannot exceed 3X the investment. In this case, the limit is $18M. Of course, the preferred shareholder can waive their liquidation preference and participation, and take their percentage ownership instead, like any other shareholder.

- 3X cap

Upon the sale of the company (Column A), the investor gets the maximum of column E or column F. The Founder gets the rest, column G.

The payoff is as follows for various sales of the company.

Column A is the sale price of the company.

Column B is the liquidation preference to the investor. For the sake of simplicity, we will ignore the effect of dividends. The investment was $6M.

Column C are the remaining assets to be distributed to common shareholders.
This is Column A minus Column B.

Column D is the participation of the investor in the remaining assets. In this case, the participation is 33.33% of Column C, the remaining assets.

Column E is the proceeds to the investor in the event the investor takes their liquidation preference plus participation. This is Column B plus Column D.

Column F is the proceeds to the investor in the event the investor waives liquidation and participation and just takes it pro-rata ownership. In tis case, this is 33.33% of Column A.

Column G The investor will take the maximum of Column E and Column F.

Column H is the money going to the common shareholders, namely the founders and employees. This is Column A minus Column G.

A	B	C	D	E	F	G	H
6	6	0	0	6	2	6	0
15	6	9	3	9	5	9	6
30	6	24	8	14	10	14	16
42	6	36	12	18	14	18	24
48	6	42	14	18	16	18	30
54	6	48	16	18	18	18	36
57	6	51	17	18	19	19	38
60	6	54	18	18	20	20	40

Note that if the company is sold for any amount between $42M and $54M (highlighted), the investor gets $18M, due to the cap of 3X invested. Hence, the investor is indifferent to any sale in that range.

However, the Founder gets more if the company is sold for $54M than if the company were sold for $42M. Hence the Founder wants a bigger sale, whereas the investor doesn't care. So, there is a conflict between the entrepreneur and VC in the highlighted rows, the Zone of Indifference.

Note that if the company were sold for a gigantic amount, greater than $60M, the interests of the Founder and investors are aligned. They both take their pro-rata ownership and ignore liquidation preference entirely.

TAKEAWAYS

Not every clause of a term sheet is important or controversial. Some points are more important than others. The important ones are:

- Valuation. This determines the percentage of the company you own after the investment.

- Board. This determines the composition of the Board of Directors and your participation in it.

- Liquidation preference. Most experienced investors well only asked for 1X liquidation preference. If an investor requires 2X liquidation or more, then make sure you have non-participating preferred or you may have to look elsewhere for an investor.

- Participating or non-participating preferred. This determines whether investor has "double dipping" privileges. See the clause on participating preferred. However, in the majority of cases, the investor will insist on participating preferred. Excessive haggling on this point (by the issuer) may jeopardize your negotiation.

- Protective provisions. There may be case specific clauses requested by the investor, such as the spending cap imposed on first time entrepreneurs.

Other clauses such as dividends, use of proceeds, redemption, registration rights and the like are usually not worth arguing about for Series A. These causes could be important in later rounds, but not early on.

EXERCISES

For the following questions, use the Coldwater Circuits Series A term sheet presented in this chapter.

Question 1:

If the company is sold for $30,000,000, how much does the Founder get? Assume all the employee options have been allocated to employees and 1 year of dividends are to be paid to the investors.

Question 2:

Assume the Founders push back on this proposed term sheet. Instead they are able to negotiate a $20 million pre-money valuation. Assume $6,000,000 is invested, the Founders have 7,000,000 shares and the option pool is 20%. Only the valuation changed.

Later the company is sold for $30 million. All one year of dividends and all employee options are allocated. How much does the founder get?

Question 3:

What is the minimum sale price of Coldwater that is required for the Founders, (exclude employees and investors) to get $2 million? Assume all of the shares in the employee option pool are distributed and one year of dividends are paid to the investors at the time of sale.

Question 4:

The Use of Proceeds clause ensures that the entire amount of the money raised stay within the company to fund grow. However, there may be occasions when the Series A investor would permit cashing out prior investors. Under what conditions would that happen?

Answer #1:

Event	Amount	Explanation of Amount
Sale of the company	30,000,000	Given
Less liquidation preference	6,000,000	Series A investment
Less dividends	420,000	7% of $6m for one year
"Remaining Assets"	23,580,000	Left to distribute among all shareholders
Founders' Ownership	46.67%	From the cap table
Founder pre-tax proceeds	11,004,786	46.67% of $23,580,000

Answer #2:

Since the Investors invest $6m on a $20m pre-money, their ownership percentage is 23.08% ($6m/$26m). The Founders' ownership is 100% - 23.08% (investors) – 20% (pool), or 56.92%

Event	Amount	Explanation of Amount
Sale of the company	30,000,000	Given
Less liquidation preference	6,000,000	Series A investment
Less dividends	420,000	7% of $6m for one year
"Remaining Assets"	23,580,000	Left to distribute among all shareholders
Founders' Ownership	56.92%	From the cap table
Founder pre-tax proceeds	13,421,736	56.92% of $23,580,000 Or an increase of $2.4m due to an increase in pre-money valuation

Answer #3:

Then, solve for Sales Price where

0.5692*(Sales Price − 6,000,000 − 420,000) = 2,000,000

where 0.5692   = % ownership held by Founder
    6,000,000   = liquidation preference to the investors
    420,000 = one year of dividends paid to investors
    2,000,000   = target amount desired

    Sales Price   = $10,705,378

Answer #4:

There are a couple of motivations for permitting investment cash to flow out of the company immediately to prior investors. First, is to get rid of problem investors or clean up the cap table by reducing the number of shareholders. The second would be a good will gesture to prior investors or to the Founder. There may be need for a gesture to the Founder's family and thereby curry some favor with the Founder. Or the new investor may simply want a bigger share of the company.

In any case, careful thought must be given, especially at early stages of financing, to limit the leakage of cash out of the company.

(Kicking the can down the road)

In Chapter 12 we identified key deal points the entrepreneur and investor must agree to before executing a term sheet. In the case of Coldwater Circuits, discussed in the prior chapter, the investor proposed that a $6,000,000 investment would buy a 33.33% ownership of the company.

However, the entrepreneur may feel that a 33.33% ownership is too much for the investor and that the investor should only get 25% of the company. This yields a post-money valuation of $24,000,000, not $18,000,000. If the parties reach an impasse on valuation, what happens then?

An alternative is for the entrepreneur to find other investors who will advance a <u>Convertible Note</u>. A convertible note (or simply a <u>Note</u>) is a financing instrument that provides cash to the company without specifying a valuation. How does that work?

A convertible note postpones the need for a term sheet by providing a small amount of cash in the form of a loan that converts to equity on the subsequent equity round, at which time there would be a valuation. Since so little is known about the company at the earliest stage of the life of the startup, neither the investors nor entrepreneurs are comfortable with setting a valuation. By using a note, the investors postpone the valuation discussion to see what progress can be made with a little bit of money (and thereby 'kick the can down the road'). Then, presumably, there will be more information upon which to base a valuation.

The sequence of events is:

- The <u>Noteholder</u> advances a loan to the company. Like any business loan, there is an interest rate, collateral and maturity date.

- Eventually, typically less than 2 years, the company is able to raise an equity round which has a pre-money valuation. This is called a <u>priced round</u> since it establishes a price per share. Let's say this is the Series A round, although notes can precede Series B and even later rounds. In fact, Spotify issued a convertible note before their IPO in 2019.

- The Noteholder converts the face value of the note, plus accrued interest, into shares of the Series A round, thereby becoming a member of the Series A syndicate. Since the Noteholder invested *before* the Series A, the Noteholder took a greater risk than the Series A investor and will expect a lower price per share than the Series A price.

- The discount the Noteholder enjoys is either explicitly stated or is a function of a mysterious, negotiated item called a <u>Valuation Cap,</u> which is a key provision of the note. We'll discuss how this number is used later in this chapter.

- When the priced round occurs, the Noteholder surrenders the Note to the company and receives shares at the discounted rate specified in the Note. This event is called <u>conversion.</u> No further cash is required of the Noteholder to receive Series A shares.

- Upon conversion, the Note is extinguished and no more interest accrues. Since the ex-Noteholder has Series A shares after conversion, he enjoys all the preferences the Series A enjoys, like dividends, with one possible exception we'll discuss in a section later this chapter called <u>Noteholder Liquidation Preference</u>.

The number of shares the Noteholder gets upon conversion is the amount of the Note, plus interest, divided by the price per share the Noteholder converts at. In the exercises that follow, we denote the conversion price as PPS(N) (price-per-share of the Noteholder). For example, if the Note has a face-value of $600,000 and there is a 6% interest accrued after one year, the Noteholder gets $636,000 worth of Series A stock. The number of shares the Noteholder receives would be $636,000 divided by PPS(N).

This begs the question, what is the conversion price of the note, PPS(N)? To illustrate Note conversion, here are some examples.

Example 1: A Convertible Note with no Valuation Cap

Assume the Noteholder advances a Convertible Note with these terms:

- Loan amount of $600,000
- Interest rate on the Note of 6% per year
- Explicit discount of 20%.

Then, assume there is a subsequent Series A priced round from another party with these terms:

- Conversion occurs exactly one year later.
- Pre-money valuation of $12,000,000.
- $2.00 per share paid by Series A, denoted as PPS(A).

What is PPS(N), the price per share to the Noteholder?

Since the price per share paid by the Series A is $2.00 and the Noteholder gets a 20% discount. The Noteholder price-per-share, is $1.60 per share.

How many shares will the Noteholder get in the Series A round?

The number of shares the Noteholder gets is the face value of the note, plus interest, divided by $1.60 per share. In this case, the Noteholder converts $636,000, which is the face value of the Note plus one year of interest at 6%.

$$\text{Number of shares the Noteholder gets} = (\$600,000+\$36,000) / \$1.60$$
$$= \$636,000 / 1.60$$
$$= 397,500 \text{ shares.}$$

Example 2: Impact of a Valuation Cap

In Example 1, the Noteholder gets 397,500 shares regardless of the Series A pre-money valuation whether it is valued at $12,000,000 or $100,000,000. This seems unfair to the Noteholder who has no way to participate in the upside valuation of the company if it goes to $100,000,000. After all, the company became wildly successful on the $600,000 Note when no one else believed in the company.

The Noteholder participates in that upside by way of a new term in the Convertible Note called a <u>Valuation Cap</u>. The Valuation Cap is the maximum valuation of the company that the Noteholder will convert at. This is best illustrated by example:

Assume the same case as example 1, with the addition of Valuation Cap of $3,000,000:

- Loan amount of $600,000.
- Interest rate on the Note of 6% per year.
- Explicit discount of 20%.
- Valuation Cap of $3,000,000.

The Valuation Cap means even if the valuation of the company is $100,000,000, the Noteholder converts as if the valuation were only $3,000,000

Then, assume the same priced round as in example 1 above. That is:

- Conversion occurs exactly one year later
- Pre-money valuation of $12,000,000
- $2.00 per share paid by Series A, denoted as PPS(A).

The price per share paid by the Noteholder is equal to the price per share paid by the Series A multiplied by the Valuation Cap divided by the Series A pre-money. Or,

PPS(N) = PPS(A) * (Valuation Cap / Series A Pre-money valuation)

In this example,

PPS(A)= $2.00   {from the Series A term sheet}
Valuation Cap = $3,000,000   {from the Convertible Note}
Series A Pre-money = $12,000,000   {from the Series A term sheet}

Therefore, PPS(N) = $2.00 * ($3,000,000/$12,000,000)

PPS(N) = $0.50

That's correct, the price-per-share paid by the Noteholder is $0.50 a share, while the price-per-share paid by the Series A investor is $2.00 per share. The Noteholder gets a 75% discount off the price paid by the Series A investor. This is due to the huge increase in valuation of the company prior to Series A, using the cash supplied by the note. You will notice that that without the Valuation Cap, the Noteholder converts at $1.60.

Next, we compute the number of shares the Noteholder gets.

That would be ($636,000) / $0.50, or 1,272,000 shares.

So, without the Valuation Cap, the Noteholder receives 397,500 shares, but with the Valuation Cap, the Noteholder receives 1,272,000 shares.

Of course, if the ratio of Valuation Cap to pre-money valuation is such that the explicit discount is more beneficial to the Noteholder, the Noteholder can, and will choose the explicit discount.

In the Example 2, if the pre-money valuation of Series A were $3,500,000, then PPS(N) would be $2.00 * $3,000,000/3,500,000) or $1.71 per share, which is more than $1.60. Therefore, the Noteholder would prefer the 20% explicit discount and ignore the Valuation Cap.

What's the rationale for this benefit to the Noteholder?

The Noteholder is taking a greater risk than the Series A investor because the Noteholders commit cash to the startup earlier than the Series A investor. To compensate the Noteholder for that increased risk, the Valuation Cap allows for a greater discount in the event of a huge increase in valuation. One can debate the fairness of the discount, but without the Valuation

Cap, the company may not get a Note at all. If the startup management can get a Note without a Valuation Cap, more power to them.

How much should the Valuation Cap be?

In the case above, the face value of the Note is $600,000 and the Valuation Cap is $3,000,000. This is 5 times the face value of the note, which is relatively common. The Valuation Cap is subject to negotiations and, of course, entrepreneurs will ask for a higher multiple. But if the entrepreneur holds out for an excessively high Valuation Cap, that could cause a breakdown in negotiations.

Isn't a Valuation Cap just like a valuation for a priced round?

We said before that a Convertible Note postpones the valuation exercise of a priced round. Doesn't a Valuation Cap look like a priced round valuation?

The response is, sort of. The Valuation Cap is not strictly a valuation of the company. It is only the upper limit of valuation that the Noteholder uses to compute price per share upon conversion. The valuation may, and usually does, come under the Valuation Cap, in which case the explicit discount is used.

What is a Simple Agreement for Future Equity (SAFE)?

SAFEs constitute a simpler variation of Convertible Notes. These variations make SAFEs more favorable to the company than a regular Convertible Note because SAFEs sometimes have neither collateral nor a maturity date. Imagine getting a loan with no collateral provision and no maturity date!

These instruments were introduced by YCombinator in 2013 https://www.ycombinator.com/documents/ and have proven to be a popular form of early stage investing.

Investing in a SAFE makes sense if you *know* there will be a conversion. But otherwise, the SAFE investor can be left hanging. If you are an entrepreneur and can get a SAFE, take it. But be sure there is a good faith attempt to convert.

What if the Note matures and there is no conversion?

The company will simply repay the Note, with interest, upon maturity like any other loan. This is not a win for the Noteholders. They took a lot of risk for just a few percentage points of interest. Noteholders don't want to make a habit of investing in notes that don't convert. They are better off investing in real estate.

Here are some pros and cons of a Convertible Note from the entrepreneur's point of view.

Pros	Cons
Fast. No negotiation of valuation or other difficult provisions.	Dilution upon conversion caused by the explicit discount or application of the Valuation Cap.
	However, if the Valuation Cap is used, the entrepreneur's net worth has increased substantially
No immediate loss of control. Noteholders have no shares until conversion and normally don't take board seats.	The Noteholder is a creditor and is senior to shareholders in the event of bankruptcy. Therefore, the Noteholder can take possession of company assets, like patents.
No immediate dilution	Some Noteholders may not be acceptable to later Series A investors (perhaps due to prior experience), which can complicate the formation of the Series A syndicate
	Negotiation of Noteholder Liquidation Preference can get complex. This will be discussed in the examples below.

Table 13-1. Pros and Cons of a Note from the Entrepreneur's Viewpoint

On the other hand, the Noteholder has no rights normally accorded to preferred shareholders, like board seats or liquidation preferences, since the Noteholder has no shares before conversion. Many venture capitalists avoid Notes and go straight to a priced term sheet. They want the control and the preferences immediately.

LLCs With Convertible Notes.

A complicating factor for members of LLCs occurs when the LLC issues a Convertible Note. The conversion of the Note into equity can create a tax problem for Members of an LLC who are US taxpayers. This is a complex point, to be read only if you are interested in LLC accounting issues.

When a Note is converted into equity, the loan goes away, and is treated as if the loan were being paid off. The conversion would add to the capital account of the Member and be considered taxable income upon conversion. This could be a nasty surprise to the Member.

The point is that Members of an LLC should think twice about obtaining financing through a Note[1].

---

1   https://blog.vcexperts.com/2019/07/16/llcs-and-convertible-debt-too-good-to-be-true/

Here is a sample annotated Note issued by Coldwater Circuits. The Note is being funded by Fund2000, as the Lead investor, with unspecified co-investors completing the financing of $600,000.

COLDWATER CIRCUITS
CONVERTIBLE NOTE

This term sheet summarizes the principal terms with respect to the proposed investment by Fund2000 Ventures and/or one or more of its designees and/or affiliates (collectively, "Fund2000" and this term sheet is not intended to be and does not constitute a legally binding obligation of the parties, except as provided in the last paragraph herein. No legally binding obligations on the parties will be created, implied or inferred until documents in final form are executed and delivered by all parties, together with the other investors in the Series A stock, the "Investors") in Coldwater Circuits.

	Fund2000 Ventures[2]	$ 250,000
Investors:	Co-investors	$ 350,000
	Total	$ 600,000

Type of Security:

Promissory Notes ("Notes"). Notes bear cumulative annual interest at Libor + 2.0% or 8%, whichever is greater[3]. These notes convert to equity as stipulated in the "Conversion Rights" section of this term sheet.

Security:

The Notes will be a secured senior obligation of the Company, secured by all assets of the Company.

Principal Amount of Notes:

Up to $600,000, to be provided in tranches called by the Company. Approval by at least 51% of Noteholders is required to advance each tranche.

---

2   As with priced term sheets, there usually is a Lead Investor

3   Various forms of interest rates can be used. Libor is used here. U.S. prime or treasury rates can also be used. Whatever interest rate is used should be publicly and unambiguously determined.

Term of Notes:

The Notes shall be fully due and payable, with accrued interest, on December 31, 20xx. A 60% majority of Noteholders is required to extend the due date.

Conversion Rights:

The face value of the Notes, plus accrued interest to the date of conversion, may be converted, at the sole discretion of the Investor, into Series A Preferred Shares at a 20%[4] discount, up to a Valuation Cap of $3,000,000 pre-money[5].

Prepayment:

Not permitted[6]

Use of Proceeds:

Working capital needs of the company only[7].

Expenses:

The Company and the Investors shall each bear their own legal and other expenses with respect to the transaction, provided that if a sale of the Notes occurs, the Company shall pay the reasonable fees and expenses of one counsel to the Investors.

Existing Notes:[8]

All promissory notes issued by the Company for funds advanced to the Company previously shall be amended to provide that the terms of such notes will be the same as the Notes and shall provide for conversion in accordance with their terms in the event of conversion by the holders of a majority principal amount of notes of like tenor.

---

4   This is the minimum discount the Noteholder will get.

5   Establishes the maximum pre-money valuation at which the Noteholder will convert. If the pre-money valuation of the next round exceeds this amount the discount rate to the Noteholder increases.

6   If pre-payment of the Note is allowed, the Note could be paid off one day before the Series A. That would be very bad for the Noteholder.

7   Similar to a priced term sheet, the proceeds of a Note cannot be used to pay off prior investors like friends and family.

8   This would need to be reconciled with other liens that have other obligations. Could be a sticking point.

Purchase Agreement:

The purchase of the Notes will be made pursuant to a Note Purchase Agreement drafted by counsel to the Investors. Such agreement shall contain, among other things, appropriate representations and warranties of the Company, covenants of the Company reflecting the provisions set forth herein and other typical covenants, and appropriate conditions of closing. Until the Purchase Agreement is signed by both the Company and the Investors, there will not exist any binding obligation on the part of either party to consummate the transaction. This Summary of Terms does not constitute a contractual commitment of the Company or the Investors or an obligation of either party to negotiate with the other.

Closing:

On or before 90 days from the date of this term sheet.

This term sheet is non-binding and subject to negotiation of mutually satisfactory definitive documentation and to the satisfaction of each closing condition set forth above. The enforceability of those provisions is not conditioned on further negotiations or the successful outcome of any further negotiations.

The Company: Coldwater Circuits

By:_____

Date:_____

Example 1:

Let's apply the Coldwater Circuits Note just described with the Coldwater Circuits Series A term sheet in Chapter 12 to calculate the cap table for Series A, which includes the Noteholder.

The relevant provisions of the Note are:

- $600,000 face value
- 20% discount
- 8% interest rate
- $3,000,000 Valuation Cap

The relevant provisions of the Coldwater Circuits Series A are:

- Series A investor is acquiring 33.33% of Coldwater
- $1.20 per share
- Pre-money valuation of Series A is $12,000,000
- The unallocated option pool specified in Series A is 20%

Given these, what is the cap table of the Series A after the Noteholder converts?

Solution:

The general approach is,

1. Calculate the price per share paid by the Noteholder, PPS(N), upon conversion of the Note into Series A shares
2. Then calculate the number of shares the Noteholder gets.
3. Finally, once we know the number of shares the Noteholder gets, we deduct those shares from the founders (from whom all shares flow), and compute the cap table.

The price per share the Noteholder converts at uses either the explicit discount or the (Valuation Cap/pre-money valuation).

Step 1. Calculate PPS(N)

Using the explicit discount of 20%
$$PPS(N) = \$1.20 * 0.80$$
$$= \$0.96 / \text{share}$$

Using the cap, PPS(N) = $1.20 * ($3,000,000/$12,000,000)

$$= \$1.20 * 0.25$$

$$= \$0.30 \text{ per share}$$

Naturally, the Noteholder will choose to pay $0.30 per share.

Step 2: Calculate the number of shares the Noteholder gets.

The number of shares the Noteholder get upon conversion is
= Amount invested by the Noteholder divided by $0.30

Number of shares = $600,000 +$48,000 (1 year interest)/ 0.30
= 2,160,000 shares.

Step 3: Calculate the cap table with the Noteholder.

	Common Equivalent	Percent Ownership	Comment
Series A Investors	5,000,000	33.33	Given, from the Series A
Noteholder	2,160,000	14.40	From the above calculation
Founders	4,840,000	32.27	What's left over after the investors, Noteholders and the unallocated option pool is calculated
Unallocated Options	3,000,000	20.00	Given, from the Series A
Total	15,000,000	100.00	

Table 13-2 Cap Table Upon Note Conversion

The company got $600,000 when no one else would invest and developed the company to the point where is was able to raise $5,000,000 in Series A. The company grew to a $15,000,000 valuation. The company raised $5,600,000 and the net worth of the Founders is over $4,800,000.

Is this really so bad for the Founder?

Well, it could get slightly worse due to a problem called Noteholder Liquidation Preference, also known as Liquidation Preference Overhang.

What's the Noteholder Liquidation Preference?

This is a fine point, which can be skipped, but which has been the subject of some negotiation and misunderstanding.

When Noteholders convert into the next round of stock, they presumably get the same shares as the subsequent round, at a discount. However, a peculiar situation arises regarding liquidation preference. Recall the intent of liquidation preference for the Series A investor is to get their money out first. So in the Table 12-1, the Series A invested $6,000,000 and claimed $6,000,000 off the top as liquidation preference.

In the example case above, the Noteholder presumably gets the same shares that the Series A bought, including the liquidation preference. That would mean Noteholder gets a liquidation preference of 2,160,000 shares multiplied by $1.20 (Series A price) or $2,592,000 in the event of liquidation. But the Noteholder only invested $600,000, with interest. Should the Noteholder's liquidation preference be $600,000 (the amount invested), rather than $2,592,000? If the Noteholder *doesn't* get $2,592,000 in liquidation, then the Noteholder is *not* getting the same shares as the Series A. How is this resolved?

One answer is to give the Noteholder full liquidation preference rights, as if $2,592,000 were invested. The other is to issue a slightly altered form of Series A stock, which is called a shadow Series A.

Shadow Series A would be identical to Series A shares in every respect except for liquidation preference. In that clause there would be explicit language that limits the liquidation preference of the Noteholder to the face value of the note.

Who wins this argument (the Noteholder or founders) will depend on their relative bargaining positions.

TAKEAWAYS

- Convertible notes are loans which convert equity at the next price round. This eliminates the immediate need for a valuation.

- Setting a Valuation Cap is a similar exercise to negotiate pre-money valuation.

- Notes are quicker to execute than priced rounds because there is no negotiation of some key controversial provisions but can be highly dilutive to the entrepreneur.

- Noteholders have the opportunity for significant upside benefit but do not have the control that equity shareholders have.

Question

Assume a Coldwater Circuits Note with the following provisions:

- $1,000,000 face value
- 20% discount
- 8% interest rate, compounded
- $8,000,000 Valuation Cap

Two years later there is a Coldwater Circuits Series A term sheet as described in Chapter 12. The relevant provisions of the Coldwater Circuits Series A are:

- Series A investor is acquiring 33.33% of Coldwater
- $1.20 per share
- Pre-money valuation of Series A is $12,000,000
- The unallocated option pool specified in the Series A is 20%.

Given this Note and Series A term sheet in Chapter 12, what is the cap table of the Series A after the Noteholder converts?"

Answer

Step 1. Compute the conversion price per share the Noteholder. That would be the lesser of:

a. Price per share of Series A * 0.80 {due to the discount of 20%), or
b. Price per share of the Series A * (Valuation Cap divided by pre-money of the Series A)

Under (a), price per share of Noteholder is $1.20 * 0.80 = $0.96 per share

Under (b), since the Valuation Cap is $8M and the pre-money of Series A is $12M, the price per share of for the Noteholder is $1.20 * ($8M/$12M) = $0.80 per share.

Naturally, the Noteholder converts at $0.80.

Step 2. Determine the number of shares the Noteholder gets upon conversion.

Number of shares = A divided by B, where

A = face value of the Note plus interest, and

B = conversion price per share.

First, A = $1,000,000 * 1.08 * 1.08, since the 8% interest is compounded for 2 years

    A = $1,166,400

    B = $0.80

Therefore, number of shares = 1,166,400/0.80 = 1,458,000.

Step 3. Now for the cap table:

	Common Shares	Series A	Common Equivalents	%	Comments
Series A		5,000,000	5,000,000	33.33	$5M invested. $15M post-money
Noteholder	1,458,000		1,458,000	9.72	Shares computed from Step 2
Founders			5,542,000	36.95	What's left over After the Series A, the Noteholder and the pool get their shares
Option Pool			3,000,000	20.00	Given. Required by Series A
Total			15,000,000		

Chapter 14 – Term Sheet, Series B and Beyond

(When you need even more cash)

It is very rare for any large startup to be fully funded on a single round of investing. Uber, Facebook and nearly all major companies you've heard of needed up to 7 rounds of financing, and that's before their IPOs, which is another dilutive event.

Each time there a new round of investment, investors in the later round may insist on rights that are senior prior investors. For example, a Series B investor may demand that its rights are senior to the Series A with regard to liquidation preference. This means the Series B will get its liquidation preference back in full before the Series A gets any liquidation preference. Or the Series B may want Board seats and ask the Series A step off the Board. There is nothing permanent or sacrosanct about the rights of the Series A when the Series B comes along. Likewise, there is nothing permanent or sacrosanct for Series B when Series C comes along. Everything is negotiable at each round[1].

Certainly, existing shareholders will defend their rights. They can always say "no" to the next round of investors. But does the company and its investors have the leverage to do so? Then comes the question, "do you want the money, or don't you?".

Negotiations between rounds is about leverage. How is the company doing? How desperate does it need the new round of cash? Are there other investors willing to step up with more friendly terms? Leverage or not, to provide some insight into these negotiations, the entrepreneur should be aware of new terminology of what happens in later rounds.

WHAT HAPPENS AFTER SERIES A?

There are terms and concepts in later rounds which are not included or not important in Series A. Among these provisions are:

- Anti-dilution

---

1 Many investors prefer investing larger amounts in later rounds. Late stage funds have more capital to deploy. Larger amounts per deal means monitoring fewer deals. Later stage deals have a smaller percentage upside, but there is a lot less risk than Series A investing.

- Pari passu provisions
- Senior Rights
- Venture debt

SERIES B TERM SHEET

We begin this chapter by explicating a Series B term sheet. Before doing so, we present the Series A terms that preceded this deal. Referring to the example of Coldwater Circuits from Chapter 12, we have the relevant terms of the Series A as follows:

| Amount of Investment: | $6,000,000 Purchase price equal to $1.20 per share of Series A Stock (as defined below). |
| Shares: | Series A Convertible Preferred Stock (the "Series A Stock") of Coldwater Circuits, a California corporation (the "Company"). |

Investors:	fund2000 ventures	$ 2,500,000
	co-investors	$ 3,500,000
	Total	$ 6,000,000

Capitalization Table

	Common	Series A Preferred	Common Equivalents	% Ownership
Series A		5,000,000	5,000,000	33.33%
Founders	7,000,000		7,000,000	46.67%
Unallocated Options	3,000,000		3,000,000	20.00%
			15,000,000	

After Series A, the company uses the $6,000,000 to make progress. Let's assume the company hires enough employees so that the Unallocated Option pool is depleted. A new investor syndicate offers a Series B term sheet the following terms:

- Series B is acquiring 25%
- The pre-money is $20,000,000.
- There is a new option pool of 10%

There will be a Series B syndicate consisting of a lead (named Carson Road Capital) and another VC, called FBN Ventures, to complete the round. Carson Road, the Series B lead investor, wants 15% of the company, post Series B.

What is the Series B cap table?

We'll use the following framework to help guide the discussion. The highlighted rows are the Series B shareholders.

	Series A	Series B	Common Equivalents	%
Carson Road Capital (lead)			3,461,539	15.00
FBN Ventures			2,307,692	10.00
Series A investors			5,000,000	
Founders			7,000,000	
Series A employees			3,000,000	
Series B options			2,307,692	10.00
Total			23,076,923	100%

Table 14 - 1. Series B Cap Table

Step 1: We know the common equivalents of the Series A shareholders. The Series B investors are buying 25% of the company and the Series B option pool is 10%. We therefore know that the Series A shareholders collectively own 65% of the company since the Series B shareholders collectively have 35%.

Step 2: Since the Series A shareholders own 65% of the company and they own 15,000,000 shares, the total number of shares post Series B must be 15,000,000 divided by 0.65. Total number of shares is 23,076,923.

Step 3: Since the Series B investors are acquiring a 25% ownership and there is a 10% option pool, the common equivalents for the investors and the option pool are easily derived from the total number of shares. The Series B investors have 25% of 23,076,923 or 5,769,231 shares. The Series B option pool is 10% of the total shares or 2,307,692 shares.

Step 4: Compute the ownership of the Series A shareholders. For example, the Founders have 7,000,000 shares out of a total of 23,076,923, or 30.33%.

We know the pre-money valuation was $20,000,000 and the Series B owns 25% post-money. Since

- post-money = pre-money + investment {definition of pre and post}

and

- investment divided by post-money is 0.25 {Series B is buying 25%}

With a little algebra we calculate the post-money as $26,666,667.

The investment is $6,666,667.

Since the Series B syndicate invested $6,666,667 and they received 5,769,231 shares, the Series B price per share is $1.1556.

Carson Road Capital, the lead investor in Series B, is purchasing 3,461,539 shares at $1.1556 per share. Therefore, Carson Road is investing $4,000,000. FBN Ventures is putting up the balance of the Series B cash.

Now we can look at the entire term sheet.

SERIES B CONVERTIBLE PREFERRED STOCK[2] FINANCING TERM SHEET

This term sheet summarizes the principal terms under which Coldwater Circuits, Inc. (the "Company") will issue 5,769,231[3] of its Series B Convertible Preferred Stock to Carson Road Capital, FBN Ventures and Series A shareholders (the "Investors").

Investors:	Carson Road Capital	$4,000,000
	FBN Ventures	$2,666,667
	Total	$6,666,667

Securities: 5,769,231 shares of the Company's Series B Convertible Preferred Stock convertible into an equal number of shares of Common Stock at $1.1556 per share.

Post-Closing Capitalization: Set forth below is the pro forma capitalization of the Company on a fully diluted basis.

	Series A	Series B	Common Equivalents	Ownership Percentage
Carson Road Capital		3,461,539	3,461,539	15.00%
FBN Ventures		2,307,692	2,307,692	10.00%
Series A investors	5,000,000		5,000,000	21.67%
Founders	7,000,000		7,000,000	30.33%
Series A employee options granted	3,000,000		3,000,000	13.00%
Series B Unallocated options		2,307,692	2,307,692	10.00%
	15,000,000	8,076,923	23,076,923	100.00%

Upon closure of the Series B Preferred, the authorized number of shares of Common stock in the Company will be 30,000,000[4].

---

2   As with Series A, these are preferred shares which convert to common. Series B denotes the second time the company raised an institutional round.

3   This odd looking number is derived from the Series B cap table. It's the total number of shares purchased by Carson Road Capital and FBN Ventures in Table 14 – 1.

4   The "authorized number of shares of Common Stock" is identified in the documentation submitted to the state in which the Company is incorporated. The limit is a shareholder protection measure. It prevents the management from arbitrarily issuing lots of shares, which would diminish the percentage ownership of existing shareholders. In this case, the Series B increased the number of shares, thereby requiring that Coldwater inform the State of California that it intends to increase the number of authorized shares to 30 million.

| Valuation: | Pre-money: | $20,000,000 |
| | Post-money: | $26,666,667 |

Use of Proceeds: All proceeds received at the Closing shall be used to fund working capital requirements of the Company.

Closing: December 31, 20xx or as soon as possible. A second closing may be held subsequent to December 31, 20xx to the extent necessary to allow participation by existing shareholders. The closing is subject to completion and execution of all final documentation.

Liabilities: Current liabilities at the time of Closing shall not exceed an amount to be mutually agreed upon between the Investors and the Company.

Description of Series B
Preferred Stock:

1) Dividends:

The holders of Series B Preferred Stock shall be entitled to receive non-cumulative dividends, when and if declared by the Board of Directors.

2) Liquidation Preference:

Upon liquidation, dissolution or winding up of the Company, proceeds shall be distributed ratably to the holders of Series A&B Preferred and the Common Stock until such time as the holders of the Series A&B Preferred have received an aggregate amount equal to their Original Purchase Price per share[5] (subject to appropriate adjustments for stock splits, stock dividends, combinations or other recapitalizations) plus declared but unpaid dividends for each share of Series A&B Preferred Stock. The remaining assets of the Company shall be distributed ratably to the holders of the Common Stock.

A consolidation, merger or re-capitalization of the Company, a sale by the Company of all or substantially all of its assets, or a sale of 50% or more of the Company's stock, shall be treated as a liquidation for these purposes.

3) Conversion:

---

[5] This states that the Series B and Series A would each take their pro-rata ownership of the company in case of liquidation. Series B is not senior to Series A. This is a win for the Series A investors.

Each share of Series B Preferred Stock and all declared but unpaid dividends shall be convertible at any time, at the option of the holder, into Common Stock of the Company on a one-for-one basis subject to the adjustments described below. There will be an automatic conversion on the vote of greater than 60% of the holders of Series B Preferred Stock.

Each share of Preferred Stock will be automatically converted into Common Stock at the then-applicable conversion price on the closing of a firm-commitment underwritten public offering at an aggregate offering amount of not less than $25 million.

4) Anti-dilution Provisions:

The conversion price of the Series B Preferred Stock shall be subject to weighted average adjustment in the event that the Company issues additional shares in an equity financing at a purchase price less than the price paid for Series B Preferred Stock.

5) Voting Rights:

Series B Preferred Stock shall have the right to that number of votes equal to the number of shares of Common Stock issuable as if conversion of the Series B Preferred Stock had taken place exclusive of dividends.

6) Protective Provisions:

For so long as at least 50% or more of the shares of Series B Preferred remain outstanding, the consent of the holders of at least 60% of the Series B Preferred Stock[6], voting as a separate class, shall be required for any action which (i) alters or changes the rights, preferences or privileges of the Series B Preferred Stock, (ii) increases the authorized number of shares of Series B Preferred Stock, (iii) causes a consolidation, merger or re-capitalization of the Company, a sale by the Company of all or substantially all its assets or a sale of 50% or more of the Company's Stock, or(iv) causes sale of stock senior in liquidation to the Series B Preferred Stock.

---

6   Since Carson Road owns 60% of the Series B, it can approve any of the protective provisions in this section.

A 51% majority of Series A and B Preferred[7] shareholders voting together as a class will be necessary to increase the authorized number of shares of Common stock.

If the Company proposes to issue equity in a subsequent capital-raising transaction, all shareholders shall be offered an opportunity to participate pro rata in accordance with the terms of the Company's existing Investors Rights Agreement.

7) <u>Information Rights:</u>

So long as any Investor continues to hold equity securities of the Company representing at least 5% of the Company's outstanding common stock equivalents, the Company shall deliver to such Investor internally prepared unaudited monthly and quarterly financial statements and annual financial statements audited by nationally recognized independent public accountants, if requested. Investors shall be entitled to standard inspection rights, provided that all rights above shall terminate upon an underwritten public offering of the Common Stock of the Company.

Registration Rights[8]:

Series B Preferred Stock shall have the right to one demand registration and unlimited piggyback registrations, subject to underwriter's restrictions. In addition to the Demand Registrations, at any time after the Company will be eligible to register securities on Form S-3 in accordance with the Company's existing Investors Rights Agreement. Underwriter will be designated by the Company. The registration rights shall terminate on the date five (5) years after the closing or three (3) years after the Company's initial public offering, whichever is earlier, or with respect to each holder, at such earlier time as (i) the Company's shares are publicly traded, and (ii) the holder is entitled to sell all of its shares in any 90 day period pursuant to SEC Rule 144. All registration demands are subject to customary delay provisions of up to 90 days at the discretion of the Board of Directors.

---

7   The <u>class</u> of preferred shareholders consists of Carson Road, FBN and Fund 2000 (from Series A). Collectively they own 10,769,231 preferred shares. This clause states that only 51% of the preferred shares are needed to increase the number of common shares. This means that FBN and Fund2000 could approve such an increase without the consent of Carson Road, even though Carson Road is the lead investor in the Series B.

8   Series A shareholders had their registration rights. The Series B can request similar rights.

Election of Directors:	The initial number of Directors of the Company will be five. Carson Road Capital shall be entitled to a Director seat so long as Carson Road retains 10% of the common stock equivalents[9] ; the Company shall be entitled to one Director and the remaining directors shall be elected by joint vote.

It shall be the intention of the parties to elect up to two additional outside directors with industry experience. Any additional directors shall be elected by joint vote and shall be mutually acceptable to the current and Series B representatives.

It is anticipated that upon closure of the Series B Preferred financing, the Board of Directors will consist of Dick Tracy, Art Carney, Ben Franklin, George Abe and Woody Zelig[10].

The Company agrees to fully indemnify all directors[11] to the maximum extent permitted by applicable law.

Key Person Insurance[12]:	Until all Series B Preferred Stock have been redeemed or converted, the Company will obtain and maintain key-man life insurance with proceeds payable to the Company in the amount of $2 million on the life of the Company's Chief Executive Officer

Right of First Refusal and Co-Sale Agreement:

The shares of the Company's securities held by the Key Shareholders (Dick Tracy, Sherlock Holmes) shall be made subject to a right of first refusal and co-sale agreement with the Investors such that the Key Shareholders may not sell, transfer or exchange their stock unless the Company first, and each of the Investors, second, has an opportunity to purchase such shares, which purchase with respect to the Investors shall be on a pro-rata basis, and if such rights are not exercised, then each Investor has an opportunity

---

9   Carson Road owns 15% of the common equivalents of the company. Entitlement means it can't be voted off without a revision to some legal documents as long as Carson retains at least 10% ownership.

10   In this case the five members of the Board of Directors were named individually. This expresses the intent to retain some of the existing board members from the Series A the company and the outside board member. Identifying board members by name is not good practice.

11   Indemnification requires a Directors and Officers (D&O) insurance policy to be paid for by the company.

12   Since the company has already made progress, it's a good idea to indemnify the company in case something happens to the CEO

to participate in the sale on a pro-rata basis. This right of first refusal and co-sale shall not apply to certain permitted transfers, including transfers to family members and relatives, trusts and pledges, so long as the transferee is similarly bound.

The Series B Preferred shareholders will be pari passu with the Series A shareholders[13] with respect to restrictions on transfer as defined in the current Investor Rights Agreement.

Sales by current Common shareholders shall be subject to a right of first refusal such that Common shareholders may not sell, transfer or exchange their stock unless the Company first, and each of the Investors, second, has an opportunity to purchase such shares, which purchase with respect to the Investors shall be on a pro-rata basis. This right of first refusal will not apply to certain permitted transfers, including transfers to family members and relatives, trusts and pledges, so long as the transferee is similarly bound

These rights of first refusal and co-sale also shall not apply to and shall terminate upon a Qualified IPO or upon an acquisition, merger or consolidation of the Company.

Lockup:

All existing shareholders and all new shareholders agree not to sell Company shares still owned for a period of 180 days or longer as required by underwriter restrictions following the effective date of the Company's initial public offering.

Employee
Reserve:

A Stock Option pool shall be authorized at the time of the closing of the sale of the Series B Preferred Stock (the "Closing") as set forth under "Post-Closing Capitalization" above. A portion of the Option Pool will be allocated to key employees, consultants, directors, and advisors of the Company as determined by the discretion of the CEO during the first year of operations; and subject to approval by the Compensation Committee of the Board of Directors. Additional shares may be authorized for the Option Pool resulting in a pro rata dilution of all shareholders.

---

13 Right of first refusal and Co-sale are examples of pari passu provisions. The Series B stipulated to the terms in Series A. Provisions such as these are not highly contested.

Proprietary Information and Inventions Agreement

Each officer and key employee of the Company enter into a proprietary information and inventions agreement[14].

Salaries/ Officers: All salaries must be reviewed and approved by the Compensation Committee appointed by the Board of Directors.

Due Diligence: The Investors and Company shall have the right to conduct legal investigation prior to Closing. Closing will be subject to satisfaction by the Investors of such investigation.

Expenses: The Company shall bear its own legal fees and other expenses with respect to the transaction and shall pay for all reasonable fees and expenses of the Investors in the transaction, if the Closing occurs. Disbursements of a single special legal counsel for the investors upon closing are not to exceed $20,000.

Stock Purchase Agreement: The investment shall be made pursuant to a Stock Purchase Agreement, which shall contain, among other things, appropriate representations and warranties[15] of the Company. THIS TERM SHEET IS A NON-BINDING SUMMARY OF TERMS DISCUSSED BY THE PARTIES. THE CLOSING IS CONTINGENT UPON, AMONG OTHER THINGS, THE NEGOTIATION AND EXECUTION OF A MUTUALLY SATISFACTORY STOCK PURCHASE AGREEMENT AS CONTEMPLATED ABOVE.

The parties below agree to the aforementioned terms as of December 31, 20xx

Coldwater Circuits, Inc.   **Carson Road Capital:**

_____   _____

By: Dick Tracy, CEO   By: George Abe, Venture Partner

---

14   Since the company has been in existence for a while, it may be the case that employees of the company have developed new inventions. This clause ensures that all such inventions have become the property of the company.

15   The representation and warranty letter is similar in form and content to a similar letter in Series A.

This concludes our sample Series B term sheet. We now move on to certain provisions in greater detail.

ANTI-DILUTION

When anyone buys shares on a public stock exchange there is a risk that the price of the shares may decline. In that case the investor is out of luck.

The situation is slightly different for preferred investors. The purpose of anti-dilution is to provide some protection for preferred investors in case the price per share goes down in a later round. The lower round is called a <u>down round</u>. Some protection is provided by repricing the original shares or by providing more common equivalent shares by adjusting the conversion ratio.

Anti-dilution is found in Series A term sheets, but its effects are not calculated until the next round. Anti-dilution provides no protection for common shareholders, this is a preference granted to preferred shareholders.

Example: Coldwater down round

- From the prior Coldwater Circuits Series A case in Chapter 12,

  - Series A bought 5,000,000 shares at $1.20 per share, for a total investment of $6,000,000
  - $18,000,000 post money valuation; Series A owns 33.33%
  - 15,000,000 shares outstanding (fully diluted);
  - Series A conversion ratio 1:1
  - Anti-dilution "broad based weighted average"

- After the Series A, the company needs money but the valuation of the company drops to the point where Series B investors offer the following terms:

  - Series B investors offer $3,000,000 at a $9,000,000 pre-money. The company went from an $18,000,000 post money after Series A down to $12,000,000 post money after Series B. The down round happened because the company failed to make significant progress with the Series A money

  - Series B demands a new Series B Option Pool of 15%

Given these provisions, what is the Series B Cap table?

Step 1: Recall the Original Series A Cap Table ($18,000,000 post money)

Shareholder	Post A Round (000)	Common equivalents (000)	Percent ownership	Comments
Series A investor	5,000	5,000	33.33	1:1 Conversion from Series A term sheet
Founders	7,000	7,000	41.67	From Series A
Option pool	3,000	3,000	20.00	Required by Investor
Total	15,000	15,000	100.00	

Table 14-1. Original Series A Cap table of Coldwater Circuits in Chapter 12

Step 2: Compute the Series B Cap Table with the Original Conversion Ratio of 1:1 for Series A

Let's start with a Series B skeleton Cap table. We know that the Series B purchased 25% of the company, since they invested $3,000,000 with a $12,000,000 post-money valuation. The Series B option pool is 15%, given. Therefore, the Series A shareholders jointly own 60% of the company with their 15,000,000 shares.

Shareholder	Post A Round (000)	Post Series B common equivalents (000)	Percent ownership	Comments
Series B investors		??	25.00	$3,000,000 invested at $12,000,000 post money valuation
Series A investor	5,000	5,000	??	Assume no Antidilution protection
Founders	7,000	7,000	??	From Series A
Series A employees	3,000	3,000	??	Series A option pool depleted
New Series B option pool		??	15.00	Required by Series B investor
Total	15,000	????	100.00	

Table 14-2. Series B Cap Table, With Missing Pieces

The first order of business is to compute the Post Series B common equivalents, denoted by ????."

Since the Series A shareholders own 15 million shares and this is worth 60% of the company, the total number of shares must be 15 million divided by 60%, or 25 million shares total after Series B.

Once you have the total number shares, the rest is easy. Given that there is no change in conversion ratio for Series A, the various percentages owned by the Series B and the various share counts owned by the Series A, the Series B Cap Table is computed as:

Shareholder	Post A Round (000)	Post Series B Common equivalents (000)	Percent ownership	Comments
Series B investors		6,250	25.00	$3,000,000 invested at $12,000,000 post money valuation
Series A investor	5,000	5,000	20.00	From Series A, assuming no anti-dilution protection
Founders	7,000	7,000	28.00	From Series A
Series A employees	3,000	3,000	12.00	Series A option pool depleted
New Series B option pool		3,750	15.00	Required by Series B investor
Total	15,000	25,000	100.00	

Table 14-3. Series B Cap Table Without Adjusting for Series A Anti-dilution

What's wrong with this cap table?

Nothing especially but Series A preferred investor doesn't like it. The Series A investor went from 33.33% to 20% and is not happy about that. This is the reason for anti-dilution. Anti-dilution adjusts the conversion ratio of the Series A preferred to provide more common equivalents.

How do we do that?

Step 3: Compute a new conversion ratio.

Let X = number of fully diluted common equivalent shares before Series B

Y = number of preferred shares sold in Series B

Z = hypothetical number of shares to get $3,000,000 at old price ($1.20)

New Conversion Ratio = (X + Y) divided by (X + Z), where

X = 15,000, fully diluted shares before Series B

Y = 6,250, computed in Table 14-3

Z = 2,500, computed as 3,000/1.20. If the Series B price were $1.20, then only 2,500,000 shares would have been sold to raise $3M

The new conversion ratio is (15,000 + 6,250) / (15,000 + 2,500) = 1.214

The Series A conversion ratio was 1.0. Now it's 1.214 after Series B. Note that as X increases, conversion ratio drops. That's what we mean by weighted average. It gives recognition to the number of shares before Series B. Entrepreneurs want X as big as possible. If Series B were an up-round, the conversion ratio for the Series A would still be 1.0.

Step 4: Apply the new conversion ratio to the Series B cap table

Recall from our discussion of series term sheets that common equivalent shares are equal to preferred shares multiplied by conversion ratio.

Shareholder	Post A Round (000)	Post Series B Common equivalents (000)	Percent ownership	Comments
Series B investors		6,696	25.00	$3,000,000 invested at $12,000,000 post money valuation
Series A investor	5,000	6,070	22.66	1.214 Conversion ratio multiplied by 5M shares
Founders	7,000	7,000	26.14	From Series A
Series A employees	3,000	3,000	11.20	From Series A. Series A option pool depleted
New Series B option pool		4,017	15.00	Required by Series B investor
Total	15,000	26,783	100.00	

Table 14-4. Cap Table With the New Conversion Ratio

The Series A no longer has 33.33% of the company but anti-dilution provided some benefit. The Series B investor gets exactly what it wants, namely 25% ownership.

Another way to calculate the effect of anti-dilution is to compute the conversion price of Series A by multiplying the Series A original price per share by the reciprocal of the ratio above. Namely take the Series A price per share and multiply by $(X+Z)/(X+Y)$. But the example using the conversion ratio illustrates the complexity and impact of anti-dilution calculations and helps clarify the meaning of conversion ratio.

This anti-dilution calculation may seem a bit brutal to the Founders. They are now down to 26.14%. But it could be worse. There could be Full Ratchet.

What about Full Ratchet?

Entrepreneurs will occasionally see the term <u>Full Ratchet</u>. Full Ratchet simply means X = 0. That is, no recognition is getting to the number of prior shares. This means there is no recognition is given to previous progress made by the company. To see how the computation works, we use the data from Step 4 and 5 above.

- New Conversion Ratio = (X + Y) divided by (X + Z)
- Full Ratchet means X = 0
- New Conversion Ratio = (0 + 6,250) / (0 + 2,500)

$$= 2.5$$

This is very punishing to the company. And because of that, Full Ratchet is rarely used. Investors rightly believe Full Ratchet is too demotivating for the Founders. The above computation where X=the number of shares prior to Series B is called weighted average anti-dilution. Weighted average anti-dilution is common, if there is anti-dilution at all. In fact, in some cases, Series B will ask Series A to waive anti-dilution in order to protect the ownership of the Founders.

Now we turn our attention to other provisions of later round term sheets.

Pari Passu Provisions

In later rounds, entrepreneurs will see the term pari passu. In Latin means roughly "Side by side; on equal footing; at the same rate". In this context this means later shareholders stipulate to provisions of earlier shareholders. It applies to less controversial provisions of the term sheet, such as Information Rights, Co-sale, standard Registration Rights, etc. Most people understand what these mean and there is little room for negotiation. It's not worth wasting a lot of time on boilerplate issues like these.

Of course, various "pari passu" clauses do not affect the Founders who have common stock and thus are subordinate to both Series A and Series B shareholders. It affects rights only among investor groups.

Pari passu also indicates joint participation with prior shareholders on some provisions, especially Liquidation Preference, as opposed to "Senior Liquidation Preference".

Senior Liquidation Preference

Earlier, we presented a discussion on seniority in the chapter on entity formation. Our purpose here is illustrate the impact of senior rights on liquidation preference.

Preferential rights of a preferred shareholder are said to be senior over other shareholders if they can be exercised over other preferred shareholders. Here are examples of seniority and pari passu with respect to liquidation preference.

- Assume Series A invests $3,000,000 and Series B invests $5,000,000. Later the company is sold for $4,000,000 (a bad outcome for the company).

  - If Series B is <u>senior</u> to Series A, Series B gets the entire $4,000,000 since it invested $5,000,000. There is nothing left for Series A.

- Alternatively, if Series A is pari passu with Series B, then Series A exercises its rights along side the Series B

  - Series B gets 62.5% ($5,000,000/$8,000,000) of the sales price; Series A gets 37.5%

  - Series B gets 62.5% of $4,000,000 or $2,500,000 and Series A gets $1,500,000

  - So, Series A got $1,500,000 by being pari passu with Series B, whereas with seniority for Series B, the Series A gets nothing.

The computation of ownership of startup companies can get very complicated. Conversion of convertible notes, seniority between rounds and anti-dilution calculations can lead to complex, high-stakes discussions of who owns what upon exit. We presented a simple calculation for a Series B that showed the computations can get complex. But these examples were simplified for instructional purposes. In reality, when there are multiple new shareholders on each round, each with seniority rights and conversion provisions, you have the recipe for misunderstandings and lawsuits about who owns what.

Venture Debt

Venture debt is a form of debt financing which is, unlike a convertible note or a SAFE, has no conversion to equity. Except for warrant coverage, venture debt is essentially non-dilutive. Some characteristics are as follows:

- (almost) Non-dilutive financing after Series A and usually before Series D. Only warrants are attached to the Note on the order of 2% to 5% of the face value of the loan. Warrants are often negotiated out or replaced by a nominal success fee.

- There is no explicit discount or Valuation Cap.

- Venture debt is collateralized

- Usually needs a name brand venture capitalist in prior rounds. This is to provide comfort to the venture debt holder that there are deep pockets in back of the company.

- Face value of the debt is limited to 20% - 40% of prior equity funding

- Closes quickly, as compared with equity rounds or convertibles.

- Is offered by venture debt funds or specialized banks, such as Silicon Valley Bank or AvidBank

- Relatively low history of default[16]

Venture debt requires the prior backing of a significant institutional investor like a venture capitalist which has provided cash to the company relatively recently. Thus, the startup is borrowing largely on cash it already has.

But the value proposition to the company and existing investors is to extend the runway for the company to achieve further milestones and hence increase its valuation on subsequent equity rounds. If the startup wants to augment its cash position in anticipation of some future major cash requirement, this can be an attractive form of financing. In fact, current shareholders may encourage the management to raise venture debt as opposed to convertible debt to protect them against future dilution.

Debt or Equity?

If the entrepreneur has a choice between debt and equity financing, here is something to consider. Equity investors have shorter term goals. To get their money back, the company must exit either buy a sale or an initial public offering. Therefore, the minute an entrepreneur has taken a dollar from a venture capitalist, the entrepreneur has more or less agreed to sell the company. The only question is when and what price.

---

16   https://www.anderson.ucla.edu/faculty-and-research/anderson-review/venture-debt.

Bankers, on the other hand, want you to stay in business. They want to lend you again and therefore have a vested interest for you to stay in business under your management. They don't want an exit. They want a long-term relationship. But bankers can't take the risks of startup companies. The risk/reward ratio is too high. They can only lend after the company has made substantial progress. So, to avoid equity investors at an early stage, you must grow organically.

TAKEAWAYS

- Later stage financing involves different instruments, new terminology and complicated spreadsheets.

- Each Series of investment is a different event. This means later Series investors can ask that prior investors waive certain rights. Prior investors can, of course, reject these requests. Hence, obtaining funds in a later investment round involves negotiation with prior investors

- Most entrepreneurs can expect to have more than 2 rounds of investment.

- The calculation of ownership gets complicated quickly after a few rounds of investment, given the impact of convertible notes, later round investments, anti-dilution, seniority rights and new employee option pools.

("The secret to success in business is to know something no one else knows."
Aristotle Onassis)

Startup companies have very little in the way of assets. In many cases, intellectual property is the only asset the company. Creation, acquisition or monetization of intellectual property can be a key element of entrepreneurial success. Various forms of intellectual property are:

- Patents
- Trade secrets
- Copyrights
- Trademarks
- Trade dress

This chapter will deal with patents and trade secrets, primarily from a United States point of view.

PATENTS

A Patent is a monopoly granted by Governments to inventors to promote sharing of inventions. Inventors get a monopoly in exchange for full disclosure of their invention. It is interesting to note that patent rights are in Article 1 of the United States Constitution. It precedes the right to bear arms, the Bill of Rights, due process and other familiar constitutional protections. The Founding Fathers thought patent rights (and copyrights) were key to the establishment of the new nation.

Article I, Section 8

Clause 1: The Congress shall have Power To lay and collect Taxes, Duties, Imposts and Excises, to pay the Debts and provide for the common Defence and general Welfare of the United States; but all Duties, Imposts and Excises shall be uniform throughout the United States;

Clause 2: To borrow Money on the credit of the United States;

Clause 3: To regulate Commerce with foreign Nations, and among the several States, and with the Indian Tribes;

Clause 4: To establish a uniform Rule of Naturalization, and uniform Laws on the subject of Bankruptcies throughout the United States;

Clause 5: To coin Money, regulate the Value thereof, and of foreign Coin, and fix the Standard of Weights and Measures;

Clause 6: To provide for the Punishment of counterfeiting the Securities and current Coin of the United States;

Clause 7: To establish Post Offices and post Roads;

Clause 8: To promote the Progress of Science and useful Arts, by securing for limited Times to Authors and Inventors the exclusive Right to their respective Writings and Discoveries;

Etc.

+++++++++

From the language of Article 1, a patent is the deal between the inventor and the public. The deal is the inventor gets monopoly use of the invention for a limited time. In return, the public gets training on new technology which it can use after the patent expires. To be granted a patent, the inventor must fully disclose the mechanism of the invention and best mode of operation. Without full disclosure, the language that provides for promoting "the Progress of Science and useful Arts" would have no meaning. So the patent must teach "someone skilled in the art" as much about the invention as is known by the inventor. Upon expiration of the "limited Times" of the patent (meaning patent expiration), the public has full use of the intellectual property.

A patent is property like any other tangible asset. It can be bought, sold, leased, licensed or inherited. Even though a patent is an intangible asset, it can have great value. In fact, for some investors, a precondition for investment in a company is that the company have patents. The investor wants a monopoly position for their invested product. Also, in case of bankruptcy, the creditors or shareholders can seize the patent, just as they would any other asset.

For some inventors, the requirement to disclose their "secret sauce" is a bad idea. Even while the monopoly protection is still in force, it may be technically possible to circumvent provisions of the patent and create something similar to, but not identical with, the invention using the information in the published patent. Often upon reading the patent, outsiders an get an understanding of the theoretical basis of patent and work around it. Therefore, some inventors will resort to trade secret protection to avoid the disclosure requirement of patenting. We'll discuss trade secrets later in this chapter.

Patents may be filed in part and then later a "continuation" filed. The canny inventor can use this to deliberately delay the patent grant date, providing a potential benefit because the patent is not issued, and made public, until it is granted. This technique is called "submarining".

Over the decades and centuries, different types of patents have been codified in United States Federal Law. These are:

- Utility
- Provisional
- Foreign patent
- Design patent
- Plant patent

Utility Patents

The patent protection most people think of as a patent, and was probably contemplated by the Founding Fathers, is referred to as a <u>Utility Patent</u>. It is granted by the United States Patent and Trademark office (USPTO.GOV) and provides for 20 years of monopoly protection.

The patent process begins with the inventor filing a patent application. This is normally done with the assistance of a lawyer so that the language of the patent can be carefully crafted to ensure the broadest possible protection and the least possible ambiguity. When the patent is filed with the USPTO an important date, called the <u>priority date</u> or <u>filing date,</u> is established. The filing date is important in the event that two inventors file patents on the same invention. The applicant with the earlier filing date has priority.

First to File Versus First to Invent

The priority date established by the filing date is a relatively new legal development in the US. This changed in 2011. Prior to 2011, the priority date was established by the first to invent. Establishing an invention date was, and is, a contentious process. The question of who invented something first meant keeping careful lab notes, emails and test results. Even then, competitive inventors could challenge your notes with their notes. This extended the patent application process and increased expense. Therefore, the Leahy-Smith America Invents Act (AIA) of 2012 changed the US from a first to invent country to a first to file country, which brought the US into alignment with the rest of the world. This was legislation introduced by Senators Patrick Leahy (D-Vermont) and Lamar Smith (R-Texas) and signed by President Obama in September 2011. Bipartisanship was at work.

After the inventor submits a patent application, it is assigned to a patent officer who will then put it on a big stack of other patent applications from prior inventors. The United States has a few thousand patent officers, organized by discipline. However, there are hundreds of thousands of patent applications. The result is that it can take 2 to 5 years and thousands of dollars to get an application through USPTO.

After the patent officer gets around to reading your application (after a few months), in all likelihood your application will be rejected. Typically, the rejection we'll be based on the existence of prior art, which undermines your novelty or non-obviousness. You or, more likely your patent attorney, will review this rejection letter and respond, typically by altering the application. This round-trip is called an office action (OA). A patent application can take 2 to 5 OAs with each OA taking months to complete.

Eventually the patent is granted, with a given <u>Grant Date</u>. Regardless of the Grant Date, the 20 years of protection starts from the Filing Date, not the Grant Date. After the Grant Date, there are various dates at which the inventor must make periodic maintenance payments to the USPTO to keep the patent in force. Failure to make these payments means the patent goes to the public domain. Sometimes this is acceptable if the patent has lost its commercial value after a few years in force, which can happen in fast-moving industries. The entire process from filing a patent application, through the various office actions to the final granting of the patent is a process called <u>patent prosecution</u>.

After 20 years from the filing date, the patent expires and the intellectual property goes to the public domain. There are techniques that inventors can use to extend the life of a patent but these are fine points left best to instruction by patent lawyers.

Once granted, a patent gives the patent holder the exclusive right to manufacture, sell or otherwise practice the invention in the United States, and only the United States. Foreign patents with protection in other countries will be discussed shortly.

A simplified schematic of a US patent is depicted as follows:

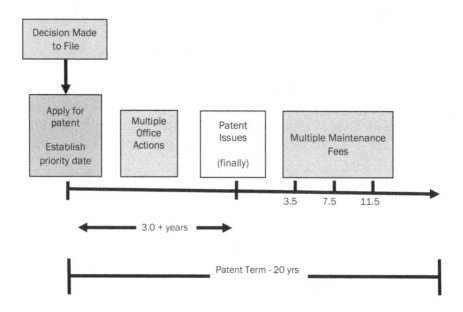

Figure 15-1. Simplified Schematic of a Utility Patent

This schematic omits provisional and foreign patenting which will be discussed later and depicted in Figure 15-3.

Expedited Patent Prosecution

Patents take a long time to complete and are processed in order received. However, the USPTO has instituted provisions which can expedite the process. The first provision allows for inventors over the age of 65 or in poor health to go to the front of the line. The concern is that patent prosecution can take so long that the applicant may die during the process. A simple verification of age or health condition is required. If the patent application fraudulently contains the name of a person who doesn't qualify, the application is denied.

For younger and/or healthier inventors, there are other mechanisms to get to the head of the line. Under current law there is the Prioritized Patent Examination Program. It provides for final disposition of a patent within 12 months.

In order to qualify for prioritized handling, the patent application must be relatively simple. That means there must be a small number of claims so that the examiner can get through all the claims quickly. In addition, there is a fee charged and there is a limit on the number of expedited applications allowed per year. When this legislation was originally enacted, the limit was 10,000 per year and the fee was $4,000. These limits are increased by small amounts from time to time. See https://www.uspto.gov/patent/initiatives/usptos-prioritized-patent-examination-program or search online for "USPTO track one" for current information on rules, limits and fees.

What is Patentable in the USA?

Most anything made by humans (as opposed to nature) is patentable provided 4 tests are met. The tests are:

- Novelty. The invention must not be known or used by others, patented, or described in a printed publication. This is where a prior art search is important.

- Non-obviousness. An "invention" may be novel, but if it simple-minded, it won't get a patent. That means it must not be easily deduced from the current body of knowledge nor obvious to "one skilled in the art". This is the subject of most patent challenges.

- Usefulness. The invention must have a legal and moral use. For example, a new way to refine cocaine would not be patentable. More seriously, for some inventions the utility is unclear. For example, some genomic inventions may lack clarity on specific uses.

- Enablement. It must be real. The inventor must have reduced the invention to practice. That means they need more than just an idea or know-how. Know-how or skill is not patentable. A concept is not patentable. You must demonstrate to the public, and the patent officer, that your invention is real.

The following types of inventions are patentable in the US, provided the tests above are met.

- Software
- Devices (machines, components)
- Composition of matter (for example, therapeutic or diagnostic drugs or compounds harder than diamonds)
- Genetically modified life forms. (for example, Chakrabarty's oil eating microbes (US patent 4,259,444))
- New use of known substances

- Business methods are technically patentable but since the U.S. Supreme Court ruling in the case of Bilski v Kappos[1], the bar was raised very high on business methods so they are now tough to get.

What is not patentable in the US?

The following are neither created by humans nor enabled and thus are not patentable.

- Scientific discoveries. A natural phenomenon existed before humans knew about it and thus is not patentable. E=MC**2 is not patentable.
- Mental processes, algorithms. Skill or know-how.
- Non-functioning products.

How to ruin a patent application (in the USA)

- Fail to conduct a proper Prior Art Search

In order to establish novelty or obviousness, it is necessary uncover has been done or published previously. Such prior art searches are performed by the company, the company lawyers and the USPTO. If your lawyers are doing a lot of prior art searching, that increases your legal bills. Do as much of it as you can. During the patent process, the USPTO will conduct its own prior art search.

Prior art search will look at prior patent applications and written articles, both in the US and overseas. Even if you want just a US only patent, there can be disqualifying prior art from outside the US. Prior Art will not only uncover interference but will also help narrow claims of your patent application to avoid interference.

On the other hand, even if the entrepreneur finds prior art, it may still make sense to proceed with patent prosecution. A prior patent may be overly broad and could be rejected upon litigation. Or you may craft your claims to circumvent prior art. At the very least, a prior art search can provide an understanding of what other companies are investigating and hence be a good source of market information.

- Offer the invention for sale, public use or experimentation.

Let's assume you have an invention then decide to sell some product without obtaining a patent. You have created prior art which precludes getting a patent. Even if you sell the

---

1   US Supreme Court ruling in Bilski v Kappos regarding business methods
    https://www.supremecourt.gov/opinions/09pdf/08-964.pdf

product with a non-disclosure agreement, the sale qualifies as prior art. Moreover, even if you only offer the product for sale without actually selling anything, you have created prior art. Before you sell anything, if you want a patent, you should start patent prosecution before you even try to sell.

Some fine points may arise as a result of testing or experimentation. For example, what if you offer a sample of your invention to a 3rd party for validation? Does that qualify as prior art? If could if you take payment for the sample. You will need to check with you patent lawyer to determine the risks to your patent application for experimentation and test. In any case, be sure you have a solid non-disclosure agreement with any party that is experimenting with your product.

- Describe the invention in a publication or public presentation anywhere in the world in enabling detail.

If you provide details of your invention prior to making a patent application, your enabling publication will qualify as prior art. If you have made an enabling publication, you have one year to file a patent application. If you miss the one year deadline to file, you can't get a patent on the invention related to your publication in the United States. Other countries have different rules on what grace period is provided, if any, if there is a publication or public presentation. The question then arises as to what is a "publication"? After a number of legal proceedings, the following can qualify as publications.

- Journal article, online or printed
- Abstract produced online or distributed publicly.
- Verbal presentation, with open attendance.
- Student dissertation.
- Speaking in private to one knowledgeable person

There are exceptions for presentations in academic or research settings. If you are a researcher presenting results to peers or your funding agency, that would not be a prior art problem. In any case, an inventor should be careful to determine the venue of publication, audience and amount of material presented or order to preserve patent rights. An attorney may come in handy.

Problems of software patents

Software presents particular problems for the inventor since infringing software could be hard to detect if it's embedded in a computer or semiconductor integrated circuits. If you invent a software program, how do you know someone is infringing if it's buried inside a computer?

In addition, recent United States Supreme Court decisions, such as the Alice v CLS Bank[2] case, raised the bar on obtaining software patents. In particular, simple automation of a manual process with a general purpose computer generally won't qualify for patent protection. There's insufficient novelty or failure of the obviousness test in some of these patents. Here's a list of patents which were granted by USPTO but subsequently invalidated by the courts.

- 6,585,516 A computer to help users plan meals around dietary goals
- 6,398,646 The management of a bingo game via computer
- 7,627,509 Linking a mortgage line of credit to a checking account
- 8,313,023 Computer to convert reward points between stores
- 6,055,513 System to upsell customers to buy other products

If an inventor is going to improve a manual process, then use something other than a general purpose computer, or, better yet, do something substantial that can't otherwise be done manually.

The final and perhaps more crucial problem for software patents is that the inventor must disclose. Disclosure of software makes it relatively easy for others to circumvent the patent even for broadly worded patent applications.

The software developer must address further questions about the code before considering intellectual property protection.

- Did you use software modules from prior art? If so, you may be precluded from getting a patent at all.

- What about Open Source? If you use Open Source code, the Open Source license agreement may preclude a patent.

- What about integrated circuit masks? Semiconductor circuits are subject to other forms of protection apart from the normal patent process. Search online for "integrated circuit layout design protection".

---

2   https://www.supremecourt.gov/opinions/13pdf/13-298_7lh8.pdf. This was a unanimous decision of SCOTUS. Clarence Thomas and Sonia Sotomayor, normally not on the same side of any judicial decision, wrote the majority and concurring opinions.

If patenting doesn't seem like an attractive way to protect software, then copyright, trade secret or licensing protection may preferable.

Inventorship versus Assignment

An inventor is the scientific or engineering genius who creates something new. However, the inventor may not have property rights to the invention because the inventor may have signed over, or <u>assigned</u>, those property rights to his or her employer, who is the <u>assignee</u>. Assignment of patent rights is usually part of the employment agreement the inventor signs as a condition of employment. The assignee will then commercially exploit the patent by licensing or sale.

Conversely when a startup company wants to monetize an invention it created, it must be sure to obtain control from their employees who invented it.

Example of a Utility Patent

We close this discussion of utility patents by annotating the abstract and first claim of US Patent 5,960,411, easily accessible at the USPTO website. This is the Amazon 1-click patent filed by Hartman, Bezos, et al., arguably the most valuable single patent of recent decades.

United States Patent   **5,960,411**[3]

Hartman , et al.   **September 28, 1999**[4]

Method and system for placing a purchase order via a communications network[5]

Abstract

A method and system for placing an order to purchase an item via the Internet. The order is placed by a purchaser at a client system and received by a server system. The server system receives purchaser information including identification of the purchaser, payment information, and shipment information from the client system. The server system then assigns a client identifier to the client system and associates the assigned client identifier with the received purchaser information. The server system sends to the client system the assigned client identifier and an HTML document identifying the item and including an order button. The client system receives and stores the assigned client identifier and receives and displays the HTML document. In response to the selection of the order button, the client system sends

---

3   Patent number

4   Date patent was granted by USPTO

5   Name of invention with Abstract of invention.

to the server system a request to purchase the identified item. The server system receives the request and combines the purchaser information associated with the client identifier of the client system to generate an order to purchase the item in accordance with the billing and shipment information whereby the purchaser effects the ordering of the product by selection of the order button.

Inventors:	Hartman; Peri (Seattle, WA), Bezos; Jeffrey P. (Seattle, WA), Kaphan; Shel (Seattle, WA), Spiegel; Joel (Seattle, WA)[6]
Assignee:	Amazon.com, Inc. (Seattle, WA)[7]
Family ID:	25457073
Appl. No.:	08/928,951
Filed:	September 12, 1997[8]

We claim:[9]

1. A method of placing an order for an item comprising:

under control of a client system,
displaying information identifying the item; and in response to only a single action being performed, sending a request to order the item along with an identifier of a purchaser of the item to a server system;

under control of a single-action ordering component of the server system,
receiving the request;

retrieving additional information previously stored for the purchaser identified by the identifier in the received request; and

generating an order to purchase the requested item for the purchaser identified by the identifier in the received request using the retrieved additional information; and

---

6 List of inventors, which must be complete and accurate. If you knowingly provide an incorrect list of inventors, that would be cause to invalidate the patent application.

7 Rights to invention are assigned to Amazon by the inventors, presumably by employment agreement

8 Date the patent application was filed. Note it took a little over 2 years for USPTO to approve.

9 Claims identify the value the invention provides the public. Claim #1 is the main claim. In this patent there were a total of 26 Claims. Claims are listed in descending order of generality. The most general claim is #1.

fulfilling the generated order to complete purchase of the item

whereby the item is ordered without using a shopping cart ordering model.

Figure 15-2. The Abstract and Claim #1 of Patent 5,960,411

Is this invention obvious? At the time, there was discussion in the software community as to whether or not this should have been granted a patent since it was "obvious". USPTO thought this invention was not obvious and Jeff Bezos became a billionaire.

Provisional Patents

Because obtaining a utility patent is time consuming and expensive, inventors are well advised to do a little marketing before they spend that time and money. Enter the provisional patent.

Provisional patents are lightweight applications in that there is no full prior art search performed by the USPTO and is not subject to OAs. It's basically a placeholder to establish a filing date. The provisional patent must provide for a complete description of the invention in the event the provisional is converted to a full utility patent. The applicant cannot have a claim in the utility patent which is absent from the provisional.

Provisionals are inexpensive but require that the provisional be converted to utility patent in one year. If the provisional is not converted in a year, it can't be converted to a utility patent and the subject matter cannot be patented. The one-year protection is best used to determine the commercial viability of the invention. If, after one year, the inventor decides there is no market, then the inventor saves a lot of time and money by not converting.

Provisional patents are allowed in the USA, but this form of protection does not exist everywhere. Should you seek similar protection in another country, you need to check with the patent authorities in your country of interest.

Details about provisional patents can be found at
http://www.uspto.gov/patents/resources/types/provapp.jsp
or by searching for "USPTO provisional patent".

For American inventors, or any other inventor who can take advantage of provisional patents, they are largely a must. The inventor gets an extra year of protection. The inventor can also have broader claims that would be in a utility patent. For example, if you think you are nearing an invention but don't quite have final lab results, you can file a provisional and continue experimenting. If you can complete your lab testing while the provisional is in force, but before patent prosecution, you can safely claim the invention in your utility patent application, even though you didn't have final results before the provisional.

Foreign Patents

Everything we discussed so far addressed how to get a patent in the United States. However, patents are country specific. Just because you have protection in the United States doesn't mean you have protection in any other country.

If you want international protection for your patent, you can fly to each country in which patent protection is sought, hire a local attorney and apply. There was a time in which this was done. However, today the process of worldwide patenting is streamlined through the Patent Cooperation Treaty (PCT), ratified by the United Nations in 1970. The PCT is administered by the World Intellectual Property Organization (WIPO, wipo.int). WIPO continues as a self-funding agency of the United Nations.

Here is a depiction of the international patenting process using an instructional schematic provided by the UCLA Technology Development Group.

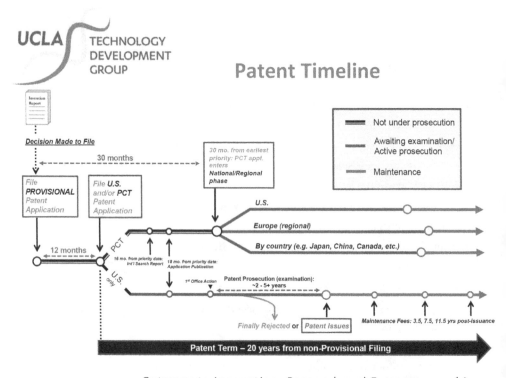

Figure 15-3. Global Patenting Using a Provisional Patent and PCT

To begin the process of international patent application, the applicant converts the provisional application to a PCT application or, absent a provisional, makes a PCT application directly. Patent lawyers do this routinely.

Once a priority date is established, either with a provisional or utility patent, the applicant has 30 months to enter what is called the <u>National Phase</u>. In the National Phase the applicant decides which countries to get patent protection. The applicant may, for example, want protection in Spain but not Portugal. Applicants may forego some countries because more countries means more cost to the patent applicant. The applicant will go through a process similar to a US-only application in each country. The applicant will pay legal fees, filing fees and language translation fees. This is very expensive so there is an incentive to limit the number of countries.

Some countries are excluded from the PCT process, largely for geopolitical reasons. Taiwan, for example, is precluded because of its relationship with China. However, the vast majority of countries are signatories and the patent applicant is well advised to go through the PCT process. The PCT provides the following:

- Mechanism to file, search, publish and administer a worldwide patent filing with one application.

- Time for the inventor to consider countries of interest and expenses.

- Sixteen months after the priority date, WIPO will publish its own prior art search. This is the International Search Report. This report is sent to the applicant prior to the initiation of National Phase to help the applicant determine if they should go ahead with National Phase.

- Eighteen months after the priority date, WIPO will publish your PCT application before National Phase. This is not a service to you but rather to the rest of the world. It puts the world on notice that your patent may be headed for National Phase and that competing inventions may have prior art problems due to your application. Publication presents a problem called "No Man's Land", which we discuss in "Trade Secrets", below.

- PCT provides no patent prosecution in any country. Each country decides what is patentable. WIPO only provides an administrative step to file, search, publish and administer globally but doesn't provide patents.

- WIPO oversees the process from its headquarters in Geneva, Switzerland.

It is possible to go through the process shown in Figure 15-3 without having a provisional patent. The process would merely begin at the box entitled "File U.S. and/or PCT Patent Application". National Phase would begin 30 months after this date.

Also note that Figure 15-3 also applies to patent applications for the U.S. only. That is, no foreign patents requested and therefore no PCT filing. Simply take the lower path at the box entitled "File U.S. and/or PCT Patent Application". In this case, patent prosecution is the same as described above under "Utility Patents".

Global Patent Strategy

Having made the business decision to pursue a patent and that you need global protection, here is a list of steps to be taken in chronological order.

- Get experienced IP counsel to map out a strategy
- File a provisional patent in countries where it is permitted.
- Do market research and business planning during the provisional period.
- Identify cross-licensing options or monetization strategies.
- If it's a "Go", file a PCT application.
- Get the WIPO opinion letter and decide if you can work around the objections.
- Select the countries where you want your patent filed.
- Set aside a (big) budget. You will be paying language translation fees, lawyer bills and filing fees with multiple countries.
- Monitor changes in patent legislation worldwide.

The decision to patent or not should not be treated as a technical or legal decision. It is a business decision. For each invention, the entrepreneur must ask "Does patenting make sense at all?". Are the protections provided by patents worth the time, money and disclosure that patenting requires?

The benefits of global patenting:

- You get a monopoly in as many countries as you're willing to pay for.
- Establishes technical credentials.
- Restricts freedom to operate for others.
- Enables cross-licensing, or exchange of patents.
- Has some liquidation value in bankruptcy.
- Has public relations value.
- Provides a source of income via licensing.
- Differentiates you from your competition.

The negatives of global patenting are:

- You are disclosing your best practices and novelty.
- It takes management time and money to get and defend one. Defending a patent costs more than getting a patent.
- If you are a startup company, your opponents have more lawyers than you.
- Getting the patent may take longer than the product life.
- Trade secret protection or copyright protection, where applicable, may be better alternatives and not just for cost reasons.

We close our discussion of patents by briefly describing 2 lesser used but nonetheless interesting form of patents. These are Design Patents and Plant Patents.

Design Patents

In 1879, a French sculptor named Auguste Bartholdi was granted a <u>Design Patent</u> for the Statue of Liberty. In theory, anyone who wanted to create trinkets or clothing or anything else bearing the likeness of the Statue of Liberty must have obtained a license from Bartholdi. Who knows whether this was done or not, but this case illustrates that visual ornamentation can be patented and that American citizenship is not required to obtain a US patent.

Design patents provide protection for "Visual ornamentation applied to an object". As of 2013, a Design Patent had a life of 15 years. The process is simple. Just submit your design to the USPTO and demonstrate that it is different from other designs.

Other design patents are Grand Baroque design for flatware, iPod Shuffle, Crocs shoes and iPhone designs.

Search online for "USPTO design patent" for the last word on eligibility and process.

Plant Patents

For inventors in horticulture or botany, there is the <u>Plant Patent</u>. It protects plants, algae and fungi which require assistance for propagation. Some of these organisms can be commercially useful, such as algae that convert into biofuels or microbes that clean oil spills.

Plant patents, however, raise the sensitive question of the patentability of naturally occurring life forms. As cloning of animals in particular becomes technically feasible, there are ethical questions raised as to patentability.

At any rate, for documentation of the simple case of plants, algae and fungi, search for "USPTO plant patent".

The intention of the Founding Fathers of the US Constitution was to encourage invention and have the knowledge <u>shared</u> throughout the economy.

Trade secrets are intended to do the exact opposite. With trade secret protection, inventors do not teach the public. Trade secrets are protected primarily by state law but the various states are largely in alignment on how to get and keep trade secrets. Search online for "Uniform trade secrets act".

Benefits of Trade Secrets

- Provides legal protection and remedies. If someone steals your trade secret, you can sue for misappropriation.

- Offers a broader scope of protection than patents. See list below.

- It's inexpensive, powerful and quick. No need to work through the patent office.

- There is no time limit, unlike patents. Trade secret protection exists for as long as the information is held secret.

Problems of Trade Secrets

- You lose protection if you don't have a process to identify or protect your trade secrets. It's not just a matter of keeping quiet. You need some paperwork.

- Protection is lost when a patent is published. You can't have both a patent and a trade secret on the same invention.

- Does not protect against reverse engineering. If someone figures out what you are doing, they can copy it without penalty.

Trade Secrets protect more than patentable inventions

Valuable information which is not subject to patent can be protected by trade secrets. The following information can be valuable and thus should be kept secret. In fact, the value of these is derived in part because of their secrecy.

- Technical data, such as experimental results. Failed tests can be especially useful.

- Formulas, drawings, and flowcharts.

- Software

- Processes and methods.

- Anything patentable, like machines and components.

- Recipes

- List of customers, sales prospects, due diligence results, and financials.

Trade secrets require a formal secrecy policy

- Trade secrets must be identified. For example, employees must know that the formula for Coca Cola is a trade secret, without knowing the formula itself. Employees and outsiders must know what is or is not a trade secret so they know whether or not they are in violation.

- Restrict access to those who need to know.

- Keep records on who has access.

- Enforce non-disclosure agreements with 3rd parties and employees.

- Have employees acknowledge a trade secret agreement.

- Have destruction and return clauses when supplying samples to third parties.

If you do all these and someone steals the trade secret, you can sue.

Most trade secrets are betrayed by current or recently departed employees. Employees are more mobile and use the cloud which makes it easy to leak information. The exit interview is important. At that time employers should ask departing employees to reaffirm respect for trade secrets.

Here's a comparison between patents and trade secrets:

	Patents	Trade Secrets
Protections	For novel, non-obvious, useful and real inventions	Much broader than patents. Includes business information, test results
Disclosure required	Full	None
Cost to obtain	Expensive. Plan on more than $100,000 for global protection	Only administrative cost. Little legal expense. Much cheaper than patents.
Needs a lawyer?	Almost always	Almost never
Duration of protection	20 years, 21 if there's a Provisional Patent	Indefinite, possibly forever
Time to obtain	Years to get a patent	Immediate protection
Protection against reverse engineering	Yes	None. But if this was done, your invention wasn't that inventive.
Availability worldwide	Almost every country has patent protection of its own definition	Some countries have no trade secret laws or a record of enforcement. The inventor must do the research.
Can be licensed?	Yes	Yes
Oversight and monitoring required	Constant lookout for infringers	Constant lookout for infringers Constant enforcement of employee agreements, non-disclosures, record maintenance.

Table 15-4. Comparison of Patents and Trade Secrets

- Patents are an expensive and time-consuming way to protect inventions. However, in some situations they are necessary and thus the entrepreneur needs to set aside adequate time and money to get patent protection where indicated.

- Some patents have literally been worth billions by enabling the patentee to hold a monopoly position and establish leadership while maintaining a large moat around the invention.

- Trade Secrets are an inexpensive and quick alternative to patents, with wide application and longer time duration than patents. However, they may not be available or sufficiently protective. Also, some investors may require patents.

- The choice of IP protection is a business decision, not a legal or technical one.

("I dyed my hair this crazy red in a bid for attention. It has become a trademark
and I've got to keep it this way."
– Lucille Ball, comedienne)

Apart from patents and trade secrets, other forms of IP protection are copyrights, trademarks and trade dress, which are meant to protect other ideas and form a brand. We begin with copyrights.

COPYRIGHTS

As with patents, copyright law emanates from Article 1, U.S. Constitution.

It gives exclusive rights to creators of certain tangible works. Under current US law copyright protection lasts much longer than the 20 years of a patent. The life of a copyright also depends on whether the creation was done on behalf of oneself or an employer, termed "work for hire". Search online for "USPTO copyright policy" or go to copyright.gov.

Copyright law does not protect the concept or the idea of a work, only the tangible expression. For example, if you publish an article that outlines a cure for cancer only the article itself is protected by copyright law, and not the cure.

What is copyrightable?

- Writing, books, articles, poetry

- Software, which are considered a form of writing, hence copyrightable

- Music, which can have a very broad definition

- Plays, pantomimes, choreography

- Paintings and sculpture

- Movies, trailers for movies

- Architectural works, buildings, renderings of buildings

What is not copyrightable?

- Individual words, abbreviations, slogans. An element of creativity is required. Slogans are more likely to be trademarked.

- Lists or compilation of facts. Some value or creativity is required.

- Ideas, not reduced to tangible form. Thoughts are not copyrightable.

- Domain names. URLs are granted by ICANN. (icann.org). The world is not limited to the familiar .com, .net, .gov etc. There are hundreds of generic top level domains (gTLD) which are administered by different authorities worldwide. Top level domains such as .food, .basketball, .tokyo exist but don't necessarily have a large number of websites.

- Government publications, since they belong to the public.

What are the Rights granted to the holder of a copyright?

- Reproduction (electronic or otherwise)

- Distribution (electronic or otherwise)

- Public display or performance (dance or pantomime)

- Rights to derivative works, including language translation, dramatizations, abridgement, condensation, musical arrangement.

How to get a copyright?

- Simply reduce work to tangible form. Copyright is conferred automatically upon creation. There is no need to register or notify the government.

- But if you want to sue somebody for infringement or prevent importation, you must register the work with the government. This is a simple, inexpensive process. You ask for a registered copyright and submit a copy of the work. Search for "USPTO copyright registration".

- Another way to get a copyright is to buy or license one. Copyrights are property that can be bought, sold, licensed and inherited.

- Hire someone to create for you. "<u>Work for hire</u>" belongs to the employer.

What about audio and video piracy?

Under US copyright law, there is a doctrine called <u>fair use</u>, which allows copying for personal use. This issue came to a head in a 1984 ruling in favor of Sony in the Betamax case[1]. In that action movie studios and TV producers were concerned that the newly invented video tape-cassette recording (VCR) systems would erode sales of original content as consumers started to use them to make copies of TV shows and the like. The content creators argued that Sony should not be allowed to sell the video recorders. The Supreme Court of the United States (SCOTUS), in a 5–4 decision, ruled in favor of Sony thereby preserving the right of consumers to record content for private use.

It is interesting that the entire infrastructure of consumer content distribution today is built on a decision upheld by a single vote in the US Supreme Court in 1984.

Tests of Fair Use

The cases of Napster/Kazaa/BitTorrent and the like have raised the issue of fair use many times in the court system. Case law has more or less ruled on behalf of fair use if;

- the purpose is for personal use, such as the time-shifting of video

- the nature of the original work is largely factual

- the amount of copied material is minimal, and

- the market effect or value is minimal. If there is profit to be made, it's likely not fair use.

---

1   https://www.copyright.gov/fair-use/summaries/sonycorp-universal-1984.pdf

All this is argued in expensive legal proceedings by an army of well-paid copyright attorneys who work in content litigation.

Apart from fair use, copyright law also permits copying for criticism, satire, comment, news reporting, teaching and research.

Government publications are not subject to copyright on the presumption that they have been paid for with tax dollars and therefore belongs to the public.

What about "Work for Hire"?

"Work for hire" is content created while employed. Your employer will typically have the copyright to the content you created on the job. This is often conveyed in your employment agreement. The key point about work for hire in the USA is that it changes the lifetime of the copyright. If you create something on your own, while not employed, there is one duration of copyright. If, however, you create work as an employee, the life of the copyright could be different.

Go to https://www.copyright.gov/help/faq/faq-duration.html or search for 'copyright duration' for information on the duration of copyrights.

Special issue of software copyrights

Software is considered like a literary work, like a novel or movie, and hence subject to copyright protection. To get a copyright, you only have to create it in tangible form. But if you want to sue someone, you need to register your software program. See "https://www.copyright.gov/circs/circ61.pdf" for procedures. If your program contains trade secret material, there are provisions in the copyright application which allow you to redact the trade secrets. There are also special processes for user manuals, object code, HTML, video games and screen shots.

Should you patent or copyright software? Here's a framework to help decide.

	Software Patent	Software Copyright
Protections	Novel, non-obvious and useful inventions	Doesn't need to be useful but should be novel
Level of protection	Protects software concept	Only protects the copy of the code
Disclosure	Full	Can be redacted
Cost	Expensive. Plan on more than $100,000 for global protection.	Nominal. Only fees to USPTO.
Needs a lawyer?	Almost always	Almost never. But you will need a lawyer to prosecute infringement

Duration of protection	20 years, 21 including a Provisional Patent	Much longer than patents
Time to obtain	Years to get a patent	Immediate protection
Can be licensed?	Yes	Yes

Table 16-1. Comparison of Patents versus Copyrights for Software

Since software copyrights are relatively cheap, there generally isn't harm in registering software. But most developers are more comfortable with maintaining trade secrets for software.

TRADEMARKS

Arguably the most valuable form of intellectual property for a non-technical business is its trademark(s). A company's most valuable asset is its brand and trademarks protect the brand. That's why Lucille Ball didn't change her hair color as she aged.

Trademarks differ conceptually from patents, trade secrets and copyrights.

While patents, trade secrets and copyrights protect the creator of the work, a trademark protects not only the creator of the work but also the consumer of the work. For example, when a consumer purchases a bottle of Coca-Cola, the design of the bottle (trade dress) and the logo (the trademarked Coca-Cola script) provides the consumer with confidence that there is real Coca-Cola inside. It is confidence for the consumer which is key to the value of a trademark.

Trade dress is a derivative of trademarks in that it protects the visual appearance or packaging of a product to give assurance to the buyer of the identity of its contents. The layout and design of a retail store can qualify as trade dress.

A trademark or trade dress protects the names and symbols associated with a business entity. Trademarks can include logos, sounds, color/design schemes, sounds and other markers used to associate goods or services with a particular provider.

Trademarks can be licensed (e.g. UCLA sweatshirts, which is a multimillion dollar annual royalty business) or otherwise conveyed to other parties. If your trademark is licensed out to another vendor, the licensor must be sure to monitor the products of the licensee to protect your reputation. UCLA, which licenses out its logo to shirt manufacturers, needs to ensure that those manufacturers produce quality product.

Trademark Requirements

- To get a trademark, you must register it with the USPTO in the US. If you want a trademark operative in another country, you must register the trademark in that country. A trademark registered in the USA does not confer protection outside the US.

- You must have a product in use to designate with the trademark. You can't just design a logo and have it registered. The mark must be associated with a real product and be in commercial use.

- The mark must be distinctive; it can't be "common", "generic", or "ordinary". And the mark must be distinct from any other trademark that is protected (not "confusingly similar"). This is the subject of most forms of trademark litigation.

What happened to "Kleenex" and "Xerox"?

Some trademarks become part of the language to such an extent that they lose their value as trademarks. For example, when one needs bathroom tissue paper, they often refer to the tissue as "Kleenex", even though the tissue paper may be made and distributed by Scott or some generic brand. Likewise, with "Xerox". When one makes a copy of a document, you hear someone making a Xerox copy even though the copier machine is made by Minolta or other competitor of Xerox. When a trademark becomes a generic term, the trademark is said to have suffered genericide.

Other famous trademarks that have suffered genericide are cellophane, aspirin, escalator, trampoline, videotape, zipper[2].

Trademark Issues

- Choose your trademark wisely. You will be stuck with it for a while. Trademarks are expensive to change and a change confuses customers.

- Be aware of geographic limits. What is trademarked in one country is not necessarily trademarked in another.

- Maintain continuous use of your trademarks. You can lose your trademark if there is no product associated with it for a lengthy period. As of this writing, this period is 3 years. But go to https://www.uspto.gov/trademark" or search for 'uspto trademark maintenance' for rules on maintaining trademarks.

---

2   https://www.consumerreports.org/consumerist/15-product-trademarks-that-have-become-victims-of-genericization/

The Case of CaliBurger

In 2011, an entrepreneur in California was checking a list of trademarks in China and noticed that In-n-Out (the popular hamburger chain in California) had not registered its trademarks there. So, the entrepreneur started a hamburger stand in Shanghai, bearing the yellow, white and red look of In-n-Out's restaurants. One of the menu items was a cheeseburger "Animal Style", from In-n-Out's menu.

The entrepreneur was an intellectual property lawyer who knew how far to push the envelope, so he called his hamburger business "CaliBurger" rather than and In-n-Out. The name aimed to evoke the California lifestyle on Nanjing Road, in the heart of Shanghai.

His business idea was that Americans, particularly those from California, would be craving an In-n-Out burger while away from home. However, as is often the case in entrepreneurship, the market took another turn. The main customers were local Chinese who were attracted to the lifestyle. They also liked the idea that the hamburger meat was imported, which allayed fears about food safety. The restaurant rapidly became successful and a second one was opened in another part of Shanghai.

Naturally, In-n-Out was not impressed and soon sent CaliBurger a cease and desist notice. However, CaliBurger's had a strong case since In-n-Out had no defendable trademark in China. But instead of fighting the larger In-n-Out, CaliBurger settled with In-n-Out and left Shanghai. However, CaliBurger as part of the settlement, CaliBurger was allowed to survive in other parts of the world, including California. This case illustrates the power of trademarks.

TAKEAWAYS

- Copyright protection is an important and inexpensive way to protect certain creative work. There are limits to what you can protect and what you can potentially use from others under the doctrine of 'fair use'.

- Trademarks and trade dress are important and inexpensive ways to protect your brand. They must be chosen to last a long time and be in continuous use.

- Depending on the characteristics of what is to be protected, you may need to consider copyrights, trademarks and design patents.

Questions

Which of these is a Trademark violation?

What would be the defense of each company if McDonald's, Starbucks and Pizza Hut came after them with a Cease and Desist Order?

Answer:

The defense would assert that customers are not confused by these and these are obvious satire. This argument may or may not hold up.

However, if any of these establishments made money off because of these signs, that would likely be a violation.

Whether an entrepreneur monetizes or acquires Intellectual Property (IP), the contractual vehicle to do so is the license agreement. A license agreement is a contract in which the licensor grants the use of IP of any type (patent, trade secret, copyright or trademark) to a licensee, who receives the right to use the IP in exchange for some consideration, like money, equity, other IP rights, or some other asset. Note that what is licensed is only the right to use the IP, not a transmission of ownership, which is possible through a sale. This chapter only discusses licensing.

Since the license is the vehicle by which IP is monetized or acquired, it is one of the most important contracts an entrepreneur will enter into, particularly for high technology entrepreneurs where the IP is the foundation upon which an innovative company is to be built.

Figure 17-1 is a schematic of the flow of rights and consideration for a patent license. Licenses for trade secrets, trademarks and copyrights follow a similar schematic but we use the patent case as illustrative.

Intellectual Property Licensing

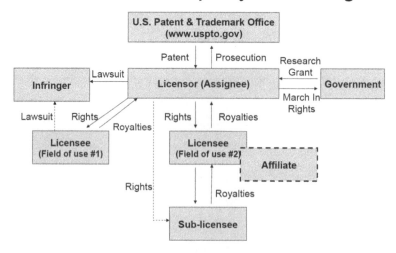

Figure 17-1. Intellectual Property Licensing Schematic

We will explain the key clauses of a patent license agreement. The same structure can be modified for trade secrets and copyrights.

Key transactions in this schematic are described as follows.

- The patent is issued by the patent office to the entity, called the Licensor, that will in turn license the patent to a Licensee. The Licensor is the Assignee listed on the patent application.

- In this schematic there are 2 licensees, each with a different field of use (application). Both licensees obtain rights to the patent in return for royalty payments. There can be other forms of payment, such as fees or stock.

- Licensee #1, notices that there is an Infringer who is violating the patent. Either the Licensee #1 or the Licensor can initiate a lawsuit against the Infringer. The License Agreement will determine who gets to initiate the lawsuit first.

- Licensee #2 issues a sublicensee to an entity, which practices the patent. One example of a sublicensee is a business that exploits the patent in a foreign country.

- It is possible that Licensee #2 can sell product to an Affiliate. If so, the Affiliate must pay for product to Licensee #2 in an arm's length transaction, so that royalties to the Licensor can fairly track with market rates.

- If Licensee #2 no longer honors the license agreement, either voluntarily or due to insolvency, the dotted line indicates that the sublicensee may enter into a direct relationship with the Licensor, at the discretion of the Licensor. There are situations in which the Licensor would not want that particular sublicensee to have continued access to the IP in which case the sublicensee cannot use the IP. Perhaps there is another principal licensor pending or perhaps the sublicensee may not be viable. It is also possible that the Licensor will impose additional terms on the sublicensee so that the Licensor can be compensated for the loss of the original Licensee.

- If the discovery made by the Licensor is financed by a research grant from the U.S. Federal Government, the Government is granted for March-In-Rights. These rights are limited use rights to use the invention, with or without a royalty agreement, typically due to a national emergency. For example, if the Licensor is a pharmaceutical company who created a drug to combat a serious contagious disease, then, for public safety reasons, the Government can march in and use the invention, without spending time negotiating. This situation is very rare so March-In-Rights have rarely been exercised by the government.

For brevity and clarity, many provisions are removed from this sample. Typical license agreements are at least twice the length of this sample. Our interest here is in highlighting terms that are germane primarily to licensing rather than standard boilerplate type language.

LICENSE AGREEMENT

This Agreement is made and is effective this day _____, (the "Effective Date") between INTERGALACTIC RESEARCH, INC ("Licensor"), a California corporation having its corporate offices at (address, city, state, zip) and Fledgling Corporation, Inc. ("Licensee"), a corporation having its principal place of business at (address, city, state, zip).

The parties agree as follows:

1. DEFINITIONS

1.1   "Licensor' Patent Rights" means the Licensor's interest in any of the patent applications listed in Appendix A attached to this Agreement description of invention[1] and any corresponding foreign patents or patent applications[2]; all of which will be automatically incorporated in and added to Appendix A and made a part of this Agreement.

1.2   "Licensed Product" means any article, composition, apparatus, substance, chemical, or any other material covered by Licensor' Patent Rights or whose manufacture, use or sale would constitute an infringement of any claim within Licensor' Patent Rights.

1.3   The "Field of Use" refers to domain or application in which the intellectual property is to be applied.[3] ....

---

[1]   The description of invention must be a complete and unambiguous identification of what intellectual property is being transferred. For example, a patent number(s) or case number or copyright. A general description won't do.

[2]   Foreign patent applications on the same intellectual property are included, however, improvements are not. If the licensor makes improvements, those rights are not transferred in this license. If the licensee makes improvements, those are the property of the licensee. Therefore, the description of invention must be carefully crafted to avoid future problems. One way to avoid future problems would be for the licensee to sponsor continued research with the licensor, in which case the licensee would normally have rights of first refusal to improvements made by that sponsored research.

[3]   For example, a therapeutic drug may be used against both kidney cancer and liver cancer but the Licensee may only want the Field of Use to be kidney cancer. This frees the Licensor to negotiate another license with another Licensee for liver cancer.

1.4   "Affiliate" means any corporation or other business entity in which Licensee owns or controls, directly or indirectly, at least 50% of the outstanding stock or other voting rights entitled to elect directors.

1.5   "First Commercial Sale" means the first sale of any Licensed Product by Licensee or any Affiliate or Sublicensee.

1.6   "Net Sales" means the total of the gross amount invoiced for the sale of Licensed Products by Licensee, or by any Affiliate or Sublicensee, less the following deductions: _list of discounts agreed to[4]._ Where Licensee or any Affiliate, Joint Venture or Sublicensee is the Customer, then Net Sales shall be based on the gross amount normally invoiced or otherwise charged to other Customers in an arm's length transaction[5] for such Licensed Products.

1.7   "Sublicensee" means any third party sublicensed by Licensee to make, have made, use, sell, offer for sale or import any Licensed Product.

1.8   "Sublicensing Income" means income received by Licensee on account of Sublicenses. Sublicensing Income includes income received by way of license issue fees, milestone payments, and the like but specifically excludes royalties on the sale or distribution of Licensed Products or the practice of Licensed Methods. Not included in the definition of Sublicensing Income is income received by Licensee as payment or reimbursement for research costs conducted by or for Licensee, including costs associated with materials, equipment or clinical testing.

2. GRANT

2.1   Subject to the limitations set forth in this Agreement, The Licensor hereby grants to Licensee an exclusive license[6] (the "License") for the expressed Field of Use.

2.2   The Licensor expressly reserves the right to use Licensor' Patent Rights and associated technology for sponsored research by another entity, academic research, education, and

---

4   Deductions could include cash discounts, quantity discounts, tariffs, excise taxes, credits for returns, insurance. This is all negotiable.

5   Sales to an Affiliate could represent a conflict of interest. This language is necessary so that royalty income is not undercut by an artificially low Net Sales figure to a related company.

6   Exclusivity means there is only ONE licensee for the Field of Use. It is possible for either the Licensor or Licensee to prefer a non-exclusive license. For example, the Licensor may want multiple Licensees to create a competitive environment or establish an industry standard. The Licensee may opt for a non-exclusive license to reduce cost.

non-commercial clinical purposes including publication[7] of research results and sharing research results with other non-profit institutions and allowing other non-profit research institutions to use Licensor's Patent Rights and associated technology for the same purpose.

3. SUBLICENSES

3.1   The Licensor also grants to Licensee the right to issue exclusive or nonexclusive sublicenses ("Sublicenses") to third parties to make, have made, use sell, offer for sale or import Licensed Products.

3.2   Licensee must pay to Licensor _____% of all Sublicensing Income.

3.3   On Net Sales of Licensed Products sold or disposed of by a Sublicensee, Licensee must pay to The Licensor an earned royalty in accordance with Article 5 (Royalties) as if these were Licensee's Net Sales.

3.4   Licensee must provide to the Licensor a copy of each Sublicense within 30 days of execution, and a copy of all information submitted to Licensee by Sublicensees relevant to the computation of the payments due to The Licensor under this Article 3.

3.5   If this Agreement is terminated for any reason, all outstanding Sublicenses will be assigned by Licensee to the Licensor, at the option of the Licensor.[8] The Sublicenses will remain in full force and effect with the Licensor as the licensor or sublicensor instead of Licensee.

4. FEES[9]

4.1   In partial consideration for the License, Licensee will pay to the Licensor a license issue fee of $_____within 30 days of the Effective Date. This fee is nonrefundable and is not an advance against royalties.

---

7   This enables the Licensor to continue research. This clause is a core provision for university-based research licensing. See https://www.autm.net/AUTMMain/media/Advocacy/Documents/Points_to_Consider.pdf

8   For example, the Licensee could be an American company which goes out of business, but the Sublicensees could be in Asia and still be viable. In that case, it is in the interest of the Licensor and Sublicensees to continue the business relationship. In other cases, the Licensor may not want rights transferred to a sublicensee. The transfer of rights to a sublicensee is not automatic and would be a matter of negotiation.

9   Fees are a way for the Licensor to collect payments without having to track Net Sales.

4.2 For each Licensed Product reaching the milestones[10] indicated below, Licensee would make the following payment to the Licensor within 30 days of reaching the milestones:

    4.2a   XXX
    4.2b   XXX

4.3 Licensee must pay to the Licensor a license maintenance fee of $_____ beginning on the one-year anniversary date of the Effective Date of this Agreement and continuing annually on each anniversary date of the Effective Date. The license maintenance fees are non-refundable and are not an advance against royalties.

5. ROYALTIES[11]

5.1 Licensee must pay to the Licensor for sale of Licensed Products in the Field by Licensee or its Affiliates an earned royalty of _____% of Net Sales.

5.2 If any patent or any claim included in Licensor' Patent Rights is held invalid or unenforceable in a final decision by a court of competent jurisdiction from which no appeal has or can be taken, all obligation to pay royalties based on that patent or claim or any claim patentably indistinct from it will cease as of the date of that final decision. Licensee will not, however, be relieved from paying any royalties that accrued before that decision or that is based on another patent or claim not involved in that decision.

5.3 *There will be other detailed provisions regarding currency conversion of products sold outside the U.S. and other issues regarding foreign sales of licensed products.*[12]

---

10 Milestones could include product or market or financial events, such as the completion of a clinical trial, or raising venture capital or sales of a specified amount.

11 Royalties provide an upside to the amount the Licensee pays to the Licensor. The more sales the Licensee makes, the more is paid to the Licensor. This requires a precise definition of Net Sales and requires an audit provision so that the Licensor is comfortable with the Net Sales reported by the Licensee.

12 The handling and reporting of Net Sales and Royalties for international sales can be a complex part of a license agreement. We omit that here but caution the reader that this where lawyers could spend a bit of time.

Another royalty provision could address the issue of royalty stacking. Royalty stacking occurs when a Licensee must obtain IP from 2 different companies to launch a product. For example, there could be a pill which requires both a therapeutic compound to address the disease and a proprietary protective coating for timed release of the therapeutic inside. The Licensee may be asked to pay a 4% royalty for the therapeutic and a 3% royalty for the coating. Royalty stacking could be addressed with both Licensors so that the Licensee would pay less than 7% combined royalties.

6. DILIGENCE

6.1   Upon the execution of this Agreement, Licensee must diligently proceed with the development, manufacture and sale ("Commercialization") of Licensed Products and must diligently endeavor to market them within a reasonable time after execution of this Agreement and in quantities sufficient to meet the market demands for them[13].

6.2   The Licensor has the right to terminate this Agreement or reduce Licensee's exclusive license to a nonexclusive license if Licensee fails to perform any of the milestones[14] in this Paragraph. This right, if exercised by the Licensor, supersedes the rights granted in Article 2 (Grant).

    6.3a   XXX
    6.3b   XXX

7. PATENT FILING, PROSECUTION AND MAINTENANCE

7.1   The Licensor will file, prosecute and maintain the patents[15] and applications comprising Licensor' Patent Rights. These patents will be held in the name of the Licensor and will be obtained with counsel of the Licensor's choice. The Licensor must provide Licensee with copies of each patent application, office action, response to office action, request for terminal disclaimer, and request for reissue or reexamination of any patent or patent application under Licensor' Patent Rights. The Licensor will consider any comments or suggestions by Licensee. The Licensor is entitled to take action to preserve rights and minimize costs whether or not Licensee has commented.

---

13   This may seem like an odd provision. But it is designed to protect against "squatting" or "shelving". Squatting happens when a company which has a product notices that there is a newly emerging competitive product. Squatting means the Licensor obtains rights to the IP but doesn't commercialize it to protect the market position of its original product. Universities hate this since their mission is to surface their technology for the public good. Even if they are paid by the squatter, squatting runs counter to the mission of the university.

    If the Licensee has worked in good faith to achieve a milestone but falls short, the Licensor can seriously harm the Licensee by changing license provisions, for example by converting from an exclusive to a non-exclusive license. Therefore, diligence is a contentious provision when it is negotiated and possibly more contentious when it is enforced.

14   These diligence milestones can be similar to financial or business milestones but often would include technical or development terms, such as completion of clinical trials or completion of a prototype.

15   The clause enables the Licensor to control the patent prosecution process for inventions covered by this license agreement. When a Licensor grants rights to a Licensee, it is expected that the Licensee will continue development and eventually file patents of its own. When the Licensee files its own patents, there could be overlap with the original license agreement. The Licensor wants to protect its turf as the Licensee files its own patents by carefully controlling the claims and scope of its patents. The Licensor therefore must control the patent prosecution process.

    As a minor point, having the Licensor control the process relieves the Licensee of payments to patent lawyers for the time being. If the Licensee doesn't have much money this is a benefit since the patent may not issue or the patent process can take years.

7.2 Licensee will bear all costs[16] in the preparation, filing, prosecution and maintenance of patent applications.

7.3 Licensee has the right to request patent protection on the Invention in foreign countries if the rights are available[17]. Licensee must notify the Licensor of its decision within eight months of the filing of the corresponding United States patent application.

8. PATENT INFRINGEMENT

8.1 In the event that Licensee learns of the substantial infringement in the Field of any patent in Licensor' Patent Rights, Licensee will inform the Licensor in writing and will provide the Licensor with reasonable evidence of the infringement. Licensee may request that the Licensor take legal action against the infringement of Licensor' Patent Rights in the Field. The Licensor has the right to (a) commence suit on its own account or (b) refuse to participate in a suit. The Licensor must give notice of its election in writing to Licensee by the end of the 100th day after receiving notice of the request from Licensee. Licensee may thereafter bring suit for patent infringement in its own name if and only if the Licensor elected not to commence suit[18]. However, in the event Licensee elects to bring suit in accordance with this Paragraph 8.2, the Licensor may thereafter join the suit at its own expense.

8.3 Any legal action will be at the expense of the party that brings the suit and, with the exception of Paragraph 8.4, all recoveries will belong to that party. Legal action brought jointly by the Licensor and/or Licensee and fully participated in by both, however, will be at the joint expense of the parties and all recoveries will be shared jointly by them in proportion to the share of expense paid by each party.

8.4 If Licensee undertakes the enforcement or defense of any Licensor Patent Rights by litigation, any recovery of damages by Licensee will be applied first toward Licensee's

---

16 But eventually the Licensee will reimburse the Licensor for all patent expenses, both past and ongoing. Legal expenses borne by the Licensor prior to this agreement, will be subject to a negotiated payment plan. Ongoing legal expenses we'll be accrued. The timing of total payments will be negotiated.

17 The Licensee identifies the countries in which there should be patent protection. Each country adds to the cost of the patent which will be charged to the Licensee. Recall from our part discussion of PCT, the Licensee has 30 months to decide which countries they seek patent protection.

18 This says the Licensee may not bring suit without asking the Licensor to bring suit first. This is so that the Licensor can verify the merits of the case. If the Licensor doesn't proceed, the Licensee can.

unreimbursed expenses and legal fees relating to the suit. Licensee will retain the balance of the recovery but will pay the Licensor a 25% royalty on this balance[19].

9. PROGRESS AND ROYALTY REPORTS

9.1   Beginning _____*date*_____ Licensee must submit to the Licensor semiannual progress reports covering Licensee's activities related to the development and testing of all Licensed Products and the obtaining of the governmental approvals necessary for marketing. Progress reports include the following:

    9.1a   Summary of work completed.

    9.1b   Key scientific discoveries.

    9.1c   Summary of work in progress.

    9.1d   Current schedule of anticipated events or milestones.

    9.1e   Market plans for introduction of Licensed Products.

    9.1f   A summary of money spent in the reporting period.

9.2   After the First Commercial Sale of each Licensed Product, Licensee must make quarterly royalty reports to the Licensor by February 28, May 31, August 31 and November 30 of each year (i.e., within two months from the end of each calendar quarter). Each royalty report must cover Licensee's most recently completed calendar quarter and must show:

    9.5a   Gross sales and Net Sales of any Licensed Product[20].

    9.5b   Number of each type of Licensed Product sold.

    9.5c   Royalties payable to the Licensor.

10. BOOKS AND RECORDS

10.1   Licensee must keep accurate books and records of all Licensed Products manufactured, used or sold. Licensee must preserve these books and records for at least five years from the date of the royalty payment to which they pertain.

10.2   The Licensor' representatives or agents are entitled to inspect these books and records at reasonable times. The Licensor will pay the fees and expenses of these inspections. If an

---

19   But if the Licensee proceeds and wins, then the Licensor gets some of the proceedings, even though it passed on suing the infringer.

20   This reporting will likely be subject to audit, normally demanded by the Licensor. The payment of audit expenses is normally paid by the Licensee.

error-favoring Licensee of more than 5% of the total annual royalties is discovered, then Licensee will pay the fees and expenses of these inspections.

11. LIFE OF THE AGREEMENT

11.1   Unless otherwise terminated by operation of law or by acts of the parties in accordance with the terms of this Agreement, this Agreement is in force from the Effective Date recited on page one and remains in effect for the life of the last-to-expire patent in Licensor' Patent Rights.

11.2   Upon termination of this Agreement, Licensee will have no further right to make, have made, use or sell any Licensed Product except to sell items held in inventory by the Licensee and sold within 6 months of termination. In that event, the Licensee will continue to make royalty payments and provide royalty reporting.

11.3   Any expiration or termination of this Agreement will not affect the rights and obligations set forth in the following Articles[21]:

Article 10   Books and Records.
Article 16   Use of Names and Trademarks.
Article 17   Warranties
Article 18   Indemnification.

12. TERMINATION BY THE LICENSOR

12.1   If Licensee violates or fails to perform any material term or covenant of this Agreement, then the Licensor may give written notice of the default ("Notice of Default") to Licensee. If Licensee does not repair the default within 60 days after the effective date of the Notice of Default, then the Licensor has the right to terminate this Agreement and the License by a second written notice ("Notice of Termination") to Licensee. Termination does not relieve Licensee of its obligation to pay any royalty or fees owing at the time of termination and does not impair any accrued right of the Licensor.

---

21   Even though the license agreement is terminated, there are still obligations under the license agreement. Termination simply means that no products can be sold and no more payments made but the obligations in 11.3 continue.

13. TERMINATION BY LICENSEE

13.1   Licensee has the right at any time to terminate this Agreement in whole or with respect to any portion of Licensor' Patent Rights by giving written notice to the Licensor. This notice of termination will be subject to Article 19 (Notices) and will be effective 90 days after the effective date of the notice.

13.2   Any termination in accordance with Paragraph 13.1 does not relieve Licensee of any obligation or liability accrued prior to termination. Nor does termination rescind anything done by Licensee or any payments made to the Licensor prior to the effective date of termination. Termination does not affect in any manner any rights of The Licensor arising under this Agreement prior to termination.

14. USE OF NAMES AND TRADEMARKS

14.1   Neither party is permitted to use any name, trade name, trademark or other designation of the other party or its employees[22] (including contraction, abbreviation or simulation of any of the foregoing) in advertising, publicity or other promotional activity without written permission of the other party.

15. LIMITED WARRANTY

15.1   This License and the associated Invention are provided WITHOUT WARRANTY OF MERCHANTABILITY OR FITNESS FOR A PARTICULAR PURPOSE OR ANY OTHER WARRANTY, EXPRESS OR IMPLIED. THE LICENSOR MAKE NO REPRESENTATION OR WARRANTY THAT ANY LICENSED PRODUCT WILL NOT INFRINGE ANY PATENT OR OTHER PROPRIETARY RIGHT.

15.2   IN NO EVENT WILL THE LICENSOR BE LIABLE FOR ANY INCIDENTAL, SPECIAL OR CONSEQUENTIAL DAMAGES RESULTING FROM EXERCISE OF THIS LICENSE OR THE USE OF THE INVENTION OR LICENSED PRODUCTS OR THE USE OR THE PRACTICE OF LICENSED METHODS.

15.4   Nothing in this Agreement will be construed as:

---

22   The Licensor should be careful to protects it trademarks. You never know what the Licensee will do.

The Licensee should be aware of the requirement to obtain permission for press releases, promotional materials and any other marketing materials that uses the Licensor's name.

17.4a   A warranty or representation that anything made, used, sold or otherwise disposed of under any license granted in this Agreement is or will be free from infringement of patents of third parties.

17.4b   Obligate the Licensor to furnish any know-how not provided in Licensor' Patent Rights.

16. LATE PAYMENTS

16.1   For each royalty payment or fee not received by the Licensor when due, Licensee must pay the Licensor a simple interest charge of x% per annum to be calculated from the date payment was due until it was actually received by The Regents.

17. INDEMNIFICATION[23]

17.1   Licensee must indemnify, hold harmless and defend the Licensor and the inventors of the patents against any and all liability, claims, suits, losses, damages, costs, fees and expenses resulting from the exercise of this license or any sublicense. Indemnification includes but is not limited to products liability.

17.2   Licensee, at its sole cost and expense, must insure its activities in connection with the work under this Agreement and obtain, keep in force and maintain Comprehensive or Commercial Form General Liability Insurance (contractual liability included) with limits as follows:[24]

16.2a	Each occurrence[25]	$xxxx.
16.2b	Products/completed operations aggregate	$yyyy.
16.2c	Personal and advertising injury	$zzzz.

---

23   In the event that the Licensee uses the Licensor's technology and someone is harmed, the Licensee must indemnify the Licensor. You don't know what the Licensee will do with the invention.

24   This can be a tough provision for startup Licensees. Startups often don't have money to cover insurance costs. On the other hand, one can't expect the Licensor the bear the risk of products liability of products made by the Licensee. Indemnification can be a contentious provision of a license and is often a surprise to the inexperienced entrepreneur.

25   Insurance coverage limits will normally be proposed by the risk management group at the licensor. Naturally if the IP is software for video games, coverage requirements will be minimal. If, however, the IP is a therapeutic for human use or software to control airplanes, like the Boeing 737 max, then coverage limits will be much higher. Coverage agreements will also vary depending on stage of development. For example, if the therapeutic drug has progressed to the point where there's no toxicity risk, then coverage limits may be reduced.

17.3   Licensee expressly understands, however, that these coverages and limits do not in any way limit the Licensee's liability. Licensee must furnish the Licensor with certificates of insurance evidencing compliance with all requirements. Licensee's insurance must:

   18.3a   Provide for 30-day advance written notice to The Licensor of any modification.

   18.3b   Indicate that the Licensor is endorsed as an Insured under the coverages listed.

18 GOVERNING LAWS

18.1   THIS AGREEMENT IS TO BE INTERPRETED AND CONSTRUED IN ACCORDANCE WITH THE LAWS OF THE STATE OF xxxxxx, but the scope and validity of any patent or patent application will be governed by the applicable laws of the country of the patent or patent application.

19 EXPORT CONTROL LAWS

19.1   Licensee must observe all applicable United States and foreign laws with respect to the transfer of Licensed Products and related technical data to foreign countries, including the International Traffic in Arms Regulations (ITAR)[26] and the Export Administration Regulations.

20. MISCELLANEOUS

20.1   This Agreement embodies the entire understanding of the parties and supersedes all previous communications, either oral or written, between the parties relating to the subject matter hereof, except for the Secrecy Agreement dated **MM/DD/YYYY**,[27] which continues to the extent it is consistent with this Agreement.

20.2   If any part of this Agreement is for any reason found to be unenforceable, all other parts nevertheless remain enforceable as long as a party's rights under this Agreement are not

---

26   ITAR rules prohibit the export of certain things (for example, weapons, chemical weapons, some software) to certain countries (for example, North Korea) regardless of contract terms. Search online for 'international traffic arms regulation' for export control rules. Some restrictions may not be obvious, so some advice may be in order.

27   It is always the case that the parties have a Secrecy Agreement or Non-disclosure Agreement (NDA) before completing the License agreement. The provisions of the Secrecy Agreement will remain in place after the License Agreement is signed.

materially affected. In lieu of the unenforceable provision, the parties will substitute or add as part of this Agreement a provision that will be as similar as possible in economic and business objectives as was intended by the unenforceable provision.

This sample License Agreement excludes certain clauses for brevity. However, these are less controversial and have standardized language, though the terms may be negotiated.

- Attorney's Fees
- Notices
- Assignability
- Waivers
- Mediation and Arbitration

LICENSEE   LICENSOR

By_____   By_____
            Signature   Signature

TAKEAWAYS

- There are a number of ways a Licensee can pay a Licensor for the right to use Licensor's intellectual property. These are royalties, fees, equity and patent reimbursement. Another possible consideration is cross-licensing, in which the parties exchange licenses with each other, generally without payment to either party.

- Payment is not the only negotiable item. Diligence and Indemnification are also contentious.

- There are multiple ways to limit the scope of the license, thereby reducing payments to the Licensor. Among these are restricted field of use, shortened time period, geographical limits, rights to sublicense and exclusivity.

(Build or Buy?)

If you have some cash, are you better off starting a business or buying a business? The good news for potential acquirers is that in a world of aging baby boomers, there are many willing sellers of solvent businesses. For the midcareer professional, this form of entrepreneurship, called <u>acquisition entrepreneurship</u>, offers the opportunity put management experience to quick use and thereby bypass the pains of product development and finding a product/market fit.

Acquisition entrepreneurship has a good track record for success. Businesses that have been running for years have key elements in place. There is a tangible product, paying customers and a team of employees. There are likely banking relationships to provide credit facilities. Businesses that have been established for a while have a brand in the community and a reputation built up over years. It seems like a waste to see the goodwill disappear. Enter the entrepreneur who seeks to preserve the brand and goodwill and apply some added value when the founder seeks to exit.

WHY ACQUISITION?

Pros	Cons
Key business elements in place. Product, paying customers, employees, goodwill, brand in local community, reputation	Key elements in place need fixing. Some products may need to be rebuilt. Some employees may need to be retrained or let go.
Commercial banking relationships in place. Non-dilutive financing available.	Hard to buy a business from the Founder. It's their "baby" and hard to give up. The seller increases price or otherwise complicates sale.
Most small businesses are often under managed. They often benefit from a dose of financing, marketing, strategy.	There may be hidden liabilities either purposefully or inadvertently not mentioned by the seller. Among these are environmental, employee lawsuits, tax liabilities, liens.
Existing cash flow makes valuation easier	Seller may second guess your decisions if there is seller financing. Seller may even compete eventually

Can be financed in part by the seller or leveraging assets of the company. This makes fundraising easier.	Nervous customers and staff depart. They must be retained.
MBAs skills are useful. A formal business plan may be necessary.	Misalignment of vision, KPIs at the management level. Potential clash of cultures between two firms and resistance to change
	The buyer is unable to manage the acquired company.

Table 18–1. Pros and cons of acquisition

WHY WOULD ANYONE SELL A SMALL, FUNCTIONING BUSINESS?

* Death of the proprietor

   In event of death, the business has passed to the estate of the decedent/proprietor. There is a trustee of the estate who is required to sell the business and distribute proceeds to the heirs. The trustee is a highly motivated seller since they are not equipped to operate the business.

* Retirement of the proprietor

   The proprietor retires and no one in the family or company wants to take over the business. In a world of aging baby boomers, there are a lot of businesses for sale due to retirement.

* Change in the seller's personal circumstance

   Perhaps the seller just gets tired of the business. It's no longer fun. Or the seller must move geographically. Or there may be a health problem.

* Seller is overextended

   Perhaps the seller has other businesses and must divest. Or the seller may be over extended financially and needs to reduce leverage.

Whatever the motivation, there are thousands of businesses available for sale any one time. These can be found by inquiring to small business marketplaces like BizBuySell (bizbuysell.

com) or may be acquired directly from the principals such as the trustee of an estate or even the owner directly.

PROCESS OF ACQUISITION

The process of acquisition should occur in the following sequence:

- First, get an estimate for the amount of money you want to invest. The acquisition can be self-financed or financed with partners who will acquire the business with you.

  For larger amounts, you may form a search fund. A search fund is a pool of capital raised from people who know you and who will either screen or source potential deals for you. The members of the search fund and you will agree on the business to be purchased, terms and conditions and the amount.

- Next, start your search. Limit your search to companies in which there is a strategic fit between the buyer and the business.

  Small business acquisition should not be purely financial. The buyer must add value to the business post acquisition and have a growth scenario. That means the buyer's skills and interests should complement the needs of business. This seems obvious but too many buyers are motivated strictly on price and sales potential. Make sure you bring something to the party.

- Understand the seller's motivation to sell

  Retirement, change of personal circumstances and declining health are all reasonable motives. But sometimes the seller wants to unload a problem business before it gets too bad. Or sometimes the seller is just testing the waters to see what the market is willing to pay to support a later transaction. If the founder is deceased, is there a reason the family won't take the business?

- Set Terms and Conditions (T&Cs) of sale

  After the buyer determines that there is a strategic fit, the next step is to agree on terms and conditions. For example, are there escrow or earnout provisions? Is the deal all-cash or is the seller willing to provide financing? How long will the seller stay active in the business during the transition? What fixed assets are included in the deal, such as fixtures, furniture and equipment?

- Negotiate price

You can't know price until you know the value you bring to the transaction and the terms and conditions. Only then can you get to price. The problem is that many inexperienced negotiators get to price too quickly before establishing a strategic fit or T&Cs.

When negotiating price, some considerations are:

- Premium for all cash transaction. If the buyer requires seller financing, the seller should command a higher price.

- Comparable transactions. These are difficult to find and sometimes maybe irrelevant due to changing circumstances. But if you can find numbers for comparable transactions that support your case, count yourself lucky and present the numbers.

  Public company valuation and multiples are hardly relevant to small business transactions due to differences in liquidity and available financing.

- Calculation of valuation. Here's where MBA skills are useful. Write a business plan. Forecast revenues and costs and calculate the net present value of the enterprise while considering the value add you bring to the acquisition. This is a case where valuation and a proper business plan makes sense since there is some clarity on cash flow.

  While you are negotiating the deal, you need to have a post-integration transition plan. You need to hit the ground running after the transaction to make all parties, including yourself, less nervous.

Post Acquisition Transition

Once you have bought a company, then what?

The acquirer must establish communication quickly with the management and staff. Have an all-hands meeting immediately after the transaction. Assure people their jobs are secure and provide a vision for the company. Tell them the reasons you bought the company. Do a bit of cheerleading. You can't over-promise but you must be aware that people are nervous and that such nervousness will impair the operations of the business. Introduce yourself individually or in small groups with the employees and get familiar with their daily work. Encourage questions. They will have questions you can't answer. If you don't have the answer, say so. This is a time to be self-effacing and modest. Tell them that you are in learning mode and are willing to listen.

When two big companies merge, the problem of integrating management and staff is complex because someone from the acquiring company often has the same job as someone from the acquired company.

In a small company acquisition this is less of a problem, since the acquirer usually doesn't have a complete organization to bring in which takes over the target business.

The problem in small company acquisitions is retaining key people. Often the seller will stipulate that the buyer retain specific persons, out of obligation for years of service. This should be known in advance and honored. Others may need persuasion to stay. In this case you may need a retention plan.

Contact major customers, suppliers, commercial bankers and investors quickly. These people want to meet the new boss. Many of them will have suggestions. Listen to them. In particular, customers may have suggestions which the prior management was unable to respond to. You may need to virtually sell them on the deal as well.

When taking over a small business, the management and staff are afraid you are going to fire them. In turn, you are afraid they are going to quit. To calm things down, transparency and speed are necessary. That's why you need a transition plan, even before the ink is dry on the deal.

What About The Creative Element Of Entrepreneurship?

Many would-be entrepreneurs resist the idea of an acquisition since it lacks the creative element of finding disruptive solutions. It is true that acquisitions are rarely disruptive. But there can, and should, be a creative element in growing a business. Consider the following structure.

When an acquirer buys a business, there is an existing product being sold into an existing market. The acquirer is in the upper left quadrant in Figure 18–2. If the acquirer wants to stay in the Existing Market with an Existing Product, the way to growth is to sell more product, raise prices, reduce operating costs or build a brand. This is a good near-term strategy.

At some point, the acquirer may want to grow. The company can move to the upper right or lower left quadrants. That means either sell existing products into new markets or develop new products to sell into existing markets. New products can be incremental improvements to current products or entirely offerings which have the potential of cannibalizing existing products.

Eventually the company may want to sell new products into new markets, which is the highest risk move. This is done generally by going through the other quadrants, rather than taking one big step.

	Existing Market	New Markets
Existing Product	Sell more product to the same customers Raise prices Reduce operating costs Build a brand	Geography New customer segment
New Product	New products that cannibalize existing products Incremental improvements	Most disruption, highest risk. Should be done by going through other quadrants first

Figure 18–2. Strategic Alternatives for Growing an Acquisition

The point is that there is a creative element to acquisitions by considering how the company will grow post-acquisition. It is perfectly fine to stay with existing products in existing markets. There could be a lot of value created by selling more of the same, reducing costs or building a stronger brand image. But for entrepreneurs who want a more aggressive growth story, acquisitions provide a platform for doing so.

THREE CASES

Bizou Gardens Restaurant

Alan, the buyer of Bizou Gardens restaurant, had 30 years of restaurant experience in Los Angeles. His success in business enabled him to join one of the top private golf clubs in the city. He was a good strategic fit for the potential acquisition of restaurant.

Sellers of Bizou Gardens were Philip and Jeffrey. Philip and Jeffrey had restaurants in San Fernando Valley, Pasadena and Santa Monica. All three restaurants were successful but due to declining health and a tough commute to Santa Monica, Philip and Jeffrey decided to sell Santa Monica property. In addition, the Santa Monica property had the highest cost basis due to high rents in the area.

Alan became aware of the availability of Santa Monica property by word-of-mouth. All three men were well known in the restaurant community. So, when Phillip let the word out that he was willing to sell the restaurant, word quickly spread. Because the Santa Monica restaurant was well known and Alan was well-connected, the process of diligence was relatively quick. Details of the prior operation were as follows:

- Prior-year revenue of $2.6 million
- EBITDA of $100,000
- 7,000 square feet including a 2,200 square foot kitchen
- Rent $14k per month increasing to $17k next year.
- This was the only restaurant in a large office complex consisting of three commercial buildings.
- 120 seats in restaurant plus 30 seats in the bar, with a full liquor license
- The terms were all cash, meaning there was no seller financing
- For the next year there will be no competition in the area. However, after a year there is expected to be a new restaurant across the street.
- Average dinner spend was $25. Strong lunch business with an average ticket of $18
- Zagat top rated for value
- Branding and goodwill were good
- The restaurant was closed on Sunday
- There was no active sports promotion like Monday night football.
- There was no catering business
- There was no breakfast business except for coffee service.

While the business did not generate much profit, Alan felt he could add value by opening on Sunday, promoting Monday night football, offering catering to the businesses in the adjoining office complex and opening for breakfast. The strategic fit was good.

The terms and conditions were more difficult since Alan had to deal with the owner of the office complex as well as Philip and Jeffrey. He needed that cooperation in order to get a rent reduction and possibly tenant improvements. Alan was able to get some tenant improvements as well as concessions on parking in the complex.

Now armed with a strategic fit and acceptable terms and conditions, Alan was able to discuss price. He discussed the deal with his friends at the golf club. He wanted to see what interest there was and find out how much money can raise at the club. As part of the diligence, the investor syndicate had dinner at the restaurant many times to observe the volume of business and food service operations.

Several investors got comfortable with the deal and Alan was able to raise $900,000. Since Alan needed $200,000 for improvements, that left at $700,000 for Philip and Jeffrey.

Note that $700,000 is about three months of revenue. After all the business was generating over $210,000 dollars per month. Would Philip and Jeffrey accept this offer? The valuation process was straightforward. Alan had what he had, and no more. It was basically take it or leave it. It did not matter what valuation methodology was. If Philip and Jeffrey didn't like the offer they simply have to go elsewhere. A lot of deals are done this way.

Philip and Jeffrey were motivated sellers since they wanted to devote their attention to the other two restaurants. They were in no mood find other buyers. Speed was of the essence. Partly to maintain goodwill with the sellers, Alan offered $925,000, which was accepted. Alan formed a limited partnership with his friends from the country club as the limited partners and off they went.

This case has a number of takeaways.

First, word-of-mouth is a good source deal flow for people who are well-connected in a particular business ecosystem. Secondly, motivations to sell can occur in a variety of ways. In this case, the seller's health condition and the desire to cutback helped put the business up for sale. Third, the buyer must bring improvements to the business. This is not just financial transaction. There was a strategic element as well. Finally, valuation can be a simple process. The buyer can offer no more than what they have.

Allen Lane (courtesy of Harvard Business School Publishing, Case 9-384-077)

This classic case, written by Michael Roberts and Howard Stevenson of the Harvard Business School, involves a mature professional of 45 years old who after working for 20 years in electronics distribution business decided he wanted to be his own boss. His situation was:

- MBA from a top school, Harvard in this case
- Had no innovative ideas but was a fixer and general manager
- Has a family, can't move geographically, can't take a lot of risk
- Has some cash, some contacts and industry knowledge
- Wants to be his own boss and, at age 45, can't wait much longer to do so

His first three attempts to buy companies failed but he learned valuable lessons along the way.

- Not every seller is forthcoming about the business they're selling. There may be undisclosed liabilities. Some understate revenues for years and then try to convince the buyer it's worth more than the financials show.
- The buyer can use some of the assets of the acquired company to help finance the transaction. For example, he learned how much he could borrow against accounts receivable, property and inventory.
- Estate trustees, like banks, have rules about their fiduciary responsibilities to the estate and how valuation is arrived at. For example, there is a premium for an all

cash transaction and use comparables, even public company comparables. Also, there is generally no provision for major operations improvement. You take the company as is.

- Some sellers are too emotionally attached to the business they started and ran for years. It's their baby. The seller decided he could not separate himself emotionally from the business and decided to keep it.
- There are a lot of businesses for sale. Entrepreneurs are retiring or passing away all the time. You can be patient in finding the right deal.

Eventually on his fourth attempt, Lane was able to buy a company from the estate of a deceased proprietor.

Carpenter Capital

The case of Carpenter capital involved the purchase of a bus company by a founding team consisting of 5 Executive MBA students at UCLA. These were mid-career professionals who did not have a specific entrepreneurial idea in mind but had interests in investing in and owning their own company. The idea of acquiring a business did not occur to them until they took a class in entrepreneurship in their first year of the MBA program. It was then they found a Harvard Business Podcast entitled "Why You Should Buy a Business (and How to Do It)". https://hbr.org/ideacast/2017/02/why-you-should-buy-a-business-and-how-to-do-it.

MBA programs are largely about networking and building soft skills. So, after spending more than a year together, they felt they could mesh as a group. Their team motto was "you have a fiduciary duty to each other; choose partners carefully".

When sifting through businesses to buy, their rule was that there was to be no high tech. There should be no risk of technology obsolescence. Low tech is dull, but predictable. This despite the fact that the team had backgrounds in biotech and engineering. One is an MD.

Armed with that rule, their target purchase was a school bus company in Delaware. Delaware public school systems outsource transportation services to transport young students to school. Revenues and costs are highly predictable, though not spectacularly profitable. But maybe with a dose of MBA skills, profitability can be improved. The team first became aware of the availability of the business through a business broker.

The team's initial objective was not to be involved in the day-to-day operations, but rather to target experienced military-officer veterans for their leadership skills. The problem that they had was there's no one on the team who had any experience with fleet management. One of the founding members went to West Point. One of his classmates ran an automotive pool for the Army in the Middle East. They recruited him as he had deep experience in operations, working with large teams of enlisted soldiers (which would somewhat mirror the makeup of the school bus driving work force). David, the West Point grad, moved from Southern California to Delaware to help run the company along with his Army buddy. So, the strategic fit was created by the recruitment of the Army veteran.

Most Mom-and-Pop companies are built by sheer will and hard work, motivated by a heavy dose of desperation and obligation to family. To the credit of these entrepreneurs, they make it work. But rarely do they have the information, time or money to infuse their businesses with long term business strategy. They're too consumed by day to day problems.

When Carpenter took a closer look at the company, they felt they could add value. For example, employee motivation could be improved by simple things, such as coffee and recognition for mechanics who preemptively found problems with the buses. The addition of data analytics could save on maintenance costs and anticipate mechanical failures. A marketing campaign was instituted to find uses for the buses when not transporting students, such as recreational trips to Little League games or to the casinos in the area.

When other school bus companies in the area became aware of the availability of money from Southern California, they came to Carpenter preemptively to see if they could be bought. That raises the possibility of a rollup within two years of entering the market as other school bus company entrepreneurs consider retirement.

This case has a number of takeaways.

First the founding team should be clear on commitment and objectives. In this case, 2 founders made it clear they were going to stick with their day jobs. Others would participate part-time. One would devote full-time and even moved to Delaware.

Second, the founding team lacked anyone with knowledge of vehicle fleet operations. This business was a non-starter until they found that person. To their credit, they found some domain expertise, which gave the green light to move forward.

Third, financial commitments were made clear upfront. Some of the founders offered mortgages on their homes and others invested portions of their retirement plans. Others invested nominal amounts of personal cash.

Some key points of these cases can be summarized as follows:

	Bizou	Allen Lane	Carpenter
Source of deal	Word of mouth	Trustees of an estate	Business Broker
Financing	Friends	Assets of company	IRAs
		Commercial bank	Mortgages
Strategic fit	Buyer had prior restaurant experience	Buyer had experiencing related Industries	Buyers needed to hire someone with operating experience

Valuation Method	Sellers offered take it or leave it. They didn't have any more money and wouldn't mind losing the business	Bank, on behalf of the trustee, ed public company comparables, premium for all cash, discounted cash flow	Standard valuation methodologies

Table 18-3. Comparison of Acquisitions

The point is that there is no one way to accomplish an acquisition. Personalities and needs of sellers are different. But if you think about strategic fit first and worry about price later, then have a transparent transition plan, your odds of a good outcome are improved.

TAKEAWAYS

- Though there is little opportunity for a disruptive entrepreneurial experience, acquisition is a legitimate way to become an entrepreneur.

- Acquisitions capitalize on having business management experience. There is ample opportunity to use what you've learned in HR, marketing, finance, operations and strategy. You'll need a formal business plan, at a minimum, in order to secure a loan.

- There is opportunity for creativity in devising growth strategies.

- The probability of failure is lower by acquiring an ongoing business rather than starting a business from the ground up. Therefore, acquiring a business may be more appropriate for mid-career professionals who have family responsibilities.

SELF STUDY

Questions

1. Why are trustees of estates unable to engage in asset sales?

2. When buying a restaurant, what is the acquirer taking possession of? Why are restaurants bought and sold for relatively little money?

3. If you were making analyzing the strategic alternatives of Figure 18-2, how would you decide which quadrant is the next move, if any? What key questions do you need to address?

Answers

1. Trustees can't sell just the assets. They don't operate companies. The longer the company stays in the hands of the trustees, the greater the likelihood that the value of the business declines since there is no top management. Accordingly, executors would not accept an offer that required extended payment terms and therefore would not provide seller financing. Trustees are therefore a willing sellers for all cash deals.

2. When acquiring a restaurant, in most cases the acquirer is basically acquiring just a lease and other real estate amenities, like parking. There could be some kitchen equipment left behind but the buyer may not want it. If a Chinese restaurant is taking over an Italian restaurant, who needs the pizza oven?

   The key asset the acquirer is getting is location. Moreover, when taking over a restaurant, the new restaurant has major expenses regarding tenant improvements, new décor and other elements of trade dress.

   Restaurants are bought and sold for relatively low multiples of revenue since the acquirer is getting so little.

3. If there is room for operations improvement and branding, the existing product/existing market quadrant has near term gain for low risk.

   If you are better at product development than marketing, go for the new product/existing market quadrant while you improve your marketing skills. If you are better at marketing than product development, go for the existing product/new market quadrant.

   What are competitive forces regarding new products and markets? If competitors are offering new products which could obsolete your existing products, you may need to consider breakthrough products. Be less concerned about cannibalization since others will cannibalize your product line for you.

Are growth prospects better elsewhere, due to a change in demographic or regulatory factors? Then go for new markets.

In general, acquirers should not go directly to the new product/new market quadrant without going through the other quadrants first. It's hard enough to take one step. But to take 2 steps at once can only be justified by extraordinary competitive risk.

CHAPTER 19 – SPINOFFS

{"there's a fine line between corporate entrepreneurship and insubordination"
– major CEO}

In chapter 18 we mentioned advisability of acquisition entrepreneurship, especially for people with formal business training. In this chapter we introduce a similar concept we'll call <u>spinoff entrepreneurship</u>. By spinoff entrepreneurship we mean divesting a part of a large parent company to create a new company. When we say part of a parent company, we mean something as embryonic as a research and development project or something more developed such as a business unit with complete profit and loss responsibility. We differentiate spinoffs from divestitures by size and entrepreneurial status. Spinoffs are small, whereas divestitures are generally larger and are typically mature enough to stand alone.

WHY SPINOFF ENTREPRENEURSHIP?

Pros	Cons
One or more of the following business elements are in place. Research, product, customers, brand, employees.	The parent company decided not to pursue the business. The spinoff entrepreneur needs to find out why.
Can be financed in part by the parent. This makes fundraising easier.	Complex negotiations needed to untangle the assets of the spinoff from the parent.
The parent company can continue a relationship with the spinoff by being a supplier, a customer or investor, thereby providing support.	The possibility of failed spinoff negotiations may create permanent hard feelings.
MBAs skills are useful. A formal business plan will be necessary.	Difficulty in staffing the spinoff. Some people crucial to the spinoff may want to stay with the parent. Some people who want to go to the spinoff may be not be right in a startup.

Possible win-win for the parent as well as the spinoff entity.	The spinoff promoter works for a big company and has big company experience. That person may be unable to manage a startup.

Table 19–1. Pros and Cons of a Spinoff as a Path to Entrepreneurship

WHY WOULD A PARENT COMPANY SPINOFF AN ENTITY?

Every big company wants to grow. But a spinoff removes some assets, income and talent of the parent thereby making the parent company smaller. The parent company needs a strong rationale to endorse a spinoff since it contradicts the urge to get bigger. Some reasons to spinoff are:

- Monetize a research project that won't go anywhere in the big company but could develop outside the big company. For example, the parent company could have invented a new pharmaceutical drug, but the drug addresses a small market that the company is not interested in.

- Monetize a non-performing asset or business division. If an existing unit is performing poorly, the parent company may want to shut it down. But this could be expensive and cause public relations problems. A spinoff may be a better alternative than a layoff.

- Accommodate a change in strategic direction. The business division may be performing well, but the long-term strategic vision of the parent lies in a different direction.

- Investors may insist that the company focus on core businesses.

- Accommodate anti-trust concerns. Perhaps the government requires a spinoff to accommodate an acquisition in another space.

- Signal to internal and external entrepreneurs that the parent company is entrepreneurial. It therefore acts as a recruitment and retention tool.

WHY WOULDN'T A PARENT COMPANY SPINOFF AN ENTITY?

Despite these motivations, parent companies have inhibitions to spinoffs. Chief among these are:

- The parent may be concerned that the people promoting the spinoff know something the management of the parent doesn't know. Top management can rightly ask why do these people want to go?

- A related question involves conflict of interest. The management of the spinoff will be negotiating terms of the separation with the parent while they are still employed by the parent. Who is the organizer representing? The parent company or the spinoff?

- The spinoff process is poorly understood. The process is complicated especially regarding staffing issues and untangling finances and liability. There are thorny questions regarding benefits, reporting and seniority when senior staff move from the parent to the spinoff.

- Leakage of intellectual property and key people. The parent could be concerned it is spinning off its "crown jewels", or the core capabilities of the parent company. Spinning off "crown jewels" would be more problematic for companies that are not well diversified.

- On the other hand, if a parent company has lots of products, not all of them can be "crown jewels". Thus, spinoffs happen more often from larger companies with a diversified set of products.

Eastman Kodak is an example of spinning off "crown jewels". In the 1970s, Eastman Kodak invented the technology underlying digital photography. However, they did not commercialize that technology and thus struggled to survive the onslaught of digital photography. As a survival mechanism, in 1994 they spun off their chemical division which turned out to be their crown jewels. Their chemical division became Eastman Chemical which is now traded on the New York Stock Exchange (ticker: EMN), whereas Eastman Kodak, the photography company, went bankrupt.

PROCESS OF SPINOFF

The process of spinoff can come from the top management of the parent or bottoms up from an employee who wants to be an entrepreneur. When the idea of spinoff comes top-down, there's no need to convince top management of the need for spinoff.

The more complicated case is when the idea comes from an employee. This carries obvious risks for the employee, so the motivation level must very high. Given sufficient motivation on the part of the employees, some of the following points can be made to top management of the parent:

- The business of the spinoff is not aligned with the strategic direction of the parent

- The spinoff requires capital that's the parent is unable to provide

- Pursuing the spinoff idea within the parent would be too disruptive for parent.

- Investors in the parent may want to see more focus by the parent and thus encourage the spinoff of non-core businesses

- Outside investors may like what the spinoff is doing but are only interested in financing a smaller company.

- A spinoff transfers risk of a new product or a new market away from the parent. We mentioned in Chapter 1 that a big company has reputational risk and possible loss of market capitalization by having a major product fail in the market. Exposure can be reduced by commercializing the innovation in a separate entity, then later acquiring the spinoff after the product has been demonstrated. An example of this is the Cisco/Insieme case, described below.

Nonetheless, selling the idea of a spinoff to top management is a sensitive process. The relationship between the promoter of a spinoff and top management must be strong and candid. Eventually, if there is agreement that a spinoff is the proper course of action, then the process follows these key steps:

- Write a business plan, in part to convince the management of the parent company of the wisdom of the spinoff

- Choose the spinoff team and address associated HR problems

- Arrange for financing and equity ownership of the parent

- Arrange for outside financing if necessary

- Negotiate future relationship with the parent

Write a Business Plan

This must be done early and articulate the following:

- Value proposition for the parent. The Executive Summary of the spinoff plan must provide the parent Company with the economic and organizational rationale for the spinoff. The business plan is in part a selling document to the parent company.

- Transfer of assets. What property will the parent provide the spinoff? Cash? Patents? Property? Contracts? Receivables? What equity consideration will the parent company receive?

- Transfer of intellectual property. Which patents and trade secrets are transferred? Will intellectual property be licensed to the spinoff or will title be transferred? In either case, what consideration will be provided to the parent?

  Who bears costs of patent prosecution for patents and progress?

  What rights will be retained by the parent? Will the parent continue to use the patent or will there be field of use restrictions? The parent may want to continue further research. Will that be permissible?

- Will the inventors be transferred to the spinoff? Or is just the patent/trade secret sufficient? Maybe the parent will continue basic research and inventors need to stay with the parent. What impact will this have on the spinoff?

- Transfer of liabilities. What liabilities will the parent offload to the spinoff? Payables? Debts? Pension?

- How will losses, if any, incurred by the spinoff we consolidated with the financial statements of the parent?

- Transfer of people (now and future). Who from the parent company will join the spinoff and over what time frame? What additional external staff will be required?

- Funding requirements and deal structure. What percentage of the spinoff will be owned by the parent company? What shareholder preferences will the parent have? How is valuation set?

- Will management from the parent company sit on the Board of the spinoff?

- Have a cap table and governance structure specified in the plan.

Choose the spinoff team and address associated HR problems

Staffing issues are top priority when organizing the spinoff.

- Who goes to the spinoff, who stays with the parent? Who decides who goes and who stays? In some cases, some employees of the parent may want to join the spinoff but are prevented from doing so because of their importance to the parent or their lack of suitability for working a small company.

- Salary scale at the startup may be less than the parent company. In that case, will spinoff employees accept equity compensation?

- What about benefits? With the spinoff offer the same retirement and health benefits of the parent? If an individual has partial vesting in parent company in parent company retirement or equity compensation agreements, how was the vesting be credited in the spinoff?

- The spinoff may need to accommodate employees covered by collective bargaining agreements.

- Reporting responsibilities at the spinoff maybe different from the reporting at the parent. Will this cause hard feelings?

- The promoter of the spinoff will likely be the start-up CEO. Is that a good idea?

- In any case, a definitive organization chart must be part of the plan.

Arrange for a continuing relationship between the spinoff in the parent.

A spinoff company, like any startup, must have unfair advantages. In order for spinoff to survive, its unfair advantage must include the continuing support of the parent. Support can take a number of roles:

- Act as a customer, supplier, co-signer for loans.

- Allow the spinoff to use of premises, contracts, sales agreements, supply chains, insurance, employee benefits.

- Provide access to laboratories or production facilities.

- Provide administrative support, such as security and reception, if the spinoff occupies the same facilities as the parent

- Grant rights to the spinoff for IP developed in the future

All these have a price which must be factored into the business plan and valuation.

Are Spinoffs a good idea for You?

- There are pitfalls for the Parent. The loss of crown jewels, key staff and possibly a line of business.

- There are pitfalls for the Spinoff. The spinoff is a startup, with most of the headaches of entrepreneurship.

- But for professionals experienced in dealing with business discussions with big companies, spinoffs can provide a good opportunity for entrepreneurship

  - Uses formal business skills

  - The spinoff management knows the parent's strengths and weaknesses and can capitalize on them.

  - The spinoff has a running start, like an acquisition. Odds of success are better than a startup.

ABC Defense spinning off El Segundo Optics

ABC Defense was a large aerospace Corporation in Southern California. Over the past decades the company has received millions of dollars of research funding from the government for military and aerospace purposes. A common theme for ABC and other defense contractors is the attempt to commercialize military research and development for civilian purposes. The reasons are clear. They want to

- Realize value from technology already developed. This could be done by licensing their technology to other companies or by providing technology in exchange for equity in a startup, namely their own spinoff

- Provide a retention and recruiting tool for entrepreneurially minded staff. This enhances their ability and reputation to innovate

- Develop relationships for access to commercial off-the-shelf (COTS) technology.

What Did ABC Defense Have going for it?

- World-class technology in many high-tech fields:

  - Radio Frequency (RF), InfraRed (IR), and Optical sensors
  - Communication technology (RF and Optical)
  - Semi-conductor expertise
  - Software expertise (Embedded, enterprise, security)
  - System level development and integration

- Their technologies were already implemented in defense systems. The development was well past "science experiment" stage.

- Corporate level support for commercializing military technologies.

- Support from employees and investors for spinning out technology.

After considerable analysis of the various technology options, market acceptance, investor support and employee availability, ABC concluded that a spinoff of an optical communications technology was in order.

The spinoff had both top-down support as well as support from employees and the investment community.

What was the spinoff Process at ABC?

Getting management approvals was easy part. The tactical process proved to be more complicated due primarily today sensitive nature of the technologies. Some top-secret elements of the technology had to be removed. This resulted in a complex set of approvals. The sequencing of approvals was:

- Technology and marketing management of the optics business unit
- CFO of ABC
- CEO of ABC
- Legal counsel, especially regarding top-secret materials.
- Board of Directors

The spinoff happened but ultimately was not a success.

Post Mortem

A miscalculation the parent company and spinoff made was that the technology was largely overkill for commercial markets. The requirements for defense of the United States are very stringent, thankfully. That means that in most cases, military grade high tech systems perform at a higher level than is cost-effective for commercial markets. The company went to market with a very high-performing product with limited market acceptance due to cost.

Failure to find a good product market fit was largely due to marketing inexperience. The highly skilled engineers and scientists lacked experience in startup process, sales and pricing. Defense company sales process was completely different from commercial sales process. Defense procurements can take years, often have customized solutions and based on negotiated pricing. This didn't work in the commercial marketplace.

One can surmise that great technologies still lie buried America's defense companies. But great technology are just a part of entrepreneurial success.

Computer Sciences Corporation (CSC) was a large scale software systems integrator with civilian and military contracts from the federal government. It performed system integration and operations for the Social Security Administration and the US Customs Service among other large-scale federal contracts.

Underlying many large systems in the 1980s were data communications networks which moved data between computers located worldwide. For example, for the US Customs Service, when a passenger arrived at Los Angeles International Airport, information would be sent to data repositories and returned in real time. This was a major technical achievement in the 1970s and 1980s, long before the Internet. The Worldwide Web had not been invented yet. Email was cutting edge. One can argue that these services looked very much like today's cloud computing.

CSC/Infonet installed data communications networks on protocols that predated Internet. When Cisco Systems came along with router products built on Internet protocols, CSC switched to Cisco equipment and built a global network based on TCP/IP and related protocols based on Arpanet research, Arpanet being the precursor to today's Internet. {I should add that assistance was provided by Professor Len Kleinrock at UCLA, who was the first principal investigator for Arpanet in 1969.}

CSC had originally done a lot of work with the aerospace industry in Los Angeles. That's where the company was headquartered. But over time, CSC won so much federal government contracts, that much of the work moved from Southern California to Washington DC. Roughly at the same time, it occurred to the management of the data communications group, then called Infonet Services, that CSC should spinoff Infonet into a separate entity. The Infonet staff did not want to move to Washington DC and CSC management agreed there could be a business as an Internet service provider (ISP).

The key elements of the Infonet spinoff were:

- Infonet was no longer strategic to the corporate parent. CSC saw its future as a large scale systems integrator for the federal government and large commercial clients. Operating a data communications network for individual corporate use was not in the picture.

- Spinoff was initiated bottoms up. The Infonet staff prepared the business plan.

- Outside financing arranged early in the process. Key investors in CSC were supportive of the spinoff and purchased equity in Infonet.

- Shared facilities and continued ongoing relationship. Infonet staff remained in the CSC facility.

- Infonet staff was eager to join the spinoff. They were unwilling to relocate.

- CSC took a large equity position in Infonet.

In less than 10 years after the spinoff, Infonet went public on the New York Stock Exchange (ticker: IN)

CISCO SYSTEMS SPINNING OFF INSIEME, THEN REACQUIRING IT

A variation on the spinoff is the spin-in[1].

In the case of a spin-in, the parent company funds and staffs a separate company to develop a major product and later reacquires the spinoff. This has certain advantages over developing the product in-house.

- The spinoff management could pick the very best engineers from the parent.

- It focuses the engineers on the project by moving them to separate premises thereby avoiding distractions.

- The spinoff doesn't have to worry about fundraising or exit.

- Cisco offloads the risk of project failure.

- It takes the engineers off the corporate payroll scale. That means they can be paid more and get stock options in the startup, whereas by staying with Cisco, they would be tied to the Cisco compensation policy. This happens when the principals of the spinoff have very high bargaining positions at Cisco. This was the case of Insieme. The founders of Insieme were name brands at Cisco.

Insieme successfully developed a strategic product for Cisco. Cisco later acquired Insieme for $863 million. Search online for 'cisco insieme' for details.

---

1   https://mpra.ub.uni-muenchen.de/5563/1/MPRA_paper_5563.pdf

- There is disciplined process to executing a spinoff

- A spinoff has reduced risk due to existing product, markets and team

- A spinoff uses MBA skills since a business plan is necessary.

- When properly executed the spinoff is a successful form of entrepreneurship and is a good mechanism for big companies to be more entrepreneurial

SELF STUDY

Questions

1. Why would a parent company be interested in a product yet be badly positioned to exploit it?

2. In a bottoms-up spinoff, should the staff and initiating a spinoff inform top management of their intentions? If so when, and if not, what kinds of liabilities and penalties can you expect from the Parent?

Answers

1. There are several reasons why a parent company can't exploit its research.

   - Market opportunity is too small.

   - Staff shortage. The parent company is not staffed to exploit the invention. Outside staff must be acquired.

   - Conflict with customer or supplier. A customer or supplier offers a similar product.

   - There is an existing internal business that competes.

- Financing. The parent company is unwilling or unable to fund product and market development. Outside financing is required.

2. Probably upper management should be informed.

Without consent of the parent, the spinoff management has exposure to legal action from the parent regarding violation of employment agreements, trade secret loss or the taking of employees or customers.

Also, without consent, there is little likelihood of further cooperation between the spinoff and the parent company.

There are risks of raising the possibility of spinoff with management. So before

From an astute observer of management practice:

The point Dilbert is making is that there are a lot of bad Boards of Directors. Such Boards are inattentive, not challenging to the management and don't quite understand their responsibilities are to the shareholders, not to the management.

Since first time entrepreneurs have typically never been subject to oversight by a Board or been Board members themselves, it would be useful to learn some of the terminology and practices how to interact with your Board or how to be a Board member yourself.

HOW ARE BOARDS CONSTITUTED?

Boards most often consist of a small and odd number of members. One is too few and 9 is too many at the earliest stage. One is too few since it is best to have the opinions of both an inside and <u>outside member</u>. By outside member, we mean a member who is not employed by the company. This would usually be an investor. Nine on a startup Board is too many since coordination becomes problematic. It becomes more difficult to schedule meetings, obtain signatures or simply come to agreement. Three or 5 at the beginning is about right, with 3 a preferable number.

Boards have <u>Observers</u>. These are interested parties who attend Board meetings but are not Board members themselves. They don't vote on Board matters and at certain times during a Board meeting, may be asked to leave the room. Typically, these are strategic partners, strategic investors or minor investors. They are at meetings to lend guidance and expertise or be informed about company activity.

Boards will have a <u>Secretary</u>, whose job it is to take minutes. The Secretary may or may not be a Board Member, although a Board Member can function as Secretary as well.

Boards may consist of various subcommittees. Among these are compensation, audit, executive or ad-hoc committees. It is unlikely that a small company would have all of these subcommittees, but it is useful to know what they do, for definitional purposes.

- <u>Compensation Committee</u>, also known as the <u>comp committee</u> decides pay packages for everyone in the company, including possibly the receptionist. Pay package includes salary, bonus, benefits and equity. This committee is composed of mostly, if not entirely, outside Board members on the theory that it is a conflict of interest for the CEO to be on the comp committee and pass judgement on his or her pay package.

- <u>Audit Committee</u>. Supervises the audit, selects outside auditor, approves the audit report. This subcommittee consists of at least one member from management, on the presumption that the management knows the numbers.

- <u>Governance Committee</u> is a self-policing committee to review internal Board practices. It makes sure the company is in compliance with regulatory requirements. It some foreign jurisdictions, Sweden for example, a governance committee is required. Apart from regulatory compliance, the governance committee evaluates the Board as a whole and supervises a peer review of each individual Board member.

- <u>Ad-hoc Committees</u> may be formed to address unusual events. For example, if the company initiates or is subject to litigation, the Board may create a subcommittee to address the suit. If there is a take-over attempt, a subcommittee may address that. These are not everyday events but they are significant and may require focused Board attention.

It is unlikely that the startup company will have all these committees. Generally, only the comp committee will be active and even then, the entire Board could sit on this committee. But as the company grows and some of these other considerations become important, it may be useful to consider other and active committees.

The composition of the Board is one of the most important control provisions for investors. Composition of the Board and some subcommittees will be specified in the prior round term sheet.

Formally, the control of any business entity is under the control of the owners. In a corporate setting, the shareholders delegate that control to the Board. Some duties of the Board are:

- Hire, mentor and fire CEO. CEOs may forget they work for the Board.

- Vet all management and, possibly, some staff. It is common that the Board will interview every prospective hire not only to validate qualifications but also for cultural fit.

- Approve subsequent funding rounds. If a prospective investor asks that incumbent investors waive some of their preferences, the incumbents can object and ask for better terms or walk away from the prospective deal.

- Approve material transactions. Board provisions may also require Board approval of material transactions such as the sale of assets, taking on debt, joint venture agreements, major channel agreement. These could be viewed as operational questions, but if the transaction is large enough, the Board may interject.

- Find investors, customers, suppliers, service providers and partners. Board members are chosen largely because they add value in addition to the money they invested. They provide expertise, contacts, sales leads, supply chain agreements and the like. A company that only gets cash in return for its equity is not getting the full value for its equity.

- Provide therapy. Being a first-time CEO is hard. You feel huge responsibility and sometimes it can get you down. Sometimes the CEO needs a little consoling and it's the job of the Board to provide it. This is done by providing context from someone who has been there and gotten through it, preferably one who has been a CEO or an active investor before. A Board member is an insider who has a vested interest in the success of the business. They should be relied upon to provide honest feedback and encouragement when needed.

WHAT CONSTITUTES A BOARD MEETING?

- Board meetings are required events and must be held regularly. If they are not held regularly, then arguably the company is an extension of the owners and there could be risk of piercing the corporate veil. Board meetings are held quarterly, maybe monthly for very early stage companies. This is a reason why investors in early stage companies tend to invest locally. The investors want to keep an eye on things and be physically present at Board meetings and sometimes for company visits apart from Board meetings.

- In order for a Board meeting to exist, there must be a minimum number of members in attendance. The minimum number constitutes a <u>quorum</u>. Without a quorum, you don't have a Board meeting. For example, if 2 guys get together for a round of golf and discuss some business, is that a Board meeting? Generally, no. Your company documents will stipulate the minimum number for a quorum. If some members want to attend by videoconference or phone bridge, that would be OK if it is known beforehand that they are members of the quorum.

WHAT ARE SOME BEST PRACTICES FOR THE MANAGEMENT TO ORGANIZE A BOARD MEETING?

- The management should send each member of the Board a packet of information ahead of time. Members don't want surprises when they come to a Board meeting. They should have in advance the following:

  - Agenda, prior meeting minutes for approval, key operating statistics, like shipments, sales orders.

  - Any change in headcount, job offers pending, recruitment activities, disciplinary action taken and terminations. Staffing level is a key Board level concern.

  - If there are serious personnel problems, such as sexual harassment, those should be surfaced and dealt with at the next meeting.

- Prepare members ahead of time if you expect issues. Board meetings are generally not a good time to have major disagreements aired for the first time. If management expects a controversial item, then discussion of the issue should take place beforehand. If a consensus is not reached, then it will need to be discussed at the Board meeting.

- Schedule meetings in the middle of the day to accommodate travel. If you have a company in Southern California and your investors are in Silicon Valley, make it easy for them to come to the Board meeting return the same day.

- Keep your minutes and Board packages. You may need them for legal reasons but it is also useful to know who agreed with certain decisions.

A sample Board meeting agenda is shown here.

SAMPLE BOARD MEETING AGENDA [1]

Company Update	30 minutes[2]
Sales and Marketing	30 minutes
Staffing	15 minutes
Finance	30 minutes

Company Update

- Review of minutes of prior Board Meeting
- Review of Key Performance Indicators (KPIs)[3]
- Product development
- Regulatory and legal updates
- Facilities update

Sales and marketing

- Deals closed
- Pipeline
- Lead generation

---

1   The meeting should last no more than 2 hours, usually less.

2   The company update should include bad news as well as good news. If there is only good news presented, a good Board member will ask about problems. Get ahead of the discussion.

3   KPIs should be well known in advance and tracked consistently. KPIs should include sales and operational metrics.

- Online metrics[4]

Staffing

- Current headcount and burn rate
- Offers pending
- Interviews scheduled
- Disciplinary and termination actions

Finance

- Cash flow statement, current cash on hand and burn rate
- Variances to plan
- Fundraising activities, either in process or planned.

MORE GOOD PRACTICES

- Separation of Chairman of the Board from CEO. The reason for that separation is that the jobs are different. The job of the chairman is to manage the Board. The job of the CEO Is to manage the company. For small companies it may not be practical to separate functions. Certainly, the job of the chairman is not a full-time job. There may be issues of managing Board members which the CEO may not be comfortable with.

  In some jurisdictions, in Europe for example, it may be a requirement to separate the functions. But, in any case, separation can relieve the CEO of duties not directly involved with the operations of the company.

- Prepare annual calendars for the entire Board and committees.

- Assign individual tasks to Board members between Board meetings. These tasks can include customer visits, investor visits, review test results, perform industry analysis, review sales results and help recruit new management and staff.

---

4   A standard set of website analytics should be tracked consistently. Examples include traffic, time spent on the site, which pages get the most traffic, unique users, click throughs and transactions.

- Self-evaluation. Is the Board transparent? Is it collegial? Are they able to deal with problems quickly? Is a Board afraid of conflict? The entire Board can be evaluated as well as individual members. The tricky question is how a Board evaluates itself. A Governance Subcommittee can initiate the process and review results. But often this process requires an external facilitator who interviews the Board collectively and individually. This is a tricky process but the company needs to decide whether not the Board is adding value and whether each member is engaged and interested.

- Anticipate crises. Establish a crisis playbook before a crisis happens.

  - Identify what constitutes a crisis. Sudden change in cash position? Loss of a key contract or executive? Legal action?
  - Should there be a crisis management team? If so, who is on it? How does crisis management differ from ordinary operations?
  - Does the Board need additional assistance?
  - Should there be an independent investigation organized by, and reporting to, the Board?

Being on a Board is fine if everything is going fine. But part of the responsibility of the Board is to lend experience when things aren't fine. That Board should ask itself, what are we going to do if . . .?

PEOPLE YOU SHOULD NOT HAVE ON YOUR BOARD

- <u>People not attuned to contemporary business disruptions.</u> For example, members should be conversant in cybersecurity, digitization, geopolitical risks, diversity of customers and employees, regulatory changes, changes in business models.

- <u>Industry know-it-all</u>; a domain expert who won't listen.

- <u>The Strong Silent type</u>. The Person doesn't say much and you are not quite sure if they're listening.

- <u>"I'm just a techie. You guys talk business"</u>. Sometime you have a technical genius who started the company and now sits on the Board. They have no background in, or little interest of, business issues, so they'll say "you guys talk business". Well, the Board's role is business. This person serves the company better in the technical management capacity, rather than being on Board.

- Ruthless cost cutter. Board members must believe in the company enough to make an investment from time to time. If they are only concerned about cost, then they may not simply believe in the company. In that case they should not be on the Board. You must have people who believe in the company.

- "Don't bother me with details. I'm the big picture guy". That's basically codewords for being lazy. They won't get involved with the details of sales and operations and thus may be unwilling or unable to help management solve problems.

- Non-confrontational compromiser. These people compromise all the time. They don't take decisive stands. They don't confront problems.

- Friends of the CEO. Often the initial Board members are recruited by the CEO, which may be necessary at beginning. But it is a group that doesn't challenge management and sometimes management may need some frank discussion.

If you have for members like these, you may have to replace them. Short of that, one way to get better performance is to assign each Board member a specific task and hold them accountable.

TRICKY SITUATIONS

- Board member conflict of interest. Consider a situation where an individual Board member is on the Board of Coldwater Circuits and is also on the management team or is a consultant to Fly By Night Inc. During the course of a Coldwater Board meeting, the member hears of a deal which could benefit Fly By Night. What is the proper conduct the Board member?

  The Board member must remember their Duty of Loyalty to Coldwater. They'll have to vote in the best interest of Coldwater regardless of their outside interest, or, at minimum, recuse themselves from that particular issue. Failure to do so exposes the member to personal liability.

- "Zone of Insolvency". If the unfortunate situation arises in which it appears the company could possibly go bankrupt, then at some point the Board starts to work for the creditors, not the shareholders. In the event of bankruptcy, the creditors have first claim on assets of the company. Therefore, the creditors pay very close attention to actions taken by the Board when they are concerned about recovery of assets in bankruptcy. The question becomes, at what point is the company entering the Zone of Insolvency and how does that manifest itself in decisions made by the Board?

- Who is the client of the General Counsel? In situations where the company is having problems and has an internal General Counsel, the question can arise as to who the General Counsel represents. Does the General Counsel represent the CEO, the company or the Board? In extreme cases, the Board will need its own, separate legal representation.

- Unprepared Board members. This can happen when a particular Board Members sits on many Boards. Sometimes an investor can sit on as many as 10 to 12 boards. Board members should keep in mind they have a Duty of Care. That means must be informed when making board decisions. Members who cannot honor their duty of care should step down. This is problematic when the investor has a large ownership in the company.

- Detailed Board minutes, or not? The job of the secretary is to take Board minutes. The question is how detailed should these minutes be? In most cases this is not a controversial question since the company and Board are behaving well. However, when trouble surfaces, the question arises as to how much of a paper trail to leave.

  Let's take the case the company entering the zone of insolvency. Once the company enters the zone of insolvency then detailed Board minutes become very interesting to creditors. At times like this, a quick call to the company lawyer is in order.

- Note-taking during Board meetings. Can/should an individual Board member take private notes during a Board meeting? Let's suppose there are sensitive issues before the Board. If a particular Board member disagrees with other members of the Board, there is a temptation of that Board member to take private minutes. Again, the company and Board should get legal advice.

It should be pointed out at the tricky situations such as these are rare. The most common situation is for Board member having a conflict of interest. This is most easily dealt with by recusal from a particular Board question. But in all cases, disclosure of the conflict before the Board is required.

Here is an example of minutes of a relatively uneventful meeting, redacted from an actual board meeting.

SAMPLE BOARD MINUTES

BOARD OF DIRECTORS MINUTES
FLEDGLING, INC.

A regularly scheduled meeting of the Board of Directors (the "Board") of Fledgling, Inc. (the "Company") was held on Wednesday, July 18, 20xx at the company office in Pasadena, California, pursuant to notice duly given. All of the directors of the Company attended the meeting, as follows: Elmer Fudd, Molly Thai, George Abe, and Daisy Duck (VC firm 1). Tom Terrific, (Strategic Inc., by phone)

Also present as an observer, Jon Doe (VC firm 2).

1. Call to Order; Quorum.

   The Chairman noted that a quorum of directors was present and called the meeting to order at 11:40 a.m.

2. Approval of minutes

   Elmer Fudd moved to approve June minutes. The motion was seconded by George Abe and then so passed by a unanimous vote.

3. Operational Issues.

   The CEO briefed the Board on progress made by the company since the last Board meeting. Operational matters discussed were

   • Issues found with temperature testing which induces insertion loss. Possible schedule impact.
   • Clean room preparation to begin this week. Open by September 30.

4. Recruiting

   - Contingency firms engaged for search for VP of Manufacturing. Ads generating responses. No candidates imminent.
   - Jody Beginner hired since last Board meeting as a test engineer.
   - Staff at 14

5. Trade Show

   Customers visited were Optisphere, Fujitsu, Centerpoint, Cisco, Oplink, Metrophotonics.

   Main needs expressed were ROADM and protection. Less interest in switching

6. Compensation Committee.

   Jody Beginner approved at $90K base and 50K options (0.25%).

7. Scheduling of the Next Board Meeting.

   The next meeting will be held at the company headquarters August 29, 20xx.

8. Adjournment.

There being no further business to come before the Board, upon motion duly made and seconded, the meeting was adjourned at 1:30 p.m.

_____

Dr. Elmer Fudd
Chairman and President

Approved:

_____

Daisy Duck
Secretary

WHAT ABOUT ADVISORY BOARDS?

An <u>Advisory Board</u> is a panel of outside experts who are not Board Members or employees but who are recruited to provide advice. It's a flexible arrangement to acquire expertise without costing a lot of money or equity.

- It's possible to have 2 Advisory Boards; one for technology and a separate one for business.

- Since it by Board members do not sit on the Board of Directors, there is no liability to the advisory Board member. But there's also less influence.

- Advisory members can be paid in cash or stock or not at all, if they are good friends of the management.

Advisory Boards are the subject of some controversy. Some observers like them, some don't. The controversy arises because some industry observers feel that advisory boards are waste of time and money since the advisory members have no stake in the business. There's also a risk of a loss of trade secrets or other important company information.

However, if you value their input and not too concerned by the loss of company information, advisory boards can be a low-cost way to get good information and build a network.

WHAT DOES SARBANES/OXLEY MEAN TO ME?

Sarbanes/Oxley (Sarbox), enacted in 2002, is United States federal legislation enacted after the 2000 stock market crash. Imposed new regulatory and reporting requirements for publicly traded companies, their boards and their accountants. Among these requirements are:

- CEO certification of financials
- Disgorgement of ill-gotten gains due to false statements
- Bans loans to officers and directors
- Audit committee members must be independent
- Establishes internal governance rules (Section 404)
- Mandates more record retention
- Oversight of audit firms
- Many other ....

The question is what does Sarbanes Oxley mean to startup companies? The answers is, not much. It's for publicly traded companies.

However, if you plan to go public or become acquired by a public company, then it becomes important. At the point you may need to become Sarbox compliant in order to be public or part of a public company.

DO YOU WANT TO BE A BOARD MEMBER?

This chapter so far dealt with the Board of Directors from the entrepreneur's point of view.

Let's take the other point of view. That's when you are invited to be a board member. Most believe this is very flattering and it's an honor to be asked to be on someone's Board of Directors. This is particularly true when you're asked by the CEO who is a friend or colleague.

Before accepting, there are a few things to think about.

- Compensation. It should be explicit whether you will be paid in shares or cash or a combination of both, or not at all. If paid in shares, how will vesting work?

- Are you familiar with Duties of Care and Loyalty?

- The problem of taking a Board seat is exposure to liability. Board members can be sued by various parties. For example, you could be sued personally by creditors, potential investors or even the management of the company on whose Board you sit.

  Because of potential liability, prospective board members will insist on Directors & Officers insurance (D&O). This is an insurance policy paid for by the company which indemnifies board members individually. Even if you are to prevail in a legal action, then care must be taken to be sure the D&O policy covers legal fees for your defense.

  If the company has no D&O insurance, then potential members need to think twice about whether or not to sit on Board. Companies will go bankrupt. In that case, disgruntled creditors could possibly come looking for deep pockets.

Before you accept a board position, ask questions.

- Why does the company want you? How do you add value to the company? Or, are you there to be an ally of another Board member or the management?

- Who are the other Board members? What is their added value, individually? What is their Board experience? It's generally a good idea that's someone else on the Board have some experience.

- Who are the professional advisers? Accountants, lawyers? Is the company dealing with ethical and competent professional advice?

- Who are the investors? What is the investment thesis other investors?

- What are the recent financial and operational results?

- Are there claims against the company?

- How long does a Board member serve? What are the mechanisms for removal? Are the terms staggered? That is, do all Board members leave the Board at the same time?

- What are provisions for D&O insurance or indemnification?

- Can you read recent Board packages? You should be able to read recent Board agendas and minutes.

- What are the Board processes? How often does the Board meet? What are the various committees? How collegial and transparent is the Board?

Being on a Board is not simply an honor or flattery. It's serious business and care must be taken to join an ethical and competent Board when you are asked.

TAKEAWAYS

- If you are the management, make sure the Board members take their roles seriously. They should add value and not be just rubber stamps. Challenge them from time to time. Make sure they are engaged and helpful.

- There should be no surprises at Board meetings. Board meetings should have agendas and objectives. Prepare for meetings in advance.

- If you are a prospective Board member, know that being a board member is serious business. Make sure you are protected in case of bankruptcy or misconduct by the company or a tort action. Don't join a Board just for the honor. Ask questions.

Books

Rogers, Everett M. (1962). Diffusion of Innovations. Glencoe: Free Press. ISBN 0-612-62843-4

Joseph Bartlett, "Fundamentals of Venture Capital", Madison Books, 1999,.ISBN 1-56833-126-6

"HBR's 10 Must Reads. On Entrepreneurship and Startups", ISBN 978-1-63369-438-5

"New Business Ventures and The Entrepreneur, 6th Edition" Michael Roberts, Howard Stevenson, William Sahlman, Paul Marshall, Richard Hamermesh, ISBN-10: 0073404977

"The Portable MBA in Entrepreneurship (The Portable MBA Series) 3rd Edition", William Bygrave and Andrew Zacharakis. ISBN-10: 0-471-27154-3

"Venture Capital and the Finance of Innovation, 2nd edition", Andrew Metrick, Ayako Yasuda, ISBN-10: 0470454709

"Seed-Stage Venture Investing, 2nd Edition: An Insider's Guide to Start-Ups for Scientists, Engineers, and Investors 2nd Edition" Bill Robbins and Jon Lasch, ISBN-10: 0314279725

"Creative Capital: Georges Doriot and the Birth of Venture Capital", Spencer Ante, ISBN-10: 9781422101223

"Crossing the Chasm, 3rd edition", Geoffrey Moore, ISBN-10: 0-06-051712-3

"Steve Jobs", Walter Isaacson, ISBN 978-1-4516-4853-9
   The first 85 pages are particularly instructive for entrepreneurs.

General On-line Resources

Links come and go. But these were useful in the research for this book. Apologies if they don't work anymore.

Tech Coast Angels, a rich trove of documents, templates and samples
   https://www.techcoastangels.com/for-angels/

California Management Review, UC Berkeley
   http://cmr.berkeley.edu/browse/

Entrepreneurship blog at Wharton
   https://entrepreneurship.wharton.upenn.edu/entrepreneur-resources/

National Venture capital Association
   https://nvca.org

AngelList
   https://angel.co

Angel Resource Institute
   https://www.angelresourceinstitute.org

YCombinator's Guide to Entrepreneurship
   http://www.ycombinator.com/resources/

Innovation takes a village
   http://knowledge.wharton.upenn.edu/article/innovation-sometimes-it-takes-a-village/

12 things I wish I knew before starting my own company
   http://www.cosmopolitan.com/career/a57493/things-i-wish-i-knew-started-my-own-company-bulletin/

Luck Matters
   http://www.theatlantic.com/magazine/archive/2016/05/why-luck-matters-more-than-you-might-think/476394/

Videos

California Management Review
> https://cmr.berkeley.edu/videos/

Stanford Venture Program
> https://ecorner.stanford.edu/videos/

Long Fuse, Big Bang by Andrew Hargadon, UC Davis
> http://www.uctv.tv/shows/Long-Fuse-Big-Bang-Thomas-Edison-Electricity-and-the-Locus-of-Innovation-24976

Growth of Uber
> https://www.facebook.com/pg/traviskal/videos/

Elevator pitch samples and suggestions. Go to http://ecorner.stanford.edu/ and search for "elevator pitch"
> Or go to YouTube and search for elevator pitch". There are good and bad ones there.

Podcasts

Mick Mountz and the founding of Kiva Systems
> http://www.npr.org/2013/06/28/196630096/mick-mountz-founder-of-kiva-systems

How I Built This by Guy Raz at National Public Radio
> https://www.npr.org/podcasts/510313/how-i-built-this

> > Interesting episodes for Sandy Lerner (Cisco Systems), John Zimmer (Lyft), Jenn Hyman (Rent the Runway), Perry Chen (Kickstarter), Yvon Chouinard (Patagonia), Miguel McKelvey (WeWork), Wendy Kopp (Teach For America), Alice Waters (Chez Panisse), Herb Kelleher (Southwest Airlines), Joe Gebbia (Airbnb).

Process

Entrepreneurship: It Can Be Taught
> https://hbswk.hbs.edu/item/entrepreneurship-it-can-be-taught

HBR on Lean Startups
> https://hbswk.hbs.edu/item/6659.html

Why the Lean Startup changes everything
> https://hbr.org/2013/05/why-the-lean-start-up-changes-everything

Eric Reis describes the Lean Startup
> http://ecorner.stanford.edu/authorMaterialInfo.html?mid=2329

New TV: Antithesis of a Lean Startup
> https://hbr.org/2018/08/newtv-is-the-antithesis-of-a-lean-startup-can-it-work

Startup checklist
> http://www.mbbp.com/uploads/1437/doc/Low_Down.pdf

Four VCs evaluating opportunities
> https://hbswk.hbs.edu/item/four-vcs-on-evaluating-opportunities

Why Entrepreneurs are happier than their peers
> https://knowledge.wharton.upenn.edu/article/why-mba-entrepreneurs-are-happier-than-their-peers/

The Economist asks what exactly is an entrepreneur?

    https://www.economist.com/schumpeter/2014/02/16/what-exactly-is-an-entrepreneur?fsrc=nlw%7Cnewe%7C2-19-2014%7C7842779%7C137618446%7CNA

The Team As Hero

    "Entrepreneurship Reconsidered: The Team as Hero", Harvard Business Review, May-June 1987.

How Uber, Airbnb and Etsy Attracted Their First 1,000 Customers

    https://hbswk.hbs.edu/item/how-uber-airbnb-and-etsy-attracted-their-first-1-000-customers

Thoughts on team building and interviewing from Korn Ferry

    https://www.kornferry.com/institute/10-things-job-interviewers-are-looking-for

"Ready to Take Your Startup Public? Hold That Thought"

    https://knowledge.wharton.upenn.edu/article/ready-take-start-public-hold-thought/

Ideas

Bessemer Venture Partner Anti-portfolio. Fun stuff and illuminating

    www.BVP.com, then search the site for anti-portfolio.

Why Steve Jobs Didn't Listen to His Customers

    https://www.huffingtonpost.com/gregory-ciotti/why-steve-jobs-didnt-list_b_5628355.html

How to predict if a new business idea is any good?

    http://hbswk.hbs.edu/item/how-to-predict-if-a-new-business-idea-is-any-good?cid=SPemail-spridMTg0Njc yNjAwMDIS1-spmid12351553

The Geography of Startups. The Economist talks about clustering

    https://www.economist.com/special-report/2012/10/27/something-in-the-air?frsc=dg%7Ca

Founders

Age and the High Growth Entrepreneur

    https://www.nber.org/papers/w24489 or

    https://census.gov/library/working-papers/2018/adrm/carra-wp-2018-03.html

Why corporate high performers quit to work for themselves

    https://hbr.org/2019/01/why-some-high-performers-are-quitting-big-companies-to-work-for-themselves

Founder Mistakes

    http://stateofstartups.firstround.com/2017/#founder-mistakes

Would You Rather Be Rich Or Would You Rather Be King?

    http://www.startuplessonslearned.com/2012/04/founders-dilemmas-equity-splits.html

Keep the Founder

    https://a16z.com/2010/04/28/why-we-prefer-founding-ceos/

Protecting the legal interests of the founders

    http://www.mbbp.com/news/protecting-legal-interests

Founder vesting

    https://launch.wilmerhale.com/explore/formation/founders/tax-implications-related-to-shares-that-vest

Founder problems at Snapchat

    http://www.latimes.com/business/la-fi-cofounder-disputes-20150322-story.html

Wharton on the right leadership style for the digital age

https://knowledge.wharton.upenn.edu/article/the-right-leadership-style-for-the-digital-age/

The Small Firm Effect and the Entrepreneurial Spawning of Scientists and Engineers

https://businessinnovation.berkeley.edu/wp-content/uploads/businessinnovation-archive/WilliamsonSeminar/hamilton041609.pdf

The Psychological Price of Entrepreneurship

https://www.inc.com/magazine/201309/jessica-bruder/psychological-price-of-entrepreneurship.html

Equity Compensation

Startup salaries

https://angel.co/salaries

83(b) Elections

https://blog.vcexperts.com/2016/12/13/why-founders-and-employees-of-emerging-businesses-need-to-understand-83b-elections/

Fidelity Investments discusses equity compensation

https://www.fidelity.com/go/stock-plan-services/overview

The First Deal: The Division of Founder Equity in New Ventures, by Hellman and Wasserman

https://www.nber.org/papers/w16922

409A Valuation

https://www.lexology.com/library/detail.aspx?g=78d9716c-6be2-4126-9ef5-d38dfe902064

Legal and Sample Documents

Corporation or LLC?

https://blog.vcexperts.com/2015/10/13/corporation-versus-a-limited-liability-company/?utm_source=The+VC+Expert%27s+Buzz&utm_campaign=7b58b6bcf9-Corporation_Vs_LLC_10_13_2015&utm_medium=email&utm_term=0_ee0d1cc528-7b58b6bcf9-267078189

Why Incorporate in Delaware

https://www.abi.org/abi-journal/incorporation-issues-why-delaware

Top 10 legal mistakes made by entrepreneurs

https://hbswk.hbs.edu/item/top-ten-legal-mistakes-made-by-entrepreneurs

IRS information about LLCs

https://www.irs.gov/businesses/small-businesses-self-employed/limited-liability-company-llc

IRS information about corporations

https://www.irs.gov/corporations

IRS information about S Corporations

https://www.irs.gov/businesses/small-businesses-self-employed/s-corporations

Accredited investors on the SEC website

https://www.sec.gov/answers/accred.htm

https://www.sec.gov/answers/regd.htm

https://www.sec.gov/fast-answers/answers-accredhtm.html

Cooley sample documents

https://www.cooleygo.com/documents/

NVCA sample agreements
   http://nvca.org/resources/model-legal-documents/
YCombinator sample documents
   http://www.ycombinator.com/documents/
State of California Rules
   https://www.sos.ca.gov/business-programs/
Work visas
   https://www.uscis.gov/working-united-states/working-us
Mediation
   https://aaamediation.org
American Arbitration Association
   https://adr.org
WIPO and AAA offer model arbitration clauses on their websites.
   https://www.wipo.int/amc-apps/clause-generator/
   https://adr.org/clauses

Law Firms. Good sources of data

Wilmer Hale
   https://launch.wilmerhale.com
Gunderson Dettmer
   https://www.gunder.com/entrepreneurs-emerging-companies/
Wilson Sonsini
   https://www.wsgr.com/WSGR/Display.aspx?SectionName=practice
Cooley
   https://www.cooleygo.com
Stubbs Alderton
   https://stubbsalderton.com
Fenwick
   https://www.fenwick.com
DLA Piper
   https://www.dlapiperaccelerate.com

Fundraising

Accepting Money From Friends & Family
   http://www.entrepreneur.com/article/0,4621,299420,00.html
Tutorial on Crowdfunding
   https://www.youtube.com/watch?v=8b5-iEnW70k
   http://www.thecrowdcafe.com
Regulation CF (Crowdfunding)
   https://www.sec.gov/info/smallbus/secg/rccomplianceguide-051316.htm
   https://www.sec.gov/smallbusiness/exemptofferings/regcrowdfunding
Regulation A+ for security tokens
   https://www.sec.gov/news/pressrelease/2015-49.html

Why we didn't invest in your company

https://techcrunch.com/2016/09/05/11-reasons-we-didnt-invest-in-your-company/?ncid=txtlnkusaolp00000591&yptr=yahoo

The law firm of Cooley tutorial on convertible debt

https://www.cooleygo.com/convertible-debt/

Why convertible notes are sometimes terrible for startups

https://techcrunch.com/2012/09/05/why-convertible-notes-are-sometimes-terrible-for-startups/

SEC regulations regarding regulation D

https://www.sec.gov/fast-answers/answers-regdhtm.html

AngelList says most VCs lose money

https://angel.co/blog/what-angellist-data-says-about-power-law-returns-in-venture-capital

Tutorial by the law firm of Cooley on term sheets

https://www.cooleygo.com/negotiating-term-sheets/

TechCoastAngels, angel investors in Southern California

https://www.techcoastangels.com

For Innovation Success, Choose a Corporate VC

https://knowledge.wharton.upenn.edu/article/innovation-success-choose-corporate-vc/?utm_source=kw_newsletter&utm_medium=email&utm_campaign=2016-01-27

Corporate VCs Yield Better Innovation outcomes

https://mackinstitute.wharton.upenn.edu/2016/corporate-vcs-yield-better-innovation-outcomes/

Band of Angels, angel investors in Silicon Valley

https://www.bandangels.com

Guy Kawasaki's rules for Powerpoint

https://guykawasaki.com/the_102030_rule/

Bill Reichert's Top Ten Lies Entrepreneurs Tell

https://www.garage.com/files/LiesEntre.pdf

https://www.youtube.com/watch?v=ReE44CymfF4

Bill Reichert's Top Ten Lies Venture Capitalists Tell

https://www.garage.com/bill-reichert-top-10-lies-vcs-tell-entrepreneurs/

Caps on Participating Preferred

http://www.mbbp.com/news/zone-of-indifference

Presentation Tips

Presentation Zen

http://www.presentationzen.com

Kate Mitchell on presentation

http://ecorner.stanford.edu/videos/3144/Questions-Going-into-the-Pitch

Prisoners pitching ideas

http://ecorner.stanford.edu/videos/3159/Nailing-the-One-Minute-Pitch

Startup Pitch Decks

https://attach.io/startup-pitch-decks/?ref=producthunt

Business Plans

"Ernst & Young Business Plan Guide", Jay Bornstein, Patrick Pruitt, Brian Ford, 3rd edition, ISBN-10: 0470112697
SEC handbook for some writing tips
    https://www.sec.gov/pdf/handbook.pdf
Kolchinsky's Guide to a Biotech Startup, 4th edition
    https://www.ctsi.ucla.edu/researcher-resources/files/view/docs/EGBS4_Kolchinsky.pdf

> You can also search online for business plan by type of business. For example, searching online for 'business plans restaurant' will get you lots of good and bad business plans for restaurants.

Intellectual Property

USA Patents
    https://www.uspto.gov
Google Patents
    https://patents.google.com
WIPO
    https://www.wipo.int/portal/en/index.html
WIPO on PCT
    http://www.wipo.int/pct/en/
USPTO on PCT
    https://www.uspto.gov/video/cbt/GIPA-English/PCT/
Provisional Patents
    http://www.uspto.gov/patents/resources/types/provapp.jsp
Copyrights in the USA
    https://www.copyright.gov
Software copyrights
    https://www.copyright.gov/circs/circ61.pdf
Trademarks in the USA
    https://www.uspto.gov/trademark
Statue of Liberty
    https://www.google.com/patents?id=6esWAAAAEBAJ&printsec=abstract&zoom=4&source=gbs_overview_r&cad=0#v=onepage&q&f=false
Trade Secret Identification Rule
    https://www.fenwick.com/docstore/Publications/Litigation/Trade_Secret_ID_Rule.pdf
Intellectual Property Law blog
    https://www.intellectualpropertylawblog.com
In-n-Out versus Caliburger
    https://www.latimes.com/business/la-xpm-2012-feb-10-la-fi-china-double-double-20120211-story.html
US Supreme Court ruling in Bilski v Kappos regarding business methods
    https://www.supremecourt.gov/opinions/09pdf/08-964.pdf

Licensing

AUTM (was the Association of University Technology Managers)
   https://autm.net
AUTM 9 Points to Consider for Licensing
   https://www.autm.net/AUTMMain/media/Advocacy/Documents/Points_to_Consider.pdf
ITAR regulations
   https://www.export.gov/article?id=International-Traffic-in-Arms-RegulationsInternational-Traffic-in-Arms-Regulations
Open Source Initiative on Software Licenses
   https://opensource.org/licenses

Acquisitions

Buying a business
   https://hbr.org/ideacast/2017/02/why-you-should-buy-a-business-and-how-to-do-it
A website to buy or sell a business
   https://www.bizbuysell.com

Spinoffs

The case for corporate spinoffs
   https://knowledge.wharton.upenn.edu/article/hp-and-the-case-for-corporate-spinoffs/
The case against corporate spinoffs
   https://hbswk.hbs.edu/archive/spinning-out-a-star-why-spinouts-seldom-work
Spinoffs are hot
   https://www.forbes.com/sites/steveschaefer/2012/11/02/why-spinoff-stocks-are-sizzling/#7e71ad6f24c2
Spinoffs and spin-ins
   https://mpra.ub.uni-muenchen.de/5563/1/MPRA_paper_5563.pdf
McKinsey on divestiture strategies
   https://www.mckinsey.com/business-functions/strategy-and-corporate-finance/our-insights/going-going-gone-a-quicker-way-to-divest-assets

Governance

Harvard Law School Corporate Governance Blog
   http://blogs.harvard.edu/corpgov/
Vicinity of Insolvency
   https://www.vcexperts.com/buzz_articles/1381
Indemnification of Directors
   https://www.vcexperts.com/buzz_articles/1120?utm_source=The+VC+Expert%27s+Buzz&utm_campaign=ab03eee71d-Buzz_10_25_2011&utm_medium=email

Fenwick on Corporate Governance
https://www.fenwick.com/Topics/pages/topicsdetail.aspx?topicname=Corporate%20Governance
AngelBlog Links on Director Topics
http://www.angelblog.net/index.html

CPSIA information can be obtained
at www.ICGtesting.com
Printed in the USA
BVHW010023200422
634727BV00006B/223